P-38 LIG

MW00830733

UNFORGETTABLE MISSIONS
OF
SKILL AND LUCK

Compiled and edited by

Steve Blake and Dayle DeBry

P-38 National Association

P.O. Box 6453

March Air Reserve Base, CA 92518

www.p38assn.org

This book is dedicated to all
World War II veterans and their families.
To all the pilots and crews of the P-38 Lightning fighter airplane
who proudly served their country and have left a legacy for
us to continue and uphold.

P-38 Lightning:
Unforgettable Missions of Skill and Luck
Remembrances of the P-38 Lightning by the people who were there
during World War II

©2011 P-38 National Association
All rights reserved

Compilation and editing by Steve Blake and Dayle DeBry
Chapter introductions by Steve Blake
Cover and book design by Dayle DeBry
Photo restoration by Marjorie Blake
Editing by Kelly Kalcheim

ISBN-13: 978-0615445458

P-38 National Association
P.O. Box 6453
March Air Reserve Base, CA 92518

www.p38assn.org

Table of Contents

Introduction

As President of the P-38 National Association it is with great pride that we welcome you to this first publishing of stories from our Lockheed P-38 Lightning pilots and ground crews.

Pulled from the Association's archives, these stories can now be shared for the very first time with a new generation of P-38 fans, young and old. Many of the stories you read here have not been available to the general public in book form. We believe these stories will entertain and enlighten you to the heroism and honor that our P-38 veterans carried into combat and into day-to-day operations.

Since 1987 the P-38 National Association has existed to keep the legacy of our beloved Lightning alive for future generations, and so that the performance of the Lightning and the skill and sacrifice of its pilots and crews will never be lost to history.

We would like to challenge each and every one of you to become an activist in keeping these stories alive for future generations by supporting and volunteering in your local communities. By advocating veterans' programs and activities, the rewards you reap will warm your heart and last a lifetime.

We would also like to invite you to join the P-38 National Association and become a wingman to some of the greatest pilots to ever fly an airplane. Strap yourself in and enjoy the journey as you relive the exploits of some of the members of our "greatest generation" as they pilot the P-38 through the war-torn skies of World War II.

Let's advance the throttles, pull up the gear and enjoy the book!

Bob Alvis
President
P-38 National Association

FOR THOSE WHO FOUGHT
Dr. Michael McKenzie

On the living room wall at home hangs one of my most prized possessions. It is a copy of an old black and white photo. In the picture are 30 men, standing in three rows, in front of a plain wooden building. On the back of the original, in my dad's handwriting, are these words: "Christmas Day, 1945 Atsugi Air Base, 49th Fighter Group, 8th Fighter Squadron" and the names of every man in the squadron.

I prize this picture not only because it is a link with my father (who died more than 20 years ago), but because it reminds me of how much my generation owes his. It cannot be denied that each generation has its own particular cross to bear. But my father's faced both a depression in which one in four Americans were unemployed, and a world war which resulted in tens of millions dead.

And still, those in the picture stand there, many smiling and confident. Many of them had seen friends die; all faced hardships we can only imagine today.

As I look at the picture, I ask myself what my generation can give the one which went before—respect? Well, certainly. But they (and we) need more than that. We have forgotten not only the lessons of history, but often times, history itself. In the college classes I teach, it is not all that unusual for my students to be unable to tell me even when the Second World War took place!

But we Americans need to gain not only in knowledge, but in wisdom. We need those men in that picture; we need them now as teachers. It matters little whether it is said (as they do so often) that

5

they were just "doing their jobs." To do such jobs in such a time and in such a place is what makes heroes. Our society needs such heroes.

We also need to understand that each generation gets its own turn in a crucible. To be sure, each is not called to give what that generation has given. Many is the time I wished I could turn in a P-38L, diving down to scatter a formation of Zekes and Tonys. But such dreams of glory seldom count the cost that lurks there.

Nearly 300,000 Americans never came home from the war that ended 50 years ago; 300,000 men and women, who never got a chance to raise a family, pay off a mortgage or grow old. This oddity—that the glory and the hell of war are common bedfellows—is mirrored on the faces of the young men in the picture. Confidence and smiles are accompanied by a seriousness not usually found on those barely out of high school. Many look old before their time.

It may well be that my generation's challenge is to keep alive the lessons of the past half century. In the 50 years since MacArthur stood on the teak deck of the *U.S.S. Missouri* in Tokyo Bay, America has faced internal challenges and crises of conscience. Now, more than ever, we need to know that there are many things worth fighting and dying for—a reminder that liberty and freedom come at a price.

All too often today, there are voices raised which would deny the transcendent values which nourish our society—values often paid for with the flower of American manhood. Such voices ironically live off the freedom fought for by the very people whose ideals they ridicule.

As we celebrate the 50th anniversary of the end of WWII, I for one do not intend to let despair, confusion or doubt overshadow the lessons taught by these warriors or this war. Good things came about because of this terrible war, this war whose end we celebrate. I owe the men in the picture that much.

So sound the roll call, the living and the dead: Sanders, Miners, Meckley, Chenowith, Bander, Bogert, Joslin, Tydeman, McKenzie, Stephenson, Tomasi, Brown, Watson, McCoy, Adams, Chandler, Leroy, Cagwin, Sleeper, Poston, Findley, Tomie, Anderson, Roberts, Wyatt, Martinez, Sheppard, Brooks, Traylor, Calabria. You who stand for all those who fought.

As long as there are those who understand the heart of things, who you are and what you did will never be forgotten.

Dr. McKenzie teaches at Northwest College in Kirkland, Washington. His late father, then-1st Lt. Dale McKenzie, was a member of the 8th Fighter Squadron from January 1945 to January 1946.

Photos: Page 5, the 8th Fighter Squadron gathered for a 1945 Christmas Day photo. Lt. Dale McKenzie is in the back row, third from right. (Oster) This page, Lt. Dale McKenzie, 1945. (McKenzie)

AN HONEST LOOK AT THE P-38
George Seeberg

Over the years, the Lockheed Lightning has certainly been characterized as one of the best (if not the very best) fighter/recon aircraft that was built and flown in WWII. Practically everybody who flew this twin-engine, twin-tailed aircraft dearly loved it. And I am no exception in this respect.

On the chance that I may alienate the friendship of those with whom I flew, I felt it was high time to jog our memories about some of the aircraft traits that were particularly annoying.

Remember...

• Skinned knuckles or torn flight gloves on your right hand as you tried to adjust the slide coolant temp controls of the F and early G models?

• The cockpit heater that did a great job except for your feet that just about froze at altitude?

• Single-engine on takeoff with a full load of fuel, ammo and belly tanks?

• The rare but sometimes runaway electric prop?

• Turbos that almost never cut in at the same time and made close formation flying a thrill?

• The miserable retractable ladder, especially when wearing a survival pack and chute?

• The cockpit fluorescent lights that were impossible to adjust?

• Sharp turns to the left at high speed before the advent of aileron boost (unless you were left-handed and then it was those right turns)?

• The fun of hand pumping your gear down when the hydraulic system wouldn't?

• And what about that compressibility thing before the dive flaps on the J and L models?

There are probably many more aggravating traits that can be re-membered—maybe with a sense of fondness. I'm sure we all would agree that there never has been a perfect aircraft made and, in all likelihood, never will be.

So to me, the P-38, even with its variety of faults, was one excep-tionally fine aircraft. That second engine kept me from having to make a couple of very long swims back to base, and even back then I was not a very good swimmer.

George Seeberg served with the 44th Fighter Squadron of the 18th Fighter Group in the Pacific. Photo of George on previous page.

CHAPTER ONE

DESIGN, DEVELOPMENT, PRODUCTION AND MODIFICATIONS

P-38 DESIGN, PRODUCTION AND MODIFICATIONS

In February 1937 the U.S. Army Air Corps began circulating its new "Specification X-608" among American aircraft manufacturers. It called for an interceptor capable of carrying a heavy armament to high altitudes quickly utilizing turbo-supercharged engines, and with a long range, a top speed of at least 360 mph and a tricycle landing gear for simplified ground handling. Coincidentally (or not), one of the companies, the Lockheed Aircraft Corporation of Burbank, California, was already working on such a design, thanks mainly to its chief designer, Hall Hibbard, and his assistant, Clarence "Kelly" Johnson. Designated Lockheed Model 22, it was a twin-engine, twin-boom, twin-tail design that included a separate fuselage pod on the center wing section containing the cockpit and the armament—one cannon, and four machine guns. The designers decided that snugly cowled, twelve-cylinder Allison V-1710-C liquid-cooled, inline engines (turning Curtiss Electric propellers) would be the best choice to power it. (The turbo-superchargers were to be contained in the booms just behind the wings).

The Model 22 was a radical design for its time, in many ways. For example, it would be the first aircraft to have all the flight controls covered in aluminum rather than the usual fabric. Its flush-riveted aluminum skin and sleek engine cowlings made for a very modern, streamlined appearance. It was also huge for a fighter, weighing in at over 15,000 pounds and with a wingspan of 52 feet.

Suitably impressed with its design, in June 1937 the Air Corps issued Lockheed a contract for one XP-38 for evaluation. Among the changes instituted in the XP-38 was counter-rotating propellers to eliminate the torque effect, especially during takeoff. Also, the company's special Fowler flaps were added to the wings to improve its low-speed handling characteristics.

It took over a year to build the XP-38. When completed, it was trucked from Burbank to March Field, near Riverside, California, on the last day of 1938 for its initial taxiing and flight tests. It took to the air for the first time there on January 27, 1939, with 1st Lt. Ben Kelsey at the controls. Kelsey was the officer in charge of the USAAC's Pursuit Projects Office, located at Wright Field near Dayton, Ohio, where extensive flight testing of new aircraft designs was performed.

It was soon time for Lt. Kelsey to transport the XP-38 to Wright for that purpose, which flight took place on February 11. However, when he arrived at his destination, due to the high speeds he had attained en route (averaging the desired 360 mph) it was decided that he should complete a cross-country flight instead. So after refueling, Kelsey took off for Mitchel Field on Long Island, New York. Unfortunately, due to carburetor ice, the XP-38 crashed there on final! Lt. Kelsey was basically just shook up, but the aircraft was destroyed.

Although it hadn't yet been fully tested, influential Air Corps officers, including Ben Kelsey, were convinced of the aircraft's possibilities, and in April 1939 another contract was issued for thirteen YP-38s. These were designated Model 122s, the first of which didn't fly until September 17, 1940. The "Y" stood for test and evaluation. Lockheed employees began calling them "Yippees" (for YPs), which nickname stuck for P-38s in general, at least at Burbank.

The first production models of the P-38 (now designated 222) were the P-38-LO (also the first to be delivered in Olive Drab and Neutral Grey paint), the P-38D and the P-38E. Even though P-38E's scored the Lightning's first air victories in the Aleutians in August

P-38Ds being completed outside the Lockheed factory in Burbank

during the summer of 1941. In the background are Lend Lease Lockheed Hudson bombers displaying RAF roundels. (Cecil Kramer)

1942, none of these versions were fully combat ready. They did, however, have self-sealing gas tanks and more cockpit armor, and the E was the first to receive the P-38's final armament of one 20mm cannon and four .50-caliber machine guns.

The first unit to be equipped with these early model P-38s, in late 1941, was the 1st Pursuit Group at Selfridge Field, Michigan, which utilized a few of them in that year's large scale Army maneuvers (war games).

It was while being test flown in 1941 that two serious problems with the P-38's performance became apparent, one of which did considerable damage to its reputation. This was compressibility, which took hold during a steep dive at a critical mach number, resulting in the controls locking up and the pilot often having great difficulty pulling out of it. The other was tail flutter, or aerodynamic buffet, which caused an extreme vibration which could cause serious damage to the plane. This was soon corrected by Lockheed engineers with a simple design modification—the fitting of larger wing-root fillets to improve the air flow over the plane's surfaces. The compressibility problem was partly solved by instructing the pilots regarding trim tab use and throttle retardation and, especially, restricting dives to a certain mach number, which could obviously be problematic in some combat situations.

What was to become the P-38's official name was bestowed on it by the Royal Air Force, which had placed a large order for what it called the "Lightning I" in 1940. Unfortunately, after this export version, the P-322, was evaluated by an RAF pilot at Burbank in 1941 and three were sent to England for further evaluation in early 1942, the order was cancelled. The main reason was that the British had ordered this aircraft without turbo-superchargers or counter-rotating props, its performance suffering accordingly, but they were also concerned about the P-38's compressibility and tail flutter problems.

Some early examples of the Lightning were utilized as test-bed aircraft. One highly modified P-38 called the "Swordfish" tested airfoils, and another was used to determine the efficacy of a pressurized cockpit. Others were modified for such tasks as towing gliders and launching torpedoes. Two experimental types based on the P-38 were also tested but never produced. One of them was a high-altitude fighter, also with a pressurized cockpit, designated the XP-49, and the other was the XP-58, a very heavily armed and armored twin-engine interceptor/bomber destroyer.

The P-38F was the first model that was really suitable for combat, and it and the G that followed it on the assembly line were the first to see extensive action, in North Africa and the South Pacific, in 1942. Of tremendous importance was the addition of under-wing pylons for bombs or jettisonable fuel ("drop") tanks to these and subsequent models. Although there were continuous minor improvements being made to the aircraft (more powerful V-1710 engines, for example), as evidenced by the numerous subtypes (F-15, G-13, etc.), the Fs and the Gs—and the Hs that soon replaced them—were pretty much identical, at least on the outside. The 222 designation was changed to 322 in the middle of the F and G model runs at the factory and then to 422, the aircraft's final designation, starting with the

P-38H.

Photo reconnaissance versions of the P-38, with the guns in their noses replaced by cameras, were introduced on the Lockheed assembly line at the end of 1941. The first such models were designated F-4s, which were delivered to the Air Corps from March to August 1942. They were supplanted by the F-5A until March 1943 and then by the F-5B, based on the P-38J, from September 1943 to January 1944. The latter was the last photo recon version built at the Burbank plant, the final total being 459.

It was the P-38J, production of which began in the summer of 1943, that displayed the most dramatic (and visually obvious) design changes in the history of the aircraft. The streamlined, swept-back radiator scoops under the propeller spinners were replaced with larger, flat ones, to improve cooling. The intercoolers in the leading edges of the wings were moved to these "chins" under the props, next to the oil radiators, and replaced with 55-gallon fuel tanks. As to this increase in fuel capacity, combined with huge 300-gallon drop tanks and improved pilot engine and fuel management, ultra-long-range P-38 missions of eight to twelve hours became fairly common in the Southwest Pacific during the last year of the war.

During the winter of 1943, in the middle of the J-10 run, the decision was made to dispense with the olive drab and green camouflage paint. Starting in early 1944, all P-38s would henceforth be delivered in natural metal finish (NMF), which reduced the costs and increased the plane's speed slightly.

The P-38J-25, which was the predecessor of the ultimate L model, featured electrically powered dive, or "combat" flaps and power-boosted ailerons. This new "aerodynamic braking" system increased its maneuverability and finally eliminated the threat of compressibility once and for all. The next L-1 model also featured statically and dynamically balanced ailerons with hydraulic boosters to reduce the load on the control stick, which was now approximately one-sixth (!) of what it had been, thereby both improving maneuverability and reducing pilot fatigue.

In 1944 Lockheed's new modification center in Dallas, Texas, began converting P-38Js and Ls—flown there from Burbank by ferry pilots—to later model F-5s (Es, Fs and Gs), about 1,000 in total. It also converted about 75 P-38L-5s to P-38M-6 two-seat night fighters, which carried radar and a radar operator. A few of the latter arrived in the Pacific a little too late to see any combat but did serve in Japan on occupation duty with two USAAF night fighter squadrons.

The huge demand for P-38s and the fact that Lockheed had just one factory resulted in a subcontract being awarded to Consolidated-Vultee to build them at its plant in Nashville, Tennessee. Only 113 P-38L-5-VNs were built there by VJ-Day, at which time the contract was terminated.

A total of 10,038 Lightnings were built from 1938 to 1945, during which time the basic aircraft design received literally thousands of detail changes and modifications.

LIGHTNING TECH:
High Speed Dive Prompts Canopy Modifications
Ralph Eden

If you have ever wondered why the P-38 had that strap across the top of the canopy and those cross braces on the side panels, here's the answer. Back in 1968, I was working in Burbank as an aerodynamicist for LTV (Ling Temco Vaught) on their joint proposal with Lockheed for the VSX anti-sub aircraft. While I was browsing though old files during my lunch hour, I discovered some P-38 service bulletins and made copies of a few interesting ones. As I gathered additional information later, I was able to put this story together.

According to a March 1954 historical article in Lockheed's in-plant newspaper, *Lockheed Star*, Army Air Corps test pilot Major Signa Gilkey was assigned the task of wringing out one of the first production model P-38s during the early 1940s. Starting at 35,000 feet, he rolled a Lightning over on its back and pushed the control column forward for a high-speed dive. As the plane accelerated past 350 mph indicated airspeed, it entered the region of compressibility and began to vibrate violently. He could not pull the control wheel back to pull out of the dive. Reaching forward to the elevator trim tab wheel, he cranked in "nose up" trim. The P-38 did not respond immediately, but as he approached 12,000 feet it suddenly pulled out. But the pullout was so abrupt that Major Gilkey temporarily blacked out. It is most likely that it was during this dive that the top of the canopy and one of the side panels were lost, either during the dive or the pullout.

I think this occurred in early 1942. "Why," you ask? How do you know? Two Lockheed Service Bulletins affecting the canopy were published in early 1942—one to add side window cross bracing (P-38/SB-111, dated 14 April) and the other to add the reinforcing strap to the top hatch (P-38/SB-119, dated 5 May). I believe these service bulletins had the same effect as the time compliance tech orders (TCTOs) I was familiar with during my tour as a USAF Aircraft Maintenance Officer in the late '50s and early '60s. The cross bracing effectivity was for the YP-38, P-38, P-38D and P-38E. The hatch reinforcing effectivity was for the same early types plus the P-38F and the F-4 reconnaissance ships. According to the P-38 Production Table at the back of Warren Bodie's book *The P-38 Lightning*, the last of the P-38Es and the first of the F-4s and P-38Fs were being delivered in March '42, so these ships would have to have been retrofitted after delivery.

In the first accompanying photo of a P-38E, note there are no cross braces or canopy strap (or even a rear view mirror and fairing). This photo was taken sometime after June '42, since the small red circle was removed in that month from our national insignia to avoid confusion with the red Japa-

nese "meatball" markings. The second photo (below) shows the final strap and cross brace installation as it appeared on all retrofitted and subsequent production models, in this case a P-38J.

Another account of a canopy loss in a pullout from a high-speed dive is mentioned in Lockheed test pilot Tony LeVier's autobiography *Pilot.* Tony states that he succeeded in transferring from production test pilot to experimental test pilot on 1 July 1942, and that, "On my first (P-38) test flight my canopy came off in a pullout from a high-speed dive." Obviously, he wasn't flying a ship that had the strap modification!

Our then P-38 Association President, Stan Jones, once showed me a side-window cross brace he'd retrieved from a P-38 crash site. After examining it, I told Stan, "Hey, this thing is made out of steel, not

aluminum!" Lockheed's engineers wanted to make sure that no P-38 pilot had to fly home without a canopy after a high-speed pullout.

COLD LIGHTNING
Randy Acord

During the winter of 1943-44, I was assigned an airplane that turned out to be the one that provided more information regarding problems in cold weather than most others. It was a P-38J-1, serial no. 42-13565, which was manufactured in August of 1943. It was assigned to "Cold Weather Test" and ferried to Vandalier, Ohio, near Dayton, for instrumentation.

The P-38 was specially equipped with 54 thermo-couplers located in as many places on the aircraft, and I could read the temperature of each through selectors, with a potentiometer located where the gun sight normally was mounted. This special installation enabled us to study machine gun lubrication, engine lubrication, cabin heat, carburetor heat, fuel distribution, etc. The Lockheed engineer assigned to my project was Lee Chambers, a wonderful man who was a great help to many of the project officers in the Cold Weather Test Detachment at Ladd Field, Fairbanks, Alaska.

The test program for that winter was a long, complex one which included testing of snow and ice tires, oil dilution systems, cold starting use butane, wing icing tests, and napalm and other bombing tests of many types—many completed at minus 40 degrees Fahrenheit and colder. This aircraft was equipped with the General Electric turbo-supercharger regulator as well as one of the first carburetor heat installations on a turbo-supercharger.

During the month of March, this P-38 was assigned a very special project: testing a set of retractable skis. Mr. Frank Ditter, the president of Federal Aircraft Skis, Minneapolis, Minnesota (the manufacturer) assisted in the installation and tests. His personal interest was created by some problems which occurred when another P-38 was ski

20

equipped in northern Minnesota and was damaged on the ground and never flew.

During that month, would you believe that it snowed 26 out of the 31 days, with an accumulation of 34.5 inches? The conditions were ideal for such tests, and I made 165 landings, with complete retraction and extension between each landing. The interest around the base was high, especially among the Russians based at Ladd. Every operation was successful, even the dive test up to 450 mph, but the advantages were small.

P-38J-1 #43-13565, while Capt. Acord was testing it with retractable skis. Photo on previous page: Capt. Randall Acord, Ladd Field, May 1944. He received his wings and commission in March 1942 (Class 42-C) and was unusual in that he trained as both a pilot and as an engineering officer. He was sent to Alaska in May of 1943 and remained there for the rest of the war. Another of Acord's assignments was to the 343rd FG in the Aleutians, to help modify its P-38s and to instruct its pilots in the proper use of carburetor heat. (Acord)

The ski loading was 640 pounds per square inch, and regardless of the depth of the snow, the skis went to the bottom. The propeller clearance was only 14 inches and we could plow that much snow on wheels. The skis worked well on rough snow-covered ground or ice with cracks, while on glazed ice the landing slide was 7,000 feet. With no torque involved with the engines idling at 500 rpm, it was easy to do figure eights on the ground in the width of the runway.

It was a pleasure to be the project officer on this aircraft and to do all the special things that it was capable of doing. During these tests on skis, the right engine was flown with the first synthetic oil, carrying a 165-gallon belly tank on the right side only, containing synthetic oil just to service the right engine. This unbalanced looking condition drove some of the Russian pilots up a tree, wondering how the P-38 flew with all that weight on one side.

We were able to start the Allison engines without heat and run off the battery down to −30 degrees. It was a very good cold weather airplane, and I was always first off the ground on cold mornings.

Many changes were accomplished on the P-38J and placed in production on the P-38L, such as lubrication on all the electric actuators, lubrication on armament and low temperature "O" ring seals in the hydraulic system. The most important, and probably the longest, was the testing and establishing of the carburetor heat system necessary for successful operation on extra-long-range cruise missions.

After many hours of flying to collect all the data necessary, a final test was scheduled to be made at minus 40 degrees Fahrenheit or colder, at low altitude, with power settings of 1600 rpm and 24 inches manifold pressure with carburetor heat "on" for 11 and one half hours. At the end of this test, I was to put the carburetor heat in the "off" position and apply war emergency power (60 inches mp and 3000 rpm) for five minutes. Both engines performed perfectly—no spark plug fouling had occurred due to poor vaporization and distribution of leaded fuel. Fuel consumption: 53 gallons per hour, both engines.

Lee Chambers gave a daily report of our accomplishments to his boss, Kelly Johnson, at Lockheed. General Arnold and Kelly were very good friends and all this information was passed on. In July 1944 long-range cruise was necessary for an important mission in the South Pacific. Charles Lindberg took this information to the P-38 pilots in that theater, and as you know, the rest is history.

A LOCKHEED MECHANIC'S OWN TALE

Don A. Lawless

Don Lawless was a mechanic in Flight Test at Lockheed in 1941-42, and then joined the Air Force in late 1942. He remembers that Tony LeVier used to do a slow roll on takeoff at 300 feet, and he wondered if other pilots ever tried this maneuver.

Lawless also wondered how the turbo-supercharger could turn at 26,000 rpm during preflight—which he observed on the ground from the wing of another P-38—while white-hot.

Once at Wright-Patterson Air Force Base, he remembers that Jack Towle (then chief pilot at Lockheed) and Dick Stanton (foreman of the test flight hangar) came into Wright-Patterson flying the first Constellation for "Orville Wright Day." They even took Orville Wright for a ride in the right seat the next day.

Another time at Lockheed, in an attempt to find a cause of tail flutter in the P-38, Kelly Johnson had the mechanics take a short piece of darning thread and scotch tape it to the wing surface. Then, with Kelly flying as passenger in a piggy-back P-38, he observed the air flow.

During test flights the P-38 was often subjected to high speeds which often caused the turbo wheel buckets to elongate. When this happened, Lawless explained, "We would change the turbocharger with a replacement. During this operation we would mark off the turbine wheel with chalk and mark the stationary part with chalk, and play roulette. Strictly against the rules, you know, but we got the job done!"

CHAPTER TWO

WORLD WAR II:
THE LIGHTNING STATESIDE

WORLD WAR II STATESIDE P-38s

As was true of prominent WWII American military aircraft in general, P-38s were a familiar sight in the skies all over the United States from 1942 to 1945—and, due to their unique profile, were more easily recognizable than most. But they were particularly evident in the western states, and *most* particularly on the West Coast, the 4th Air Force's domain.

Of course, the Lockheed factory that produced nearly 10,000 P-38s between Pearl Harbor and VJ Day was located in Burbank, California, a suburb of Los Angeles. Its adjacent airfield launched dozens of newly built Lightnings into the Southern California skies on an almost daily basis. Some of them were on test flights and others were being ferried from factory to military airfields around the country. They were largely flown by Lockheed test pilots and ferry pilots, the latter including Army Air Corps aviators, civilians and the quasi-military WASPs (Women Airforce Service Pilots). Many WASPs were P-38 rated, including Evelyn Sharp, the only female known to have been killed while flying a Lightning, in a crash in Pennsylvania in April of 1944.

In early and mid 1942 there were two fighter groups stationed in the L.A. area, the 1st and 82nd, both of which trained there and helped provide the air defense against an expected Japanese invasion before they departed for the British Isles and North Africa. Their temporary bases there included Glendale's Grand Central Air Terminal, Mines Field (now LAX—Los Angeles International) and the Long Beach Airport. (In late 1943 and early 1944 the P-38 equipped 474th and 479th Fighter Groups also trained in Southern California, prior to deployment to the ETO.)

Glendale continued to be a P-38 training base, and other such facilities in that general area were Van Nuys, Santa Ana, Ontario and San Diego (North Island Naval Air Station), along with Muroc and Daggett in the Mojave Desert, to the east.

The major P-38 training bases in Northern California included Santa Rosa, Santa Maria and Chico, and there were others at Ephrata and McChord in Washington State. Also, the 20th and 55th Fighter Groups trained in Washington in 1942 and 1943 before joining the 8th Air Force in England. Lightning photo recon training was centered at Peterson Field in Colorado Springs, Will Rogers Field in Oklahoma City and Coffeyville, Kansas. And later in the war Lockheed established a facility in Dallas that converted P-38s to F-5 recon Lightnings rather than continuing to produce the latter "from scratch" at Burbank. That freed up its California plant to manufacture only the fighters that were in such demand by the USAAF.

The inevitable flying accidents were rampant throughout Training

Command, resulting in hundreds of deaths and terrible injuries. P-38 pilots were no exception. Most often the victims were those who had recently won their wings and were on their final step (operational training in the aircraft they would fly in combat) before going overseas to utilize their training in the defense of their country. In other, even more tragic cases, those killed or maimed were veteran pilots who had survived their combat tours and were assigned to training duties after returning home.

An unfortunate example of the above was brought to the public's attention again 62 years after the fact. An item in Southern California's *Press-Enterprise* newspaper, dated August 16, 2005, told of munitions—.50-caliber machine gun and 20mm cannon shells—being uncovered at a construction site in Chino (whose airport is coincidentally now the home of the Planes of Fame Air Museum and two P-38s).

The lethal debris in question was part of the remains of a P-38H-1, serial #42-66693, which had crashed in what was then a tomato field on October 13, 1943. Killed in the crash was its pilot, 2nd Lt. Theodore S. Porter, age 22. Lt. Porter was a member of the 384th Fighter Squadron, 364th Fighter Group, which was then based at the nearby Ontario Army Air Base, training for eventual overseas duty with the 8th Air Force in England.

Shortly after noon that day Porter was one of a flight of four pilots scheduled to practice formation flying. He took off later than the others for some reason and "poured the coal" to his engines in an effort to catch up. Almost immediately his P-38's left engine began to malfunction, emitting puffs of smoke. According to the accident report, Lt. Porter "did a slow roll to the left, appeared to recover and then his left engine again belched smoke. He rolled over again and spun into the ground." His flight leader had called out over the radio for him to bail out, but evidently too late.

Thus died another P-38 pilot in a stateside training accident while in the service of his country, before he had a chance to test himself in combat or to live out his adult life.

THE PANAMA CANAL

Throughout WWII, considerable American military forces were stationed in the Canal Zone and in the adjoining country of Panama. (Although in Central America, the CZ, which bordered the Canal on either side, was then governed by the United States.) Their main task was the defense of the Canal, which was of tremendous strategic value, especially for the shipping of supplies and the transporting of U.S. Navy warships from the East Coast of the U.S. to the Pacific Theater and vice versa. The only actual action seen by any of those forces was spotting and attacking an occasional German submarine.

In April 1945 the five fighter squadrons of the 6th Air Force's XXVI Fighter Command in the Canal Zone and Panama—the 24th, 28th, 30th, 32nd and 51st—began converting from P-39s to P-38s. They continued to serve there until they were inactivated in October 1946.

WWII—THE LIGHTNING STATESIDE, Chapter Two photo: Ruth Dailey was one of the P-38 rated WASPs. This photo of her with P-38L-5 serial #44-25461 was taken in 1944 at Love Field in Dallas, Texas, where Dailey was assigned to the 5th Ferrying Group. (Ruth Dailey Helm)

A CROSS-COUNTRY TO REMEMBER
Jess O. Yaryan

In September 1942, while stationed at Glendale, California, as an enlisted (staff sergeant) pilot with the 96th Fighter Squadron, 82nd Fighter Group, the author participated in a cross-country flight that was typical of the type of fun you could have back then:

"The Ferry Command had been ordered to take nine P-38G aircraft from the Lockheed factory in Burbank to Middletown, Pennsylvania, for further shipment to the ETO, but discovered that no pilots in the Ferry Command had ever flown the P-38. The job was given to the 96th because we were located only three miles from the factory.

Nine of us, consisting of 1st Lt. Frank 'Baby Tank' Miller and eight staff sergeants, picked up some brand-new P-38s from the factory and headed out. Our route was to El Paso, then Dallas, Memphis, Cincinnati, Roaring Spring (Pennsylvania), and finally into Middletown.

We left Cincinnati in good order, but ran into an unexpected weather front over the mountains of Pennsylvania. Since we were operating under Ferry Command regulations, we were limited to daylight/VFR operations.

Finding ourselves on top of an overcast, with only four-channel VHF radios, we were unable to talk to anyone but our selves, as VHF was not yet installed at most ground stations. We were nine lost puppies.

Someone found a sucker hole and down we went in trail. Fortunately, we broke out in a valley—mountains on both sides hidden by

Photo: Then–Captain Jess Yaryan with a 20th FG P-38 in England, January 1944. (Yaryan)

clouds. We were really lost. We flew up and down the valley search-ing for a place to land. No luck, but we found a pass between moun-tains and flew through it—into another valley! Rats!

Suddenly, Bill Gates, one of the staff sergeants, reported that he had spotted a small strip that looked like a runway and we all scram-bled over to his search area. Sure enough, there it was. We landed okay. There was nobody there, just a shack. We parked side-by-side and got out of the birds.

After a while a Pennsylvania Highway Patrol car came by and stopped. A very surprised trooper got out and stared incredulously at the birds. 'Where are the rest of the crewmen?' he asked. We told him that this was all and could we get to the nearest town.

We were put up in an old Dutch inn—feather beds, three gigantic meals a day—all for a buck a head. We were the toast of the area. The movie house gave us free admission and the high school had a dance in our honor. We could have enlisted all the high school boys in town.

When word got out that the heroes were leaving, more than 10,000 folks came to see the event. We fired up and took off. And what did Lt. Miller decide to do? You guessed it—buzz the town! And we were all on minimum fuel. We did it anyway and a fine buzz job it was.

We made it into Middletown on the fumes and Miller comman-deered the first DC-3 airliner that landed (TWA), flashed his priority orders and we were flown back to Glendale in style.

They don't make cross-countries like that anymore!"

[Some of those 82nd FG pilots retraced their steps almost immedi-ately, sailing from the East Coast for England in October and ending up in North Africa. Yaryan, however, transferred to the 20th FG, with which he was commissioned and later flew a combat tour in England flying P-38s and P-51s. He retired from the USAF as a lieutenant colonel.]

I NEED TO LAND—REALLY.
Joe Oakley

Joe Oakley was to take a high-altitude practice mission from Will Rogers Field in Oklahoma City to San Antonio and return, without landing. Just as he was about to leave the ready room he was approached by the engineering officer, who seemed a bit embarrassed. He related that the left engine of the P-38 Oakley was to take (an H-1 model, serial #42-66642) was well overdue for an engine change, but it ran so well they hated to pull it. "Just don't let anything happen to that one," the guy said, "if you can help it." Oakley took off as planned.

"At 35,000 feet, about halfway from Austin to San Antonio, the other engine quit! No way could I get it restarted. So there I was, at 35,000 feet with one prop feathered and the other engine 'well overdue for an engine change.'

Basic Air Corps Training said: In case of engine failure, land at the nearest military base. At Austin a few minutes earlier I'd spotted a huge base, identified on the chart as Bergstrom AAB. So I headed for it and started calling them. No reply.

When I passed over the field at about 8,000 feet, still unable to make radio contact, I noticed that they had a string of C-47s shooting landings on the main runway. They were like beads in a necklace, 10 seconds apart, practicing, I found out later, for troop carrier landings. I also found out they had low and high frequency radio

32

equipment, and I had only a very high frequency radio, so no communication.

I tried to enter their pattern but failed since they flew at 90 mph and I had to maintain 150 mph for safe single-engine operation. I tried more signals as taught us in cadets: If no radio, fly in the 45-degree entry leg and waggle your wings. The tower will then communicate by Aldis Lamp. But there was no sign of life from the tower.

Next I flew under their pattern at floor level to the tower. When a man appeared on the balcony, I flew right across in front of him and pointed at my feathered prop. He waved!

At this point, wondering if the 'overdue' engine was going to hold out, I thought of dropping my drop tanks in the middle of their field to wake them up. I kept the tanks and decided to make myself obnoxious another way by going way out and making a long, low, straight-in approach.

The Gooney Bird drivers didn't like it, but a couple of them fluttered away like startled fowl. I dropped my wheels but not my flaps, thinking I might have to go around yet. Sure enough, taking advantage of the break I made, a C-47 swung onto the runway ahead of me and began to take off.

To heck with it! I opened the throttles to go around, but all it did was roll almost vertical. So I chopped the throttles and pulled up the wheel lever. Then I opened the throttles again, but no good—it just rolled again. By now I was 50 feet off the ground, at 100 mph and with no flaps—and past the center of the field!

Rather than touch down hot and roll off the end of the runway and cartwheel, I cut the throttles and leveled it out just in time to slide in like a hockey puck. When I stopped sliding, I looked up and saw nothing but fire in all directions. I left the airplane in haste.

The airdrome officer came in to visit me and said he was the guy on the tower balcony. When I hit the ceiling and asked why he didn't give me some help getting down, he said he thought I was just buzzing the place. Brother!

The next day the base C.O. interviewed me and said he was at the PX and saw me going over and around then through their field and it didn't seem to him that I was going any faster than their planes. Deliver me! I promised him I would return in a few days and fly across again—at a respectable altitude—and he'd see that the P-38 flew faster than their planes and that he would know it was me wherever he was. I never did return, but I understand that two other P-38s went down and, forgetting about the 'respectable altitude,' blew away all their flower beds!"

Back at Will Rogers AAB, his photo recon training base, one would think Oakley had had enough excitement for a while. But his squadron mates decided he needed to "jump right back in the saddle." The very next day, "My buddy Bennie from Decatur, Texas, sidled up to me and said, "Hey Oak, the hometown folks have asked me to buzz the town someday. What do you say we do it in formation?" I agree, so we got a couple of planes and headed south.

"We flew across the town at about 500 feet to get their attention. They had asked Bennie, 'How will we know it's you?' He gave the standard answer: 'You'll know!'

On our second pass, at about 200 feet, they were all out waving their newspapers, aprons, or whatever. We made our third pass just above the telephone wires. I hate to think what it was like on the ground. Anyone who has had a real buzz job by a P-38 will know what I mean!

Then we climbed to minimum legal altitude and headed home. The air was crystal clear and as smooth as a glass panel. I was on Bennie's left wing and wondering if he felt that my nerves were alright. Bennie was a very stable fellow and an excellent pilot. With the air so smooth, I decided to get in really close, just to demonstrate my calm nerves.

The '38s were as steady as if they were parked on the ground. So I moved in until my right wing tip was actually touching his left vertical stabilizer and *very* gently started scraping off his serial numbers.

I stole a glance at Bennie. He was slowly motioning me away. Having made my point, I slid out a couple of yards and glanced forward just in time to see a huge eagle coming right at me. The eagle must have seen me at the same instant. We both rolled vertical, but too late! He hit my left wing just outboard of the prop and caved in the intercooler.

The plane flew home okay but they had to pull the wing. I had to change my shorts, but the poor eagle got the worst of it."

After surviving these incidents during operational training, Joe was sent to the Pacific, where he served with the 28th Photo Recon Squadron.

A CLOSE SHAVE
Michael Koziupa

Mike Koziupa remembers well his F-4 Lightning (serial #41-2152) catching fire at 21,000 feet on a March 21, 1943, training mission out of Peterson Field in Colorado Springs, Colorado. Only 20 or 30 miles southeast of Peterson things happened fast, he says, as the plane went into a dive reaching 600 mph. Koziupa estimates that he bailed out at two or three thousand feet. He blacked out briefly but recovered only seconds before hitting the ground near the huge hole his plane had made on impact. The plane was still burning.

Koziupa walked to a ranch house about a half mile away and told the rancher he had crashed and asked him to please call Peterson. Half an hour later, an ambulance and a staff car arrived to return him to the base hospital.

Fifty years later, Koziupa was invited back to Peterson by the base museum staff. His crash site had been reopened to extricate the remaining aircraft parts for display by the museum. In August 1993 Koziupa met with Len Wallace of the Colorado Aircrash Research Group and Kai Corns, curator of the Peterson Air and Space Museum. The wreckage had been located by the rancher, who still owns the property. Koziupa was asked to help celebrate that unforgettable event and recount the fire and bailout at the base's 50th anniversary celebration.

Koziupa told how, as a 26-year-old pilot, he had climbed to 21,000 feet to photograph a section of the Rocky Mountains. While flying level at that altitude, he glanced at the left engine and saw smoke trailing. A six to eight inch hole had melted away where the engine meets the wing!

Fire poured out as well, so he shut off the fuel and the mag switch, feathered the prop and put the nose down. Building up speed, he found the controls had become useless. Compressibility had set in to the point that he couldn't move them. Black smoke came in the cockpit, and the airspeed read 600 mph. He released the top of the canopy and his harness, and tried to stand up. At that airspeed, he was immediately sucked out of the plane, only to black out. Falling head first, he recovered in time to pull the rip cord. He was headed for the fire and crash site only 500 feet away, but drifted 150 feet past it.

Koziupa completed his training at Peterson Field and was sent, via Australia, to the 26th Photo Recon Squadron at Port Moresby, New Guinea. He then flew 82 F-5 missions in the Southwest Pacific.

Photo, previous page: Capt. Michael Koziupa (26PRS) in 1944, overseas in the Southwest Pacific. (Koziupa)

ANOTHER CLOSE SHAVE
Edwin M. Weigel

Before shipping out to the Pacific in 1944, Ed Weigel trained in P-38 gunnery and tactics with the 441st Base Unit at the Van Nuys Metropolitan Airport in Southern California.

One day Ed was the last man in a four-ship flight, rat-racing through the tops of cumulus clouds over the Santa Monica Mountains. The flight leader made a sudden turn, then climbed steeply to a wingover. Weigel crammed on full power to keep up and was almost inverted at 12,000 feet when the left turbo kicked in and the right one didn't. The plane went into an inverted, nose-high flat spin. He cut power, kicked rudder and stopped the spin after a turn and a half.

Still nose high and with no forward speed, he fell into the solid cloud cover. Advancing power to pull the nose down, he hoped to gain speed and roll out. He had no visual references except the instruments. The gyro-horizon was caged. He centered the needle and ball, but the speed built up alarmingly. Disoriented, and with mountains below, he had only seconds to think. The airspeed indicator passed 575 and kept going.

Weigel realized he was pointed straight down, so he chopped the throttles and sucked back on the yoke. There was pressure on the elevator for about four inches of yoke travel, and then the wheel came back and hit him in the chest. He immediately popped it forward to where he last felt control and tried again. This time it came back about half way before flopping loose. By then he heard rivets popping. He alternately banged his head on the canopy top and was jammed back into the seat.

At 5,000 feet, still in dense clouds, he pushed the yoke forward a third time and then pulled back steadily, easing off when the elevator began to feel feathery. He shot from the base of the overcast and cleared the north slope of the mountains by only a few hundred feet.

Weigel thinks this type of experience gave rise to the tale about reversing controls.

In the Southwest Pacific, Ed served with the 9th "Flying Knights" Squadron of the 49th Fighter Group.

Photo on previous page: Ed Weigel survived his wartime training and 9FS, 49FG missions to fly on the AAF Aerobatic Team. He's seen here in June 1946, at Biggs Field, El Paso, Texas, then with the 55FS, 20FG, flying a P-51 for sheer aerobatic pleasure. (Weigel)

I SURVIVED TRAINING COMMAND
Clifford T. Wilder

In January 1943, I boarded a troop train for Jefferson Barracks, Missouri. After thirty days of basic training, we were shipped to a small training detachment in Omaha, Nebraska, where we lived in dorms at Creighton University.

Five months later we were on our way to Santa Ana, California. En route I became ill with pneumonia and ended up in a hospital at Kirtland Field in Albuquerque, New Mexico. I finally arrived at the Santa Ana Air Base on August 4th—a month off my original schedule. After preflight in Ryan PT-22s, I was sent to Taft Field in Lemoore, California, then Williams Field, Arizona, with that sweet AT-6. It was there that I saw the P-38 for the first time.

A part of the demonstration by [Lockheed test pilots] Milo Burcham or Tony LeVier (I can't recall which) at Williams was a slow roll on the deck. Halfway through the roll he came lower, clearing the runway by just a few feet! After he landed he gave us a lecture on the '38, and told us that his foot slipped off the rudder during the roll. He said that anyone with less experience would have crashed. From that day on I decided that if I ever flew P-38s in combat, I would never do a victory roll on the deck!

I graduated on May 23, 1944. From Williams I went to Ajo, Arizona, for gunnery and then to [training in] fighters at Victorville, California—ten days in some war-weary P-39s. Their throttles had been wired to prevent full throttle.

Victorville was also a base for navigators, and they flew in Lockheed Lodestars. There was a double runway. They used the left with a base leg, etc., and we used the right with a 360° approach.

So one day I'm coming in and pull up and around, and at about 250° I received from ground control (in a jeep): "P-39, you're coming onto LEFT runway!" I pushed the throttle through the wire and racked it around to the right runway and, at full throttle, leveled at about five feet off the ground. The radio operator was running away from his jeep like his pants were on fire. I slowly eased back on the throttle and the stick, and flew straight ahead for about two minutes, as my knees were knocking on the control shaft.

I survived!

It was then back to Taft Field, this time to a pool awaiting assignment to P-38 transition. After three months in that pool, with some time in a BT-13, I got a 23-day leave. I guess they got tired of seeing us around Lemoore.

In November I found myself at Ontario Army Air Field, California. I hunched in behind my instructor where the radio normally is and experienced being airborne in a P-38. What a thrill! Even more so when I took one up SOLO!

Truly, flying the P-38 was the greatest. However, I soon learned how true was the saying, "There are no old, bold pilots."

We used to go east to fly over desert areas, and coming back sometimes we would go down on the deck and then up and over the mountains. I was on a couple of flights when the instructor flew up the mountain between peaks. I was usually flying wing on the instructor and was always 15 or 20 feet higher.

After one flight, as we were returning to base, the instructor started to turn to the left and then dropped the right wing and turned into me. I popped the stick to the right and forward. It was a near miss. I came back into position in the flight about 100 feet off his wing. He waggled his wings two or three times, but I didn't tighten up.

When we came down and were back in the ready room, he asked me why I didn't tighten up the formation when he signaled me. I told him that after he turned away from me and then reversed right into me, I didn't ever want to fly his wing again. I also told him that some day, if he continued to fly like that, he was going to take one of us down with him.

I survived!

P-38s lined up on the ramp among rows of citrus trees at Ontario. (Wilder)

At a later date, after a high-altitude training flight, our instructor told us to break up and play. So, I wound up doing a few rolls, several to each side. As I was on my back, WHAM—I was in an inverted spin! I tried to recover but had no control. I called out, "May Day!"

Then I realized I was at 17,000 feet and remembered that one of the test pilots had told us that the '38 would fly itself. So I let go of the stick and took my feet off the rudders. After a few seconds I thought I sensed that the plane felt different, took the stick and felt a positive pressure. I brought it out of the spin and rolled it upright.

As I'm sitting there, my knees knocking the stick again, I saw my instructor pop up off my right wing. His voice came in with, "Wilder, you lost your nose wheel door." To top this off, when we were back on the ground, we heard that a pilot from a different flight had had an unusual experience. He had felt a vibration in flight and on landing noticed a nick in his propeller. My instructor and I just looked at each other. Who knows?

I survived!

[Cliff was subsequently assigned to the Southwest Pacific, where he flew P-38s with the 36th Fighter Squadron, 8th Fighter Group. His last flight in a Lightning was on April 12, 1946, while on occupation duty in Japan—"a two-and-a-half-hour surveillance flight alone. I wrung it out and before landing I did five slow rolls in succession at 10,000 feet. Those were MY victory rolls. I had survived World War II and Training Command!"]

I WAS A LIGHTNING CREW CHIEF
William Nickloff

I worked on P-38s at Lockheed beginning in October 1941. I as-sembled the fuselage and tail boom assemblies. I also worked on the final assembly line. I was involved with a conversion of some P-322s, which were to have been sent to the British. I had to change some rigging to conform to our format.

I enlisted in the Air Corps on October 31, 1942, and was sent to Fort MacArthur [California]. After a one-night stay there for shots and uniforms, we left the following morning by rail on a long train heading for Florida. I was dropped off, with many others, in Arizona and sent to Williams Field, a hot and dusty place at that time.

I had passed exams and had been offered a petty officer rate in the Navy; however, my wife thought that the Navy uniform, with the thirteen-button tummy flap, looked "silly," so then I checked with the Army recruiter, who promised: "With your aircraft background and your academic record you will go to tech school, make sergeant, get flight skins and, since you're married, quarters and rations, and in no time be making more money than now." However, since I came from Lockheed and knew all about P-38s, I really had no need to go to the Lockheed tech school (their words, not mine). I fell for it!

I was assigned to the 535th Fighter Squadron. My Commanding Officer was Captain Fred Baxa. All the P-322s were covered and iso-lated until the lucky guys came back from the Lockheed training clas-ses. They came back with rates. I remained Private Nickloff.

I was athletically able and joined three other members of our squadron as a commando course team representing the 535th. We competed on a hot summer day against all the other squadrons on the post. Our team won, and we all got ten-day leaves. I was also named "Soldier of the Week" and made corporal.

I once saw an accident when a cadet rolled his plane over on the runway and was killed. We also had a major who killed an engine to practice single-engine operation—and feathered the wrong engine! I was there when Tony LeVier demonstrated the P-38's capabilities, like feathering and banking on a dead engine, flap-down emergency demonstrations or killing both engines for a dead-stick landing, then rolling up to the cadets, turning in and braking for a bow! Nice show!

I moved around a lot in the Training Command; however, as the war was near the end I returned to Williams Field. We also had AT-6s for advanced training, and I frequently had to fly out into the de-sert with our squadron lieutenant to salvage/repair some ground loop accidents on remote landing strips.

I was a crew chief on several planes and had to arrive early to drain sumps and preflight the planes for the cadets. I got to be pretty good at making mag checks and "blowing out the carbon." I also spent many hours changing plugs on hot engines, with rags around my arms for protection.

I was at Williams when they started destroying the P-38s. They would hoist them up, retract the gear, lower the planes to the ground, roll over them with large tractors, then cut them up with torches!

After the war ended I returned to Lockheed and worked all over the plant: Connies, Electras, F-80s, T-33s, engineering flight test, F-94s, Kelly Johnson, Tony LeVier, Fish Salmon—some of the greatest! I worked on the first C-130, the F-104, the U-2, the SR-71 and the L-1011. Forty-eight wonderful years there; it was so much fun that I would have paid to do the job (not quite!).

Then-Corporal Bill Nickloff in the cockpit of one of the P-38s he serviced at Williams Field in 1943. (Nickloff)

REMEMBERING DICK BONG
Dick Parker

I remember a day in June 1944. I was at Rankin Aeronautical Academy outside Tulare, California, and it was hotter than the gates of hell. We Primary flying "gadgets," as some people called us, were standing Saturday morning parade and chomping at the bit to get off base and into Tulare or one of the other towns in the vicinity, find a cool bar and sip a few beers before going to the local USO for the Saturday night dance.

Our backs were turned away from the flight line, which consisted of a blacktop tarmac with eight individual runways divided by painted stripes, much the same as our highways are today. All of a sudden, the rigid, formal, military-type proceedings of the parade came to a screeching halt when the adjutant, who was directing the proceedings from the center of the parade grounds, abandoned all military protocol when he turned to his right, pointed with his right arm extended and yelled at the top of his voice for all to hear: "Bong!"

Yes, Major Richard Ira Bong was in the process of making a very low pass from the south across our airfield in his brand-new P-38 with Marge's picture on its nose. Everybody broke ranks and turned in the direction which our illustrious adjutant was pointing, to see what, exactly, he was pointing at. You see, the P-38 doesn't make much noise, and he was coming at us so fast and low that no one heard him. At midfield the major reefed it in and pulled it straight up until he was almost out of sight. As he pulled it over on his back and started to descend, upside down, the gear came out—and I suppose the dive flaps did also—and he proceeded to dive straight down and land out of this rectangular loop.

What a spectacular entrance! Needless to say, the parade ended right there, and we cadets were told to assemble in the Quadrangle. Tradition had it that no cadet could enter the Quadrangle without having soloed, but I guess they overlooked that little item for this occasion. Major Bong, a graduate of this same Primary school, was escorted to the platform, and he talked to us cadets, kind of like a father to his sons, for about an hour. (He was just 23 years old himself!) He explained how lousy he was at aerial gunnery and how he had to drive right up behind a Jap to be able to hit him. He claimed that was one of the reasons he was back in the States, to take a gunnery course at Matagorda, Texas. Of course, no one believed him on that score.

After the football-like pep talk, he was escorted away by the brass and we were free to leave the base for the weekend. I think we all had some sense of what the major had accomplished in the Southwest Pacific and recognized that he certainly was a national hero;

44

however, none of us realized at that time how much of a hero he was still to become.

Ever since that day at Tulare, Dick Bong has been one of my idols. I've read almost everything that has been written about him, have expounded on his exploits to many people while visiting the USAF Museum in Dayton, and have several models of his P-38 with his wife Marge's picture and other memorabilia displayed in my home.

It was a really sad day when I read of his demise while test hopping a Lockheed P-80 in Burbank. I am really disturbed by the lack of knowledge the younger generations have regarding the history of the greatest event to take place in the Twentieth Century—World War II. The "Blood, Sweat and Tears" our generation experienced and the unbelievable amount of guts and determination so many of us demonstrated above and beyond the call, I shall never forget.

[The author graduated with Class 44-K at Stockton, California, and became a B-29 pilot, but the war ended just before he was to be sent to the Pacific.]

June 1944: Major Bong and Major General Robert W. Harper, then assistant chief of air staff for training at USAAF headquarters, check out a P-38 at an unidentified stateside training base. During his three-month furlough, Bong visited air bases, sold war bonds and did, indeed, complete a gunnery course at Matagorda. (USAF)

ON THE LINE: FEMALE P-38 MECHANICS
Steve Blake

Most of our readers know about the Women Airforce Service Pilots (WASP) who flew P-38s during WWII, and of the many women who toiled on the P-38 assembly lines at Lockheed. But did you know that quite a few other females maintained Lightnings in the field, after the planes left Lockheed? P-38 Association member Lenora (Collins) Albericci of Sacramento, California, knows, because she was one of them—as were her three sisters, Caroline, Doris and Violet.

The Collins sisters were among many women (civilians) who worked at the Sacramento Army Air Depot at McClellan Field during the war, repairing and overhauling P-38s. According to a contemporary newspaper account, beginning in December 1942, "They all took mechanic learner courses in aerial repair at depot post schools before being transferred to actual on the job assignments in the shops." Another reported that, "So readily did they learn the rudiments of aero repair in the classroom, that at the completion of their course they were sent directly to the aircraft maintenance shops as general mechanics helpers." The former article went on to describe one of their first jobs at the depot:

"When a certain P-38 takes to the skies from the Sacramento Air Depot in the very near future, many eyes will be upon it—for many reasons. An airplane which has moved from last place up to near the front in the P-38 rehabilitation line of engineering shops is being overhauled, assembled and modernized by women—in the first all woman venture of its kind on the West Coast.

The women, all mechanic learners, work around the clock on all three shifts, under the supervision of men flight leaders, crew chiefs and assistant crew chiefs. The men give the orders, see that they are carried out and help when they are needed—but the women do the actual work.

Skeptical males in the adjacent engineering sections have dubbed the plane 'Power Puff Special' and have inscribed 'Lady Be Good,' 'No Man's Land' and other feminine nicknames on the craft's nose. These same men, however, have stood aside respectfully as the plane has moved steadily up the production line to its final goal—the head of the line and out on the runway for its trial flight.

Climbing in, over, under and on top of the ship like a swarm of bees, the women are doing everything necessary to modernize an airplane—removal and installation of fairings, cowling and inspection plates; changing and servicing motors, fitting manifolds, brackets, controls, propellers and other work incidental to engine installation; removing parts, replacing parts, adding new ones; installing and rigging control surfaces and cables; installing seats, batteries, tanks, air heater ducts and other miscellaneous jobs ordinarily done by men."

"It is no wonder, then, that many eyes will follow this P-38 on its next and important flight—the eyes of the shop officers, group supervisors, flight leaders, crew chiefs and assistants, the women themselves—and the doubting Thomases who have watched with skepticism the plane's progress.

But no matter what their inward thoughts, the eyes of all will hold praise and admiration for these women who have taken leave of absence from their homes, businesses and former occupations, to enter a field entirely new to them, to help 'Keep 'em Flying' at the Sacramento Air Depot."

Doris, Lenora and Caroline at one point took a temporary break from the P-38 overhaul line at McClellan to instruct "rigging at technical schools (a job few men can assay)." These were part of the depot's then-new "mechanic learner training center."

Kudos to Lenora, her sisters and the other women who built, repaired and maintained P-38s during WWII, thereby furnishing "outstanding proof that women [could] be highly successful in mechanical work regardless of their former backgrounds."

This publicity photo shows the four Collins sisters working on an Allison engine at McClellan Field in 1943. Left to right: Violet (Mrs. Houghton), Doris, Lenora and Caroline (Mrs. Williams). Violet's husband was in the Army and Caroline's also worked at the Sacramento Air Depot. (Albericci)

MEMORIES OF EPHRATA
Charles C. Daugherty

I was an "instant" P-38 pilot at Ephrata in late 1944. Ephrata was on the Great Northern Railroad, in the Washington desert about halfway between Wenatchee and Spokane and about 30 miles south of the Grand Coulee Dam.

While at Ephrata, my fiancée, Mary Lou Peek of Washington, Indiana, came all the way out there by rail to visit me. (We were married in November 1945, after I returned from overseas.)

I got to Ephrata by way of Moore Field, Mission, Texas, after completing advanced single-engine (AT-6) training there with Class 44-E, and of Victorville, California, with transition fighter training in the Bell P-39 Airacobra.

The P-39 had a wingspan of 32 feet and was powered by an Allison single-speed, single-stage, supercharged V-1710 engine that was located behind the pilot. It wasn't effective above 10,000 feet. The propeller was a temperamental Curtiss Electric with circuit breakers that could go out at high rpm's. When landing, you were warned not to put the flaps down until after making the final turn on the approach. In flight you might think you were turning, but the needle would be on one side of the gyro flight indicator and the ball on the other side. You weren't turning—you were sliding forward! It truly was a flying rock.

After reporting to Ephrata in the fall of 1944, we flew the Bell P-63 Kingcobra, which was a "souped-up" P-39 with all the deficiencies corrected. It was a beautifully performing aircraft. The wingspan had been increased to 37 feet, and it was powered by an improved two-speed, two-stage, supercharged Allison V-1710 (still located behind the pilot) that was effective up to 30,000 feet. It had toggle switch engine controls, a synchronized prop and throttle and the latest Hamilton Hydromatic propeller, which caused no problems. The P-63 was every bit the equal of the P-51 and a joy to fly!

The base at Ephrata had a fine basketball team with regular league play at the base gym. The physical training instructor, who was a starter on the team, was Sergeant John Agar, a good friend and a very good basketball player. His living quarters were at the gym, and one day I was visiting him in his room when I noticed a large framed photo of movie star Shirley Temple. I asked John if he knew her, and he replied, "Yes, she's my girlfriend." Later I read in the newspaper that they were married.

In November all of our P-63s were flown to Great Falls, Montana. Russian pilots picked them up there and flew them to Russia via Alaska. A few days later, after a brief ground school and a "piggyback" ride, we single-engine pilots, with no prior multi-engine flying time, became instant P-38 pilots!

It really wasn't as bad as it sounds because the P-38J, with its two improved V-1710 engines and counter-rotating propellers, was far more stable, especially in aerobatics and stalls, than the single-engine fighter. It was a fine airplane, and if you kept your airspeed above 300 mph it was the equal of—if not superior to—any other aircraft you might encounter.

One cold morning in December we reported down to the flight line before sunup for an early morning flight exercise. It was pitch dark and cold, and snow was piled high along the runways. We took off in formation, four abreast, and all you could see were red wing lights of the other planes in the formation.

We took off down the runway at full throttle, and shortly after becoming airborne and raising my wheels, I seemed to be losing power and falling behind the other planes. I looked at both the right and left supercharger impellers, which sat on the top of the engine nacelles, and they were bright red and coughing black smoke. I then glanced at the oil temperature gauges, and the heat indicators were in the deep red! Quickly and without thinking, I flipped the toggle switches controlling the oil radiator shutters, which were on "Closed," to "Open." The oil temperatures quickly returned to normal, the engines regained power, and I was able to catch up to and rejoin the flight. The engines had been an instant away from blowing up!

In retrospect, the crew chief who had preflighted the engines had apparently closed the oil radiator shutters to get some heat in the cockpit that cold morning and neglected to reopen them. However, the bottom line was that I neglected to check them myself. During the entire war this had to have been my closest call—an instant away from either heaven or hell!

Later in December we were sent by rail down to Daggett, California, in the Mojave Desert, for aerial gunnery exercises. Upon our return to Ephrata we found that our officers' club had burned down, and nothing was saved but the beer. The outside windowsills in our barracks were lined with frozen beer bottles.

Shortly thereafter we were sent to Redmond, Oregon, where we flew P-38s out of an abandoned CCC camp, and then to Salinas, California for overseas processing. I ended up in Italy in early April 1945, assigned to the 14th Fighter Group (49th Fighter Squadron).

CHAPTER THREE

PACIFIC THEATER
OF
OPERATIONS

LIGHTNINGS IN THE PACIFIC THEATER OF OPERATIONS

5th AIR FORCE (SOUTHWEST PACIFIC)

The first combat mission flown by a P-38 in the Southwest Pacific—actually the first by a Lightning anywhere—was on April 16, 1942. It was an F-4 photo recon aircraft of the 8th Photo Reconnaissance Squadron, flying the unit's initial sortie over New Guinea. Later that year three USAAF F-4s were loaned to the Royal Australian Air Force's 1 Photo Reconnaissance Unit (PRU), which utilized them very effectively during the early New Guinea campaign. These were among the very few Lightnings to see action during the war in the colors of a foreign air force.

It would be six months before another Lightning unit became operational with the 5th Air Force in New Guinea, after it was decided to re-equip three of its fighter squadrons with P-38s. Instead of doing so to one whole three-squadron group, a single squadron from each group (the 8th, 35th and 49th) was chosen for that process. They were the 80th, 39th and 9th Fighter Squadrons, respectively.

The first to see action with its new Lightnings was the 39th Sq., in October. Next was the 9th, in January 1943, and finally the 80th, in March. The P-38 was a huge improvement over their old P-39s and P-40s, and the Lightning pilots began to run up big scores against the JAAF and JNAF.

As more P-38s became available the decision was made to activate a brand-new group in Australia. The 475th Fighter Group, comprised of the 431st, 432nd and 433rd Squadrons, was formed there in May 1943 and became operational in New Guinea in August. Despite its late start, the 475th was to become *the* highest scoring P-38 group, with 552 confirmed kills. It was also the only fighter group in the Pacific and CBI to operate the P-38 solely.

The six Lightning squadrons scored heavily during the campaigns along the north coast of New Guinea in late 1943 and early 1944, and against the Japanese "fortress" at Rabaul on New Britain in October and November.

Much to the chagrin of its pilots, the 9th FS was forced to convert to P-47s for a few months (November 1943 to April 1944) due to a temporary shortage of P-38s. The 39th FS also switched to Thunderbolts when the 9th did, along with the whole 35th FG, but in its case it did not get its P-38s back.

The 6th Photo Recon Group arrived in-theater at the end of 1943 with its F-5s, and the 9th PRS joined its two original squadrons, the 25th and 26th.

By the spring of 1944 the 5th AF's top P-38 aces were becoming famous in the press back home, particularly Dick Bong of the 9th FS and Tommy Lynch of the 39th FS. Both men were reassigned to 5th Fighter Command HQ when their squadrons lost their Lightnings and began flying "freelance" P-38 missions together. Lt. Col. Lynch had 20 kills to his credit when he was KIA by antiaircraft fire on March 9, 1944. Major Bong had 28 when he completed his first combat tour the following month. As of May, Major Tommy McGuire of the 431st FS had 18 kills to his credit, as did Capt. Jay T. Robbins in the 80th.

The P-38 was also being used in the 5th AF as an interim night fighter. Detachment A of the 6th Night Fighter Squadron actually installed radar sets and created spaces for their operators in two of its P-38Gs, although no aerial claims were made by them. The 6th NFS was replaced by the 418th NFS at the end of 1943, and the latter continued to utilize P-38s, retaining several of them even after converting to the new P-61 Black Widow in mid-1944. Major Carroll Smith shot down a Val dive bomber with his P-38 (sans onboard radar) during a dusk fighter sweep on January 13, 1944. He went on to score another two kills plus a probable with Lightnings near Morotai Island in November of that year, and added four more victories while flying P-61s.

As of March 1944, and for the rest of the war, the 8th FG became an all-Lightning unit when its 35th and 36th Squadrons finally switched from P-40s and P-47s to P-38s. The 49th FG made the same change in September, its 7th and 8th Squadrons finally trading in their old Warhawks for Lightnings. So as of that month the 5th AF had three full P-38 groups.

With the de facto end of the New Guinea campaign by the late spring of 1944, V Fighter Command turned its attention to the north and west. All three of its P-38 groups moved to Biak Island off the coast of New Guinea in June and July, and the 8th Group was sent to Morotai Island, farther west off the north coast of Halmahera, in September. These bases put them in range of Japanese targets in the Dutch East Indies, in the southern Philippines and on Borneo, but they were really just biding their time before the really big show began—the re-conquest of the Philippines.

So it was that shortly after Gen. MacArthur's forces stormed ashore on Leyte in the Philippines in October, they were joined there by the P-38s of the 49th and 475th Fighter Groups to provide much-needed air defense. During the next three months these two groups racked up dozens of kills over Leyte and Luzon. (The 8th FG, now based just to the south on Mindoro, also managed to add a considerable number of victories to its score.)

Here some of the 5th AF's top aces had their final glory days. Dick Bong ran his score up to an even forty before he was awarded the Medal of Honor and sent home in December. Tommy McGuire continued to score after his rival Bong left and had reached 38 before he was KIA on January 7, 1945 (he was awarded a posthumous Medal of Honor). Col. Charles MacDonald, C.O. of the 475th, scored 14 victories from November 1944 to February 1945, bringing his total to 27, while Jerry Johnson, 49th FG Deputy C.O., shot down 10 Japanese planes over the Philippines plus a Tojo near Hong Kong in April 1945, for a total of 22.

It was during the Philippines campaign that the last night victory by a P-38 was scored, by the 547th NFS, which had joined the 5th AF in September. The 547th, in addition to its P-61s, had two P-38J-20s equipped with sophisticated air-to-air radar sets that were operated by the pilot. With one of them Lt. Frank Raidt shot down a Japanese Tess transport plane over Luzon on the night of March 9, 1945.

It was also in March that its last Lightning unit joined the 5th Air Force, when the F-5-equipped 36th PRS was assigned to the 6th PRG.

The 5th Air Force P-38s' next big show was to have been the invasion of Japan, but thanks to a couple of strategically placed atomic bombs, that did not happen. The 8th and 475th Groups moved to Ie Shima, off the coast of Okinawa, a week before VJ Day, in preparation for the missions over Japan, and the 49th was in the process of moving to Okinawa proper. Instead, all three groups would participate in the peaceful occupation of their former enemy's country. (Incidentally, a 49th FG Lighting was the first Allied aircraft to land in Japan after the surrender on August 15.)

Nowhere else was the P-38 more successful than in the Southwest Pacific. 5th Air Force Lightnings were credited with shooting down 1,364 Japanese aircraft, and that was only part of the damage they did to the Empire.

7th AIR FORCE (CENTRAL PACIFIC)

The 7th Air Force's domain was the vast stretches of the Central Pacific, from Hawaii eventually all the way to Okinawa. Its only P-38 fighter unit was the 21st Fighter Group, which never saw combat with its Lightnings. It switched to P-51s in late 1944 before moving to Iwo Jima early the next year to fly long-range B-29 escort missions to Japan. However, some of its P-38s did end up seeing considerable action.

As soon as an airfield was available on Saipan in the Marianas after its invasion by U.S. forces in June 1944, the 318th FG (19th, 73rd and 333rd Fighter Squadrons) and its P-47s moved there to provide fighter-bomber support for the ground troops and to defend the islands against Japanese air raids. Once the Marianas had been secured there wasn't much for the Thunderbolt pilots to do other

This 28th PRS F-5B, J/"Junior," serial #42-68226, was photographed at Yontan Airfield on Okinawa on July 10, 1945 (USAF)

than oppose the very infrequent air raids, as their planes didn't have the range to fly offensive missions to Japanese-held islands farther west. So in November 1944 it was arranged to transfer three dozen former 21st FG P-38s from Hawaii to the 318th in the Marianas. For the next several months the group's Lightnings escorted USAAF bombers and recon F-5s to important targets such as Truk and Iwo Jima. In the course of those missions its pilots managed to shoot down 23 Japanese planes. (The 318th re-equipped with later model P-47s before moving to Okinawa in April 1945.)

The only other 7th AF Lightning unit to see action was the 28th Photographic Reconnaissance Squadron, which did yeoman work throughout the Central Pacific. Among its most important missions were those taking pre-invasion photos of Iwo Jima, sometimes escorted by P-38s of the 318th FG.

The 41st PRS was also assigned to the 7th Air Force late in the war, and it was just about to fly its first F-5 mission from Iwo Jima when the war ended.

11th AIR FORCE (ALASKA AND THE ALEUTIAN ISLANDS)

Ironically, the first air victory scored by a P-38 took place in one of the most remote and obscure American combat theaters of World

War II: Alaska's Aleutian Islands. On August 4, 1942, Lieutenants Ken Ambrose and Stan Long of the 54th Fighter Squadron each shot down a Kawanishi flying boat near Atka Island. (The Japanese had invaded and captured the westernmost Aleutians—the most important of which were Kiska and Attu—in early June.)

Of the 39 air victories scored in the Aleutians by USAAF fighter pilots (plus one by a Royal Canadian Air Force P-40), 19 were claimed by P-38 pilots of the 54th FS. The last were four Betty bombers (plus one probable) over Attu on May 23, 1943. That was the month the Allied reinvasion of the western Aleutians began, which campaign concluded with the evacuation of the remaining Japanese forces in August. The 11th AF's top-scoring P-38 pilot was Capt. George Laven, Jr., with three victories (he added another one later with the 5th Air Force).

There were also a handful of F-5s attached to the 54th FS which performed vital photo reconnaissance duties.

After the Japanese left, the main enemy of the American fliers stationed in that inhospitable island chain was the terrible weather—strong winds, fog and freezing cold being the norm. Other than a P-

Lt. Herbert Hasenfus is about to take off on a mission in P-38 #93 of the 54th FS in the Aleutians sometime in late 1942 or early '43. (USAF)

39 unit that was TDY there during the latter half of 1942, the 343rd FG, which was activated in September of that year, was the only fighter group in Alaska until after the end of the war. (Prior to then its squadrons had been assigned to the 28th Composite Group). The 343rd Group's other three squadrons in addition to the 54th, the 11th, 18th and 344th, which had been flying P-40s and P-39s, began converting to P-38s in 1943, which process was completed the following year.

13th AIR FORCE (SOUTH AND SOUTHWEST PACIFIC)

The landings on Guadalcanal Island in the Solomons on August 7, 1942, were the beginning of the first major ground offensive by U.S. forces in World War II. The first USAAF aircraft, Bell P-39s of the 67th Fighter Squadron, arrived there two weeks later. At the end of September the 67th was split to create a new squadron, the 339th, which was chosen to be the first in the South Pacific to be equipped with P-38s. It re-entered combat with them in mid-November after relinquishing its P-39s. The 339th was to become by far the most successful P-38 squadron in the 13th Air Force, to which all the USAAF units in the Solomons were assigned when it was activated on New Caledonia in January 1943.

New Caledonia was the official "rear area" for the 13th AF, where aircrew training was done, units were re-equipped with new aircraft and pilots were rested. The 13th's units were originally part of what was called the "Cactus Air Force" on Guadalcanal. This was a multi-service, multi-national (USN, USMC, USAAF and New Zealand Royal Air Force) organization that was, and continued to be throughout the Solomons campaign, under the overall command of the Navy with the new, official name COMAIRSOLS (Command Air Solomons).

The six fighter squadrons of the 13th AF (the 12th, 44th, 67th, 68th, 70th and 339th) alternated brief tours on Guadalcanal from New Caledonia. By early 1943 there were enough P-38s available to allow the 12th and 70th Squadrons to fly missions in Lightnings as well as P-39s.

It was also in January 1943 that a vital Lightning photo recon squadron, the 17th, arrived on Guadalcanal.

The 339th FS continued to be at the forefront of the USAAF air action in the Solomons, running up a big score against the Japanese. Its C.O., Major John W. Mitchell, led four flights of pilots from the 12th, 70th and 339th Squadrons on what was indisputably the P-38's most famous mission, the Yamamoto intercept on April 18, 1943. It is still in dispute whether it was Tom Lanphier of the 70th FS or Rex Barber of the 339th who actually shot the admiral down (or whether they in fact shared the victory), though most informed sources lean strongly toward Barber.

The 339th was also successful in helping to defend Guadalcanal against some very large air raids in the spring and early summer of 1943. On June 16, 1943, Lt. Murray Shubin destroyed five enemy planes during such a mission to become an "ace in a day." His eventual total was eleven.

John Mitchell was another top 13th AF ace. He also had the distinction of scoring the P-38's first victory at night, in the early morning of January 29, 1943, when he took off from the 'Canal to help put a stop to the almost nightly nuisance raids and shot down a Betty bomber. This was his seventh of an eventual eight victories. Major Lou Kittel, C.O. of the 70th FS, did Mitchell one better by downing two Bettys on the night of May 19.

The P-38 did additional good work in the Solomons in its unofficial role as a night fighter. Detachment B of the 6th Night Fighter Squadron arrived on Guadalcanal in February with its P-70 radar-equipped night fighters. These planes' performance was not up to the task, however, so the unit borrowed some P-38s from the day fighter squadrons. By the time it was replaced by the 419th NFS in November, the 6th NFS' pilots had scored seven confirmed kills with their Lightnings. The top-scoring 13th AF P-38 night fighter pilot was Lt. Henry Meigs, with three victories, to which he added another three later with the 339th FS on daylight missions.

As 1943 progressed, the Allies slowly moved up the Solomon Islands chain, capturing some islands of strategic value and bypassing others. The P-38 was a big factor in these actions because of its high-altitude performance and long range. By December COMAIR-SOLS had established fighter bases close enough to the Japanese "fortress" at Rabaul on New Britain Island to escort the bombers all the way there and back. Thus commenced some of the biggest battles of the South Pacific air war, which lasted until the Japanese finally withdrew their air forces at Rabaul in mid-February 1944 and it was surrounded and bypassed by the Allies.

At this time there were just two P-38 squadrons in the 13th AF, the 44th and the 339th, the former having recently switched to Lightnings from its old P-40s. These two units, mostly flying top cover, scored many victories over Rabaul but also suffered heavy losses there.

The Solomons campaign was effectively over by April 1944. The top aces of XIII Fighter Command were Capt. Bill Harris of the 339th FS with 15 victories and Major Bob Westbrook and Capt. Cotesworth ("C.B.") Head of the 44th FS with 15 and 14, respectively. Westbrook had scored seven of his with P-40s, while Head added to his eight Warhawk victories six with the P-38 during the Rabaul missions before he was KIA on January 18, 1944.

A P-38G of the 339th Fighter Squadron on Guadalcanal in April 1943. (USAF)

The 13th AF's other four fighter squadrons began converting to P-38s that spring, and by July the process was complete. They were organized as follows: The 12th, 44th and 70th Fighter Squadrons comprised the 18th Fighter Group, and the 347th FG was made up of the 67th, 68th and 339th Squadrons.

There was a huge organizational change for the 13th Air Force at this time. It was moved from the South Pacific and USN command to the Southwest Pacific as part of the new Far East Air Force (FEAF), comprised of it and the much larger and more famous 5th Air Force, under the overall command of longtime 5th AF C.O. (and Southwest Pacific Theater Commander Gen. Douglas MacArthur favorite) Gen. George Kenney. It was the perception of 13th AF veterans that during the last year of the war the 5th had favored child status while the 13th was the proverbial stepchild.

In any event, the 13th's two fighter groups moved to Sansapor, in western New Guinea, in August 1944, the 347th moving again to the nearby island of Middleburg the following month.

XIII Fighter Command's two top aces had begun their second combat tours. Lt. Col. Bill Harris was Deputy C.O. of the 18th FG, while Lt. Col. Bob Westbrook held that position in the 347th FG. Although enemy air opposition was sparse, Westbrook managed to score five more victories, bringing his total to 20, before he was killed by antiaircraft fire on November 22. Harris scored one more kill for a total of 16.

From New Guinea the two fighter groups began flying "ultra-long" eight-to-twelve-hour missions to targets in Borneo and the southern Philippines.

Like the 17th PRS, the 419th NFS had moved west with the day fighter units, and although it had been re-equipped with the new P-61 Black Widow, it still retained a couple of P-38s. One of the latter shot down a Betty bomber near Middleburg on December 30, 1944— the last night victory by a 13th AF P-38. (The 550th NFS, which became operational with the 13th that month, also had a couple of P-38s in its inventory in addition to its P-61s, but didn't score any victories with either type.)

The supposed higher-command prejudice against the 13th AF and in favor of the 5th became apparent to the men of the former at the time of the invasion of the Philippines. The only FEAF fighter groups to see action on Leyte and Luzon from October 1944 to January 1945, during which they shot down dozens of Japanese aircraft, were those of V Fighter Command, while XIII Fighter Command's languished in New Guinea. Things seemed to be changing for the better when the 18th FG was sent to Lingayen in northern Luzon in January. However, those orders were rescinded less than two months later and it moved instead to the "dusty, windy, dirty island of Mindoro" in the southern Philippines.

The 347th FG had been sent to Mindoro in February but moved to nearby Palawan Island the following month. There, both P-38 groups languished in that backwater area until VJ Day, although they did fly a few rather eventful ultra-long-range missions across the South China Sea to French Indochina.

In nearly three years of combat, the 13th AF's P-38 pilots were credited with destroying 302 enemy aircraft in the air.

Chapter Three intro photo: 5th Air force, 475th Fighter Group P-38s at one of the unit's Philippine bases in late 1944 or 1945. Note their 300-gallon and 165-gallon drop tanks. (USAF)

G.I. ANNIE AND THE 80TH FS HEADHUNTERS
Steve Blake

In early February 1943, the 5th Air Force's 80th Fighter Squadron (8th Fighter Group) moved temporarily to Mareeba, Australia, from Port Moresby, New Guinea, where it had been in combat flying Bell P-39 Airacobras for six months. The purpose was to re-equip the squadron with Lightnings. A couple dozen new P-38Fs and Gs were assigned, including G-15 serial #43-2386, which was given the name *G.I. Annie.*

The 80th FS, soon to be famous in the Southwest Pacific as the "Headhunters" Squadron, was back at Port Moresby with its new P-38s by late March. Its major combat debut with the Lightning took place on May 21, near Salamaua. During a swirling dogfight, 80th Squadron pilots claimed six enemy fighters destroyed and five probably destroyed. This was also *G.I. Annie's* combat debut; 2nd Lt. John Jones, her semi-regular pilot, shot down a "Hap," a version of the Zero/Zeke. This was the first of Jones' eight confirmed and two probable victories.

Annie was in action again on June 21. Although it hasn't been determined who was flying her, it *is* known that she scored that day. Exactly one month later, with now-1st Lt. Jones as her pilot again, this dynamic duo shot down two Zekes over Bogadjim. On the August 21 mission *Annie* was flown by 2nd Lt. Cyril Homer. During a huge air battle over Wewak, Homer shot down two Zekes and a Tony (his first confirmed victories) and damaged a twin-engine fighter. "Cy" Homer, later a major, took command of the 80th FS in October 1944 and by the war's end had run up a score of fifteen confirmed, five probables and four damaged.

G.I. Annie was flown by quite a number of 80th Squadron pilots. On September 2, 1943, it was 2nd Lt. Ken Ladd, who shot down a Dinah reconnaissance plane south of Madang with her. This was Ladd's second confirmed kill; his total was 12-2-1 by the time he was killed in action over Balikpapen, Borneo, in October 1944, while flying with the 8th Group's 36th Fighter Squadron.

Annie's last victory was scored by Capt. James R. Wilson, who downed a Hap over Rabaul on October 12; this was also Wilson's third and final victory. It was during another bomber escort mission to Rabaul, on November 7, that *Annie* came to her premature end. She was being flown that day by a new replacement pilot, Flight Officer Robert M. Gentile. According to the subsequent Missing Aircrew Report:

"Pilot snafued after reaching Wide Bay, New Britain [and] asked for escort, so element leader, 1st Lt. Leland B. Blair, went along to escort airplane back to Kiriwina [Island]. Pilot flew on element leader's wing until reaching a big front, where he pulled up and started to go through it. Element leader called him on the radio and told him to get back on his wing so that he could lead and go around the front. Apparently F/O Gentile did not hear Lt. Blair, because he went into the front at approximately 130 MPH. Lt. Blair searched the area and tried to get in contact with missing plane several times. Proceeded to Kiriwina and reported the airplane as being missing."

Neither *G.I. Annie* nor F/O Gentile was ever seen again. During an extremely eventful eight months, this remarkable Lightning and her pilots had been credited with fourteen confirmed air victories.

The semi-regular pilot of "G.I. Annie," Lt. John Jones, poses with her sometime in 1943. Note the 13 victory markings, which made her at that time the highest-scoring fighter plane in the 5th Air Force. (Stanaway)

ANY LANDING IS A GOOD LANDING
Frank Savage

Frank Savage, a veteran of the 5th Air Force's 8th Photo Reconnaissance Squadron, had his memory jogged when reading the following entry from Lt. Harlan Olson's informal squadron diary, dated March 2, 1943:

"'Powerhouse' Murphy, originality-plus, landed on the beach at Hisiu, wheels down. It was an outstanding feat of aviation and one which cannot be commended too highly. He not only risked soft sand with bad weather, but had to wedge his landing gear between driftwood on the beach. After landing safely, he taxied above the high-tide line, then radioed we sweater-outers of his location."

This succinct notation stirred memories of an eventful several days spent recovering that airplane. The story according to Savage:

"Lt. Vincent E. Murphy, a band-leading trumpet player from New Jersey, returning from a photo mission across the Owen Stanley Mountains in New Guinea, was running low on fuel and dodging heavy weather which obscured the coastal landmarks used for navigation. Penned in by heavy showers, he spotted a relatively straight beach below him and made his decision to land rather than bail out in

This veteran F-4 of the 8th PRS was photographed later in the war after it had been stripped of its original green and gray paint job and been relegated to squadron "hack." (John Stanaway)

8th PRS C.O. Capt. Frank Savage and "Limping Lizzie" on the New Guinea beach just before he took off and flew her back to Port Moresby. (USAF)

unfamiliar territory, which in New Guinea was not a desirable alternative.

'Powerhouse' Murphy's decision turned out to be fortunate. The narrow beach he so skillfully landed on turned out to be near an abandoned coconut plantation housing an ANGAU (Australian-New Guinea Administrative Unit) that had radio contact with officials in Port Moresby.

The following day, arrangements had been made to ferry a recovery team to Hisiu on a small former coastal re-supply boat. The team, including Lt. Post, the squadron engineering officer, T/Sgt. Meach, and Corporal King, tool kits, 'K' rations, myself and several aviation fuel barrels, motored up to the nearest village. We were transported to the landing beach by an ANGAU truck. The aircraft, *Limping Lizzie*, was thoroughly checked, refueled with a limited amount of gas and preflighted for takeoff.

I paced off the distance of beach offered for takeoff and, in consultation with Post and Murphy, decided I could clear the ground before running out of beach. To the best of my memory, there was 900 feet of straightaway beach available. The wet portion of the sand was firm and narrow but usable."

"On March 4, 1943, we assembled at the aircraft, dug paths for the wheels in the soft, dry sand and taxied onto the 'sand runway.' I do not recall the flap setting, but I remember I used quite a bit in order to attain max lift as soon as possible.

Holding the brakes until full power started the plane to move, I released and barreled down the beach. The Good Lord helps the dumb and the innocent, and this time it was true. Post later said that I was off the sand in 700 feet!

The flight back to Schwimmer Drome at Moresby was uneventful. My flight log indicates one hour flight time, part of which was occupied in flight test of gear, flaps, etc. The recover team and Murphy returned to Port Moresby by boat on March 5, not too enthusiastic about sea travel in the tropics.

Many 5th Air Force P-38 pilots will remember March 2 and 3, 1943, as the 'Bismarck Sea Battle,' which destroyed an entire Japanese convoy headed for New Guinea. I remember the date for my 700-foot takeoff from the sand as well."

PROP WASH ON LANDING
Ralph H. Wandrey

One of the busier moments I've had in a P-38 cockpit occurred in August 1943. We were to escort B-25 strafers on a low-level raid on the Japanese airstrips at Wewak, New Guinea. We were based at Dobodura and had to cross the Owen Stanley Mountains to Port Moresby, where we would top off our tanks and then catch up to the B-25s already en route.

As we approached Jackson Drome [near Moresby], we saw the "Jolly Rogers" [90th Bomb Group] B-24s coming in from a raid on Wewak and landing on the strip. As time was of the essence, we had to land by cutting in between the B-24s as they came in on their final approaches.

I was the last to land and was nicely set up to touch down about

50 yards behind a '24, with a second one about 75 yards behind me. All was fine until I heard the tower call: "B-24, go around; you're overshooting." I saw exhaust pour from the engines of the plane ahead of me. As I was only 25 feet above the strip, I decided to finish the landing.

I braced for the prop wash and soon found myself with full left aileron and my left wing still lifting. Suddenly, it swung past the vertical and I knew I had lost control. Looking out the top of my canopy, I saw the runway and realized that my P-38G was flat on its back, wheels down and locked, full flaps and two half-full belly tanks, only 20 feet off the ground!

I reversed controls and, as the plane rolled to vertical, I jammed the left throttle wide open, then chopped it off while I pulled the wheel into my chest. The next thing I felt was the main wheels turning as the plane gently settled onto the runway—rolling right down the center line!

At the 50th anniversary of the P-38 celebration, I told [former Lockheed test pilot] Tony LeVier about this incident. He replied, "You followed the correct procedure for inver... Wait a minute; there was no procedure for inverted flight recovery when landing!"

Yes there was, Tony. I figured it out in about two seconds! [And yes, Ralph had managed a perfect roll at 25 feet while landing a heavily loaded P-38! He was serving with the 9th "Flying Knights" Squadron of the 49th Fighter Group, with which he eventually shot down six Japanese planes—five with the P-38 and one with a P-47.]

Photo on previous page: Ralph Wandrey in the cockpit of a 9th FS P-38. (Wandrey)

MY FIRST MISSION NEARLY MY LAST
Richard F. Brown

The 68th Fighter Squadron's insignia. (Brown)

My first combat mission was a short-range one—and almost my last one. We flew by a Japanese runway en route and attacked a military installation. We were dive-bombing with 1,000-pound bombs. There were eight Lightnings in the formation and I was number four in the first flight of four. This meant I was in the middle of the attack, following three airplanes with four behind me. I was a new pilot and they were taking care of me.

The Japanese shot at all of us, but I felt comfortable and was busy following my leader and aiming at the target. The only thing wrong was that the excitement of being over enemy territory with guns shooting at me caused me to forget to turn on my proper switches to release my bomb!

I still had my bomb and we were joined up again in formation, ready to go home. My leader, Captain John Hernden, said, "No sweat, you can drop it on the runway that we'll pass near on the way home."

It seemed simple enough to me, so I turned on the correct switches and rolled over into a dive-bombing attack. I lined up and aimed at the middle of the runway—only now the Japanese have just one airplane to shoot at and the sky is full of flak. I had full throttles and top speed, but it felt like I was standing still with antiaircraft shells bursting all around me. Wanting to get out of the guns' range as fast as possible, I pushed the throttles so hard I broke the safety wire and I was in the very maximum war emergency power setting.

The last shots they fired at me exploded right above my canopy, so close I felt I could almost reach out and touch them. Now I was directly above the guns, so the flak passed by me very close before it detonated, and probably a direct hit like that would have destroyed my P-38. Those antiaircraft shells have a fuse that was preset to explode at a certain altitude, but they will also detonate if they hit anything.

Luckily, they missed. I even thought one of them might have passed behind my cockpit and between the tail booms.

There were big guns protecting that runway, plus many machine guns. Later the B-25s attacked the big guns at the end of the runway and took pictures while they were at it. The pictures show the 75mm guns in a dirt revetment circle cluster at the end of the runway.

I learned a good lesson on that first mission: Always turn on the proper switches to release your bombs!

[The author served with the 68th "Lightning Lancers" Fighter Squadron of the 347th Fighter Group, 13th Air Force, in the Southwest Pacific 1944-45. The 68th's insignia was a knight standing on two lightning bolts and holding a sword in his right hand—perfect for the P-38 Lightning aircraft they were flying.]

THE P-38 PILOT'S BEST FRIENDS:
HIS LIGHTNING AND HIS DOG

This is the story of a dog named Sally, who was found in a sugar cane field by USAAF photo reconnaissance pilot Edward H. Taylor, near the airstrip at Kipapa Gulch on Oahu, Hawaii, during World War II. Sally, whom Taylor described as "a plain 'ole poi variety of pooch," was undernourished and exhausted, but he fed her fresh eggs and boned chicken and nursed her back to health.

While they were at Kipapa an ammunition dump adjacent to the airstrip exploded while Army and Navy troops were unloading torpedo heads. Body parts flew everywhere. The next morning at dawn when Taylor went to his Operations' shack desk, he found, neatly arranged at the foot of it, arms, legs, and all sorts of human anatomy which Sally had collected.

When his 28th Photo Recon Squadron deployed to Kwajalein in the Marshall Islands and Saipan in the Marianas in mid-1944, Taylor took Sally with him on a B-25 along with the squadron's "Flight Line Aces," the men who kept their P-38/F-5s flying. Sally became the squadron mascot. She was Taylor's protector, sleeping at the entrance to his tent.

Captain Ed Taylor and his dog Sally on Saipan in 1944. (Taylor)

71

After the U.S. had a foothold on Okinawa, the squadron moved to Ie Shima, a smaller island just offshore. A Marine guard dog on "Okie" consummated a friendship with Sally that produced seven puppies—part poi and part German Shepherd—with Taylor acting as midwife.

When Taylor flew his missions, Sally stayed in his jeep, which was locked and chained to keep soldiers and Marines from stealing it. On one mission he had to bail out into the East China Sea, but was rescued and returned to home base for a reunion with the well-fed and well-treated Sally—courtesy of some conscientious squadron maintenance men.

After the A-bombs were dropped on Japan, Taylor and Sally returned to the Big PX in Texas. Would you believe Sally even went on the honeymoon in 1946 with Taylor and his new bride, Cordelia Brown?

The three of them were transferred to Langley AFB, Virginia, but on a cold winter night outside the "O" Club, Sally met her demise chasing some wild ducks over Chesapeake Bay's ice-covered waters. After all, chickens and ducks were Sally's forte from her days of catching native fowl on Saipan and Okinawa.

Sally did get in a few P-38 rides with Taylor, either piggyback or sitting on his lap, on a couple of local hops. She travelled the Pacific in style with the devotion only a dog can give its master.

THE NAVY SAVES A P-38 PILOT
John Stanaway

Then-Lieutenant James E. McLaughlin, who flew combat missions with the P-39, the P-47 and the P-38 while serving with the 36th Fighter Squadron. (Stanaway)

"Double trouble—hah!" was Sergeant Joe Gigliotti's ironic comment during the first few days of P-38 maintenance in the 35th Fighter Squadron late in February 1944. The sobriquet was meant to reflect the P-38's effect on the Japanese, but the mechanics realized that whatever problems they had had with the Allison engines of their old P-40s were now doubled with the twin-engine Lightning.

The Fifth Air Force in New Guinea was still at the end of the allocation line and made do with hand-me-down P-38s. While other units were getting the newer J models by the beginning of 1944, the 36th Fighter Squadron (sister squadron of the 35th in the 8th Fighter Group) had to make do with their worn-out H models.

Partly as a result of using less than perfect combat aircraft, the 36th lost its commander during one of its early P-38 patrols over Wewak on March 15, 1944. Another brave P-38 pilot was also downed trying to save his leader and was picked up by a Navy PBY that virtually flew into the teeth of enemy fire to do the job.

Captain Warren Danson, the 36th C.O., led thirteen P-38s off the Finschhafen strip at 0835 and was over the target area a few minutes after ten. Eight Oscars and two Tonys were quickly sighted over Dallman Harbor, and Danson led his planes down into a perfect bounce.

Captain James McLaughlin was covering Danson in the bounce, but cursed the performance of his own P-38 when the Allisons began cutting out. The "perfect bounce" was ruined when the Japanese became alerted and turned on the lead flight. McLaughlin was able at that point of escaping the enemy—as he logically should have done—with the rest of the P-38 formation. However, Danson was on the spot, with several Japanese fighters attacking him, and McLaughlin got his own P-38 into the midst of the enemy to help.

It was to no avail. Danson was shot down in flames and killed just west of Kairiru Island, off Wewak. McLaughlin was in trouble himself and was soon also shot down, east of the island.

When his head broke the surface of the water, McLaughlin could see those angry enemy fighters still flying overhead. He hid beneath his brown jungle kit and seat cushion whenever one came near; it was all he could do. He managed to get ashore and found that his smoke flare was water soaked. His .45 automatic pistol rusted into uselessness within a couple of hours.

Miles away, PBY-5 #64 of Navy Patrol Squadron 34 received an encoded message from Advanced Echelon, 5th Air Force, that read: "Man down off Wewak. Can you undertake rescue with fighter cover? Answer immediately." The pilot, Lt. H. L. Dennison, answered that his PBY could indeed undertake the rescue. The plot was given to Kairiru and the Navy was soon on the way to the P-38 pilot's aid.

Meanwhile, McLaughlin was sweating like a turkey before Thanksgiving in the face of the mighty guns of Wewak. For the moment he seemed to be safe, since the Japanese did not show any sign that they knew he had survived the plane crash. He had gathered up his parachute and brought it ashore with him to avoid leaving telltale signs.

Luckily for him, the parachute served as a signal when the Catalina arrived shortly afterward and sighted the white silk on the ground. McLaughlin joyously inflated his life raft and was immediately spotted by the crew of the PBY. Dennison landed his flying boat in six-foot swells after circling the area once. He cut one engine and taxied to the raft. McLaughlin's beaming, but still incredulous face, appeared at the rear hatch and he was brought aboard.

Perhaps the very audacity of the landing in Wewak Harbor surprised the Japanese, because few, if any, guns opened up. It should be remembered that Wewak was the best defended Japanese base in New Guinea at that time, and most Allied surface units avoided the area. James McLaughlin was grateful that one Navy flying boat crew forgot about the danger for his sake.

TARGET BORNEO
John Brown

On October 7, 1944, I had just finished getting the morning mission off as Operations Officer of the 26th Photo Reconnaissance Squadron at the Mokmer airstrip on Biak Island, off the northwest coast of New Guinea, when I got a phone call from Headquarters. I picked up a cup of coffee and started up the hill, wondering what kind of trouble I was in now.

I entered the office and said, "Sergeant, what kind of trouble am I in now?" Major Armstrong, our C.O., heard my voice, called me to come right in and said, "Sit down, John."

I poured myself another cup of coffee from the pot in his office and put it on the desk. He said, "John, we have a very important mission coming up and I know you can do it. Your combat time is about up, and we will not blame you if you say no. We need to send two pilots to find Borneo and to photograph any Japanese ships there."

"Major, I have never turned down a mission yet, so give me a go," I responded. He smiled and said, "We don't have much of a map, but I know you can figure it out."

Back in Operations I checked the board to see who else I could use on this mission. Lieutenant John Beasley's name was up, and he could use a good ride like this. I called him up to the Operations office and told him what was up. "I am ready, Captain," he said. "OK," I replied; "get your hammock, mosquito net and rosary beads." I headed over to the kitchen and ordered them to make up two bags of food and water.

We took off about 10:00 a.m. and landed at Morotai (a small island off the north coast of Halmahera), taxied up to a very small Operations building and parked. We walked over and the attendant wanted to know why we landed there. I told him what we planned to do and asked for a map. He laughed, pointed his finger due west and said, "It's out that way someplace. You may be able to get some help from one of those big ships out there in the ocean."

I said, "How in the hell can I get out to those ships?" He answered, "I'll call out and tell them to send a boat in to pick up a captain that wants to come aboard and talk to your navigation officer."

A small boat came over and tied up, and the occupants climbed up on the pier. They came over to where we were standing and asked if we knew where the captain was that called for the boat. I knew that they were looking for a Navy captain (which is about three equivalent ranks higher than an Army captain). I said, "We're the ones who called to go aboard your ship."

We boarded the boat and cruised over to the large ship, boarded

An F-5 of the 26th PRS taking off from its Philippine base at Lingayen on Luzon in May 1945. (USAF)

it and were escorted to the captain's office. We saluted and told him what we needed. He smiled and said that the only map of Borneo they had was one Magellan had made when he was there (in the 16th Century!). I said that I would take anything if they could make us a copy. He said, "OK, boys, we will have some lunch and then we'll make us a copy." Afterward I thanked him and told him it was the best lunch we had had since arriving from the States. That had been almost a year now. He said they were pulling out that night and that he wished us the best of luck. I thanked him and saluted. We re-boarded that small boat and went back to the air base.

We got the fuel truck to come down and refill our tanks. We had some supper and thanked the cook, and I talked to some fighter pilots, asking if anyone had been to Borneo. They said no and that it was too far for their planes. Returning to our parked F-5s, we got into our sleeping bags and counted the stars until we fell asleep. We were up before daylight.

We put our sleeping gear away and went up to the mess hall for some breakfast with the fighter pilots, who kept telling us not to go too far or we might never get back. I thanked them for the information and told them we'd be back. We returned to our planes, lined up and took off.

We settled back at 8,000 feet at 180 miles per hour and flew for three and a half hours. My idea was to hit the north side of the island, make a circle and head back. I noticed a lot of Japanese ships and they were all headed for the Philippines.

I got John's attention with hand signals and motioned that we would go to 17,000 feet and make a big turn to the left. I would turn my cameras on first, and every two minutes turn them off and then on. We would not talk and would use only hand signals. I would signal John when to start his cameras. If either of us saw "bogies" we *would* talk, and head for home.

After a while, John signaled that he was out of film, so we headed for Morotai. We landed after completing a ten-and-a-half-hour mission. John Beasley was completely worn out.

I knew that the photos should be delivered to Headquarters immediately. I gassed up and told John to get his film mounted and put in my plane. He would stay at Morotai that night and come home the next day.

After an hour it became dark and I turned on my instrument panel. The lights on the dashboard were dead. I took some matches out of my survival kit and struck one to hold over the instrument panel. I was blinded by the match and had to close my eyes. I got another match, closed my eyes, struck it and held it over the instrument panel until it burned my fingers. I then opened my eyes and could see the panel. I continued on.

I finally saw the Biak lights and noticed that nothing was coming in to land the regular way, so I decided to come straight in the opposite way. I dropped my wheels and was about to set down when a transport turned on its lights—and was headed right for me! I poured the power to the engines and pulled it straight up.

I closed my eyes and struck another match and again held it until it burned my fingers. I waited a second or two to open my eyes. The panel was all lit up, and I came around and followed the transport. I still had no landing lights. A line crew came along in a jeep and led me back to our parking area. I got down on my knees to thank that man who took care of me.

I finished up my operational flying time with these last three missions:

October 12: Mokmer to Morotai (staging), three hours and fifteen minutes.

October 13: Morotai-Mindoro(Philippines)-Morotai-Mokmer, ten hours and fifteen minutes.

October 15: Mokmer-Ambon (a smaller island off the coast of Ceram in the East Indies)-Mokmer, seven hours and fifty minutes.

Total: 300 hours.

LIGHTNING, SKILL AND LUCK
Mary Lou Neal

The skill was there, but the P-38 Lightning and the luck were missing when young Lieutenant Jay T. Robbins made his first kill. Of course, it *was* lucky that his P-39 was one of the four able to get off the runway during the bombing at Milne Bay, New Guinea. And it *was* lucky that he and another pilot caught that Betty. But his luck gave out in the toss of a coin and the other pilot got the credit. Things were soon to change for him.

Less than a week later, Robbins was ordered to Australia to check out in the P-

Then-Captain Jay T. Robbins in the cockpit of "Jandina." (Stanaway)

38. In his own words, "After my first flight, I knew that this was one which could create havoc with the Japanese air power.'" And he was soon able to prove it.

Back in New Guinea, on July 21, 1943, he destroyed three enemy fighters and damaged two others. His 80th Fighter Squadron, having replaced its older P-39s with P-38s, became the first USAAF squadron to destroy 200 enemy aircraft in aerial combat. Robbins himself went on to score 22 confirmed victories and become the fourth-ranked USAAF ace in the Pacific.

His most exhilarating and stressful mission, complete with a dramatic rescue, was undoubtedly on September 4, 1943, when all three factors—the Lightning, skill and luck—were present. An account of his long day, from 5:10 a.m. until 3:20 p.m., is graphically recounted in the chapter, "Lightning Over Huon Gulf," in Edward H. Sims' book, *American Aces of World War II*.

78

The flight was to be routine. He was to fly from his base near Port Moresby, stage into Dobodura, then take off for the assigned area to fly cover for the U.S. forces landing at Lae and Salamaua. The Japanese had a formidable fighting force at Rabaul, to the north on New Britain, but that was 300 miles from the ground operations and similar missions had gone undetected.

Reaching the area, the sixteen P-38s flew back and forth for a while without incident. Suddenly came the cry: "Bandits—ten o'clock high!" Robbins' flight of four was in the position to be the first to challenge them and he headed straight for the enemy—30 Zekes.

At that moment another voice called "Bandits below!" and Robbins saw five Val dive-bombers at 12,000 feet, a tempting target. But the rule of aerial tactics dictated that he go after the fighters first.

In a few seconds the sky was filled with Zekes, who had the advantage not only in numbers but in altitude. Robbins caught sight of one above and to his left who passed him and started a left turn to come in on his tail. Robbins quickly entered a climbing left turn and managed to come up almost level, the powerful engines of his plane, *Jandina*, responding beautifully. He turned left again and was on the tail of the startled enemy. At this point the Japanese made the mistake of nosing into a dive, and Robbins was able to easily close the gap. One down.

The second kill was moments later, with both planes meeting head-on and each scoring hits, but the damage to *Jandina* was minor. While watching the burning Zeke plunging, Robbins was caught by surprise from behind and a cluster of holes appeared in his right wing.

He threw *Jandina* into a dive and soon he was up to 400 mph and picking up speed. Pulling away, he spotted another Zeke below him at 5,000 feet. The pullout, after roaring down from 15,000 feet, was a gamble for both plane and pilot. But the damaged wing held and, after a near blackout, Robbins caught the enemy by surprise. Victory number three.

He was now alone; no other U.S. fighters were in sight. The Zekes began closing in on him from every direction, and his calls for help were unanswered. Miraculously, he managed to fatally cripple the fourth Zeke while making a head-on pass at him and the burning wreck hit the water.

But Robbins himself now had major damage. One engine was missing and he was nearly out of ammunition. He had somehow fought his way out of the gaggle of Zekes, but now two Tonys and a Hamp closed in on him. One popped up in front of him and his only solution was to bluff. He lined up for another head-on pass and fired his last few rounds. He scored hits as the Japanese shot past and was happy to settle for that. Now he was down to 1,000 feet with the enemy on both sides of the wounded *Jandina*. If he continued on his escape run for shore he would surely be shot down, so he elected to fight, dodging every attack and simulating counterattacks.

Enemy shells ripped through his plane and it was incredible that he was still uninjured. When ditching and certain death seem inevitable, he spotted warships ahead and, turning sharply, he displayed the belly of the P-38. He prayed earnestly that his identification of the ships was correct. Then it was the U.S. Navy to the rescue as they trained their guns on his pursuers.

There was still the long flight home to Three Mile Drome, over mountains, without a radio or full use of the controls and on one engine. But he made it. His luck had not run out.

Luck played an important role in his personal life as well. What seemed at the time to be the worst possible luck turned into what he would later admit was the luckiest thing ever to happen to him.

In Australia in late 1942, an annual physical detected an erratic heartbeat. Robbins was sent to the 4th U.S. Army General Hospital in Melbourne for tests. Although restored to flight status following the tests, he had met the American nurse who became his wife and the mother of his two sons, now also Air Force pilots. Her name was Ina, which explains the name given to each of his P-38s: Jay and Ina, hence *Jandina*. Acknowledging all his good fortune, he chose as his plane's painted-on mascot "Hotei," the lucky little Chinese god who promises good fortune to those who rub his tummy.

Luck is a great ally, but ability, not luck, was the major factor in the career of Jay T. Robbins. He retired as a multi-decorated lieutenant general in 1974. Author Sims said it best: "Of all the tasks assigned to any one man in WWII, none compared to the handling of a fighter in terms of coordination, mental alertness, split-second timing, mastery of technical detail, skill, courage and judgment."

A RESCUE MISSION NEVER FORGOTTEN
William M. Gaskill

This is the author's story of the mission he flew on November 18, 1944—and its aftermath—while serving as a P-38 pilot with the 68th Squadron of the 347th Fighter Group, 13th Air Force, in the Southwest Pacific. The 347th assigned 26 P-38s to the mission, each carrying 400 gallons of gas internally plus a 300-gallon belly tank of extra fuel, a bomb and a full load of .50-caliber and 20mm ammunition. The pilots each wore a parachute, a rubber inflatable raft, a "jungle pack" and a Mae West. The jungle pack contained a large machete, a flare pistol and a money pouch with gold and silver coins and Dutch paper currency. Also carried were a first aid kit and a .45-caliber pistol. They were to fly from their base on Middleburg Island, off the northwest coast of New Guinea, to Tarakan, a small island off the east coast of Borneo, to strafe and bomb its oil fields and gun installations.

"We were to fly from Middleburg to the island of Morotai, just north of Halmahera, fuel up and continue to the target, return to Morotai, refuel and return home. It was a long mission, 300 miles from Middleburg to Morotai, plus 748 more miles past Morotai and return—about a nine-hour sortie.

My wingman was Lt. Sylvester 'Joe' Owens, but he couldn't take off for some reason. Later, he did take off and tried to catch us. Col. [Leo] Dusard [the Group Commander], I think it was, told him to go back if he didn't see us in the next five minutes, at which time there would be strict radio silence. Owens either didn't hear or disregarded the order.

The last 200 miles to the target we flew very low to escape radar detection. We encountered no enemy air resistance.

As we approached the target, all hell broke loose. Another squadron heard the distress call from Owens: 'I am hit and bloody—I am going in.' He was the last one to the target and all the remaining Japanese guns were trained on him. He also managed to turn back to sea, where he lost altitude and landed on the water. He managed to get out of the plane quickly and into his inflatable raft before passing out.

When we left the target, the smoke was up to 17,000 feet. As we left the island, there were small transport boats trying to get to port. Our flight of only three now strafed them and set them all on fire. The group destroyed or set fire to numerous fuel tanks, a tanker, three merchant vessels, nine or ten barges and small boats and a pumping installation—a large success!

Owens, as he later related, came to and rowed over to the shore of Borneo. He lay on the beach for a while, slightly in-

Lt. Gaskill in the cockpit of his P-38. (Gaskill)

jured. He awoke to see some natives coming down the beach. He drew his gun but realized that they were probably friendly, so he brought out his money pouch and offered them some of it.

The natives took him into a village and asked him to treat a native for what appeared to be athlete's foot. Owens treated him with ointment from his first aid kit. The chief or mayor got Owens a hut to spend the night. The next morning, Owens looked out to see that natives were lined up for sick call. All appeared to have athlete's foot, but one indicated that he was sick to his stomach. Owens was stumped. He gave the guy an Atabrine pill, which is only for malaria. The guy took the pill, rubbed his stomach and smiled. He thought he was cured. Word got around!

When I got back to Middleburg, the staging base, I went about seeking ways to rescue Owens. I got permission from Col. Dusard and Major [Chandler] Worley [the Group Operations Officer] to go back and search for him. I then went to Col. Ford of the air-sea rescue squadron at Morotai. What a great outfit they were! I explained that we had a man down near Borneo and would they go look for him? 'Oh no,' he replied, 'you find him, and if we are going by and you are there to cover us, we will pick him up. Look at this map.' He showed me a large map with pins in it. 'We have 60 crews out there to pick up.'

Lt. Bob Morriss, my regular wingman, and I got underway and flew to Borneo. We were searching the shoreline when Owens fired his flare pistol in the air. Talk about excited, I was that! I sent Lt. Morriss 'upstairs' to report in and ask for help.

It was too late in the day for them to come. In the meantime, I wrote a note, put it in my canteen and threw it in the water. Little native kids swam out and got it. I told him we would be back to pick him up.

I reported in to my outfit and to Col. Ford. To my delight, he said he would have someone pick up Owens if we would rendezvous with them over Horseshoe Island the next morning.

On November 22, Lt. Everett Magor and I took off. About half way to the target, a large weather front had moved it. We almost stalled out trying to climb out through it and had to go on instruments. Finally, we broke out of the weather and ahead of us was Horseshoe Island, where we met up with 'Playmate 22,' code name for our angel of mercy.

We proceeded to the area and sure enough, there was Owens and the natives on the beach. The float plane let down and landed while we circled overhead. We knew the Japanese were nearby. The natives rowed Owens out to the plane. He boarded and the PBY took off to pick up somebody else from another outfit. They surely took a lot of risks to save a lot of people.

We fueled up at Morotai and then it was on to home base. It was on our way home to Middleburg that I heard that our most respected Group Executive Officer, Lt. Col. Robert Westbrook [a twenty-victory ace] was shot down while strafing a Japanese gunboat. I was very sad about this.

About a month later, Lt. Morriss was shot down and killed off the coast of New Guinea, where he and I were strafing. Some more fine fellows were shot down about the same time. More and more, I realize the cost of war."

A WHITE-HAIRED P-38 PILOT:
How I *Got* White Hair
Arthur W. Kidder

I was on a routine mission, flying a war-weary P-38 from Attu Island's Alexai Point to Anchorage, Alaska. This particular P-38 had been reworked into a "piggyback" instrument trainer. The radio and armor plate were moved from behind the pilot—the former to the nose—making room for another pilot. It was not used much; there was some difficulty getting an instructor pilot to double-up behind a trainee instrument pilot, with no access to the controls, and give effective instrument flying instruction.

So there I was, fat, dumb and happy at 15,000 feet on top of a solid overcast, 30 minutes out of Adak Island. The sun was setting behind me as I tried to get a weather report. The generator warning light suddenly flashed ON, the props surged and the radio went dead. It was a complete electrical failure—even the battery was dead. The props were set to manual, unsynced and throbbing. I had no gyro, no instruments, no lights—no nothing.

Lt. Art Kidder (left) and another 82nd FG pilot, Lt. Charles Adams of the 95th FS, congratulate each other for a successful mission on July 8, 1944, during which they each shot down three enemy aircraft. (Steve Blake collection)

Well, Kidder, what do you do now? I had at least an hour's fuel and a solid overcast. The last weather report, two hours old, included an 800-foot ceiling, snow mixed with rain, and fog patches. I had no place to go and no way to get there.

I then spotted a dot in the sky off to the south and turned toward it. It was a Navy R4D transport, and he was letting down. It was a sloppy formation join-up; he didn't even see me as I came in high over his tail, gear and flaps down—and into the soup we went.

It turned dark. I could just see the R4D's navigation lights. It seemed like a very long letdown; it was now snowing, and I had to hold a tight formation. Suddenly there were runway lights. With power OFF and a torching turbo lighting the area, I hit the right edge of the runway with the brakes locked.

Some time later I was in the "O" Club with several empty Scotch glasses when a couple of Navy pilots came in, bent on finding a crazy Air Force type who nearly crashed into them. I bought them a round, and to this day I don't know if they realized I had been saved by those Golden Wings.

[Art Kidder had flown an earlier combat tour with the 82nd Fighter Group (96th Fighter Squadron) in Italy, April-September 1944, during which he shot down four German planes. His second tour was with the 54th Fighter Squadron of the 343rd FG in the Aleutians, November 1944-September 1945.]

TARGET: SAIGON
Ray Nish

Our target on April 14, 1945, was Saigon, the Japanese-held capital of French Indochina. It was time, the 13th Fighter Command felt, for 13th Air Force fighters based in the Philippine Islands to make a target of opportunity sweep of the China mainland. They assigned the pioneering mission to the P-38s of the 347th Fighter Group at Puerto Princesa, on Palawan.

The 347th's pilots had flown P-39 and P-38 missions from New Caledonia, Guadalcanal in the Solomons, the New Hebrides, New Guinea, Halmahera and the Philippines; and over the Coral, Bismarck, Celebes, Sulu, Molucca, Ceram and South China Seas, and the Makassar Strait to targets in Borneo—99 percent of them over water. Someone in fighter command, however, decided that the flight to Saigon should have a lead navigation plane. Previous flights to Balikpapan in Borneo took us on longer courses than this one, but still a B-25 from the 42nd Bomb Group was assigned to lead us to this new target. Officially, the mission was a fighter escort for the lone B-25.

The flight would take us 850 miles west over the South China Sea and 850 miles back on the return. The flight of eight and one-half hours would be far from the longest we had flown, but the route to the target and back was entirely over water.

The 347th put up two flights of four P-38s each for this mission—five Lightnings from my 68th Fighter Squadron and three from the 339th Fighter Squadron. Two 165-gallon drop tanks provided the range needed. Capt. Clyde D. McBride of the 68th was Red Leader. I flew as his wingman on this mission. 1st Lt. William G. Keyworth, Jr., also of the 68th, led the 339th pilots.

We got airborne and climbed out to join the B-25. After nearly an hour, two of the 339th planes had aborted, one at a time, for one reason or another. That left six '38s following a B-25. In addition to McBride, Keyworth and me, the other pilots were David W. Pruess and Robert E. Worthen of the 68th and Wayne R. Meyers of the 339th.

I was tracking the flight plan against the course on my map, and the B-25 was taking us on a more northerly heading than we had figured. I moved in behind McBride's left wing and caught his glance. Holding up my map, I pointed to the B-25 and shook my head.

Texan McBride broke radio silence: "Ahh know. Ahh'm gonna' give him five more minutes."

The B-25 pilot also broke radio silence: "Is there a problem?" McBride: "Yeah—you're off course."

B-25 pilot: "Minute, please."

Shortly, the B-25 pilot radioed: "Our nav[igator] says we're okay."

McBride looked at me. I shook my head. He nodded and six P-38s banked left and held the turn for 30 to 35 degrees before rolling out on a new heading for Saigon.

As expected, our course brought us to the southern tip of Cap St. Jacques and the Japanese airfield just to the north on the peninsula. That airfield was our primary target. We were at 10,000 feet over the mouth of the Mekong Delta under a gray overcast sky and felt cheated. Our searching eyes could not spot a single Japanese plane,

1st Lt. Ray Nish with his assigned P-38, "Lil' Steve II," named after his infant son. (Steve Nish)

in the air, on the ground, in the hangars or on the ramp. We later theorized that the Japanese had flown their planes to another field because of a limited fuel supply.

After releasing our drop tanks, we followed Red Leader into a spiraling dive for the deck and headed for the confluence of two major rivers. McBride led us onto a Japanese destroyer docked in the Dong Nai River, with steam up and firing at us. While dodging the destroyer's flak pattern, all of us managed a good strafing run at its port beam.

Pulling up and over the destroyer, we could see several ships at the docks lining the Saigon River near its juncture with the Dong Nai. They were broadside to us. There were cargo ships, some 10,000 tons, some smaller. Down to the water and up the Saigon River we went, spread and in trail. We kept below the treetops that lined the river, pulling up to clear the ships' masts.

We were getting heavy artillery and intense ground fire from both banks of the river—batteries protecting the docks and the several large fuel storage tanks flanking the river. When we ran out of docked ships, we sprayed the fuel tanks and the gun batteries. On up the river we flew, north of the city of Saigon.

Ahead we saw an explosion as McBride destroyed a Japanese amphibian plane on the river ramp next to an airfield. He led us across the field into a shallow climb for a wingover 180, and coming back down all of us got good shots at planes in front of the hangar, as well as the hangar. McBride nearly flew through the hangar while firing a blast that started it on fire. He then turned left into the river for a strafing run back down it, all of us in trail.

Now the batteries were ready for us, and we drew both artillery and small arms fire again as we made a run at the fuel tanks and gun positions we had seen on the way up the river. Soon we were back to the cargo ships. Two of them were listing, so we pumped some more shells into them.

Ahead was a large fuel tank, and I aimed a good blast into it, puncturing it and drawing black smoke. But I noticed that the last 20mm shells to leave my cannon were spiraling and losing velocity. My next firing told me why: I had burned the riflings, and, worse than that, I was now out of all ammo.

Meyers, the 339th pilot, pulled up and radioed, "I've been hit!" I could see his left rudder had been cut in half by flak and told him to get down on the river.

We were now downriver and approaching that destroyer from its starboard beam. And my ammo was gone. McBride and the other pilots strafed it again.

Back to the delta now and still on the deck, we started closing on Red Leader when he called for a run at the flak towers that lined the peninsular tip of land at the mouth of the Mekong. I couldn't do any damage but felt my safety was to stay on the water.

There were four or five gun towers in an arc-like line at Cap St. Jacques, south of the vacated airfield, and our P-38s really blasted them. All but me. As he pulled off the last tower and turned down the delta, McBride said, "Let's do it again!" Keyworth, thinking of Meyers' damage, suggested that we head out and join up.

Red Leader soon called out, "Look who's here at 10 o'clock!" Approaching us at about 5,000 feet on a southerly heading, paralleling the coast, was the B-25 navigation plane. McBride couldn't resist: "You missed the show, Baker Fox!" No response. That was our last contact with the B-25.

Our P-38s had sunk a medium freighter, destroyed a small freighter, damaged four other freighters, destroyed a seaplane base hangar and one plane and damaged a second hangar, two gun positions and two fuel storage tanks. We couldn't confirm damage to the destroyer.

We climbed to 8,000 feet and held our plotted course for home, nearly four hours away. An hour or so later, Meyers told Red Leader his fuel was running low. With the drag from his shattered left rudder, it was no surprise. McBride asked him to read out his fuel gauges. I watched mine as Meyers read his. He had more than I did! I attempted to ease his anxiety: "You've got more than I have and I plan on making it!"

Even with all the excitement of the Saigon strafing runs, time was now dragging. Nothing but the water of the South China Sea below and ahead, and a sky that was hazy.

A half-hour out of Palawan, McBride radioed Waitress, our control tower, and reported one damaged Uncle and one low on fuel. The landings were uneventful, although not totally routine for Meyers.

My plane's crew chief later reported that I had about 10 minutes more flying time. Close, but with no storms to fly over or around on our return, it was no sweat.

That was the last time fighter command assigned a navigation plane to us.

AN ALEUTIAN ANECDOTE
Bob Waggoner

I had a funny incident that happened to me at Dutch Harbor that I shall always remember when I think of the Navy.

The islands in the Aleutians have no beaches or shorelines; they are all mountains sticking straight up from the water. The USN airfield at Dutch Harbor, on Unalaska Island, was made by literally blasting off the side of a mountain.

I was leading a flight of four new replacement P-38s from Elmendorf Field at Anchorage to Unmak, which is the next island to the west of Unalaska. The weather at Unmak shut down, as did the weather behind us at Cold Bay, near the end of the Alaska Peninsula, and we were lucky to get into Dutch.

When we landed we followed the jeep to a parking place and asked the Navy ensign there where we could get some chow. He saluted us, which we thought was unique, as we did not follow that custom. After he looked us over (we had leather jackets, special arctic issue blanket-lined canvas pants, no ties or headgear and were wearing Mae Wests) he said the officers' mess required "blues" but that we could eat with the "chiefs" (USN noncoms). We did so, and the food was outstanding. This was the first time we had milk or fresh vegetables in the Aleutians, and it was topped off with ice cream! The Navy controlled the transport and they went first class.

The next morning when we were getting ready to depart, one of our guys said he thought the ensign airdrome officer had treated us second class and asked if we could just "accidentally" charge our .50s and strafe the strip before heading for Unmak. I reminded him that we didn't have any ammo, as we had stopped at Homer (southwest of Anchorage on the Kenai Peninsula) and loaded up with booze.

A '38 without ammo in the cans will hold a case of whiskey in its nose. Homer was a tiny town where they got a year's supply of what they needed in the summer because of the ice in the winter. It had a gravel airstrip, and a couple of us had picked up some nicks in our props. We were worried how we would explain that on new planes but decided that four cases of bourbon would handle any inquiries. And no questions were ever asked as we split the booze between the officers and the enlisted men.

[Bob served with the 54th Fighter Squadron of the 343rd Fighter Group in the Aleutians, 1943-1944.]

BLACK SUNDAY
Calvin C. Wire

Easter Sunday, April 16, 1944. Our mission was to escort B-24s and B-25s to Hollandia, New Guinea. This was our seventh mission softening up that general area, prior to the proposed landings by the Army and the Marines. The weather reports for the last two days had been bad, with the possibility of a hurricane moving in. The meteorologists had strongly recommended that all flights be cancelled. However, the man in charge, General Kenney, said, "The mission must go ahead as planned."

As usual, the bombers took off first, formed up and headed for Hollandia. Some fifteen minutes later, the three squadrons of the 475th Fighter Group took off from Nadzab and headed out. (Normal procedure was to take off on our main tanks and as soon as we gained some altitude switch to our belly tanks.) We flew through the normal clouds and rainstorms, catching up with the bomber formations south of Wewak.

As we closed in on the Hollandia area, Captain Dick Kimball, who was leading the 433rd Squadron, called to tell us to switch to our internal tanks and then drop our belly tanks. I was flying a P-38J, which had, besides the main and reserve tanks, two small 45-gallon tanks in the wings out near the tips. When possible, it was best to use this gas first, so that the extra weight on the outside wings is reduced prior to entering any violent maneuvers—just good sense.

When I switched from my belly tanks to my outer wing tanks, both engines died. I immediately switched back to my belly tanks and got the engines started again. This time I switched only to the left outer wing tank and, again, the left engine stopped. I switched back to the belly tanks and tried again with the right tank, with the same result. I then went to my main tanks with no problem. I called Captain Kimball and told him my problem. He replied that as we might need all the fuel we had, I was to take my wingman and head back home.

I called my wingman, Lt. Mort Ryerson, and told him I had to SNAFU and that he was to come with me. At this time I was back on my belly tanks to make sure I would have as much time in the air as possible.

We flew at about 12-13,000 feet altitude between a solid overcast and lower broken clouds. We had no problem until we were south of Wewak and approaching the edge of the Owen Stanley Mountain Range. At this time we were looking into a solid wall of clouds from the ground to as high as we could see. I had flown a number of missions in this area before and knew that some of the mountains were 13-14,000 feet high, so we climbed to 20,000 feet, looking for any

Then-Captain Cal Wire, shown here in the cockpit of his P-38, took command of the 433rd Fighter Squadron in December 1944. (Stanaway)

opening. No luck! We then headed north and went down to 12,000 feet. Again we flew east and west along the wall of clouds, searching for an opening. Nothing doing!

As we were heading back east, I saw a plane on our left, so we headed for it. There it was: a nice big B-24, heading for home. I called Mort and said, "We hit it lucky; this guy has a co-pilot, a navigator and a radioman. Let's latch on and follow him home." We snuggled in close on his right wing. He rocked that wing to let us know we were welcome and then headed in through the awful wall of clouds. We kept tucked in for about ten to fifteen minutes, when all of a sudden, the B-24 went into a sharp left turn. I told Mort to hang on and climb, and then we made a 180-degree turn and went back out.

After we were out of the worst of it, I called Mort and told him that usually along the coast, when the weather came in from the east, the clouds would rise a bit as they approached land and leave a space we could fly in and still see what was ahead. He said, "OK, let's give it a try." So then we proceeded east to the coast and headed south. My guess was correct to some degree, as we had about forty feet between the clouds and the water. As it was raining hard, our vision through the windshield was nil, so we flew by looking out the right side windows at the line of surf. I tried to maintain a minimum of twenty feet in altitude and stay about fifty feet east of the surf line.

Everything was working out OK, until the coast suddenly made a sharp turn out to sea. I pulled back on the wheel but was too late. I didn't quite make it over a tree, which I nicked with my right prop. I got back to the surf line OK, but my right engine was shaking a bit, so I feathered the prop and shut the engine off.

About this time Mort called and said, "Wire, I can't take any more of this. I have plenty of gas and recently have done a lot of instrument flying. I'd like to break off and try to climb out of this." I told him, "OK, Mort. Best of luck!" He started climbing, and I found out much later that he made it home fine.

In the meantime, I kept going down the coast, and I was getting awfully tense—and, as you can imagine, downright scared! I really had no idea just where I was, except somewhere on the east coast of New Guinea, approaching Lae.

I kept going and all of a sudden I saw a small landing field with some planes on it, just inland from the water. I immediately swung to my right to make a landing. However, I was going too fast to make the turn to the airfield, so I flew over the west side of the field and then headed out over the ocean. When I got out far enough so I could just see the field, I headed south down the coast. As I did, the clouds came down, forcing me lower and lower.

Suddenly, I saw a wave, which seemed to be higher than my wing. I hauled back on the wheel, but again too late—I hit the top of the wave! Hitting the wave bounced me up a bit and the nose started going down. I pulled back on the wheel again, to level out, and it came all the way back into my lap. I knew then that I had lost control of the plane, so I leaned back, locked my shoulder straps, cut the mixture control and dumped the canopy. All this took very little time, but by then it felt like it was a vertical dive. I was probably not vertical, but nonetheless in a dive.

I don't remember hitting the water. I could not see it coming, nor did I feel it, nor hear it. All I know is that I came to feeling as though I had needles in my ears. I unfastened my seat belt and kicked out of the plane. My clothes and parachute had enough air in them to float me to the surface. All I could think of was getting my life raft out. It took me some time and struggling to do so, and I was getting tired from trying to stay above the water. Then I thought, "You fool; you have a Mae West on!" I pulled the string and it inflated, and I laid back for a bit of rest.

I finally got my life raft out and inflated. This will show you how stupid or "shocky" I was: Here I was in the sea, with real strong winds and awful waves, trying to get into that raft over the big end! I finally figured it out and turned it around and then climbed in. It was full of water, so I spent the next fifteen or twenty minutes bailing it out. That was another mistake. With the water out, it rode high, like a big piece of balsa wood. The wind just threw me and my raft around like a balloon. It didn't take me long to push the small end under water and fill the boat so it would ride better.

I think I was about a half-mile off the coast when I crashed. All went well after I got the water in the raft. The wind in the meantime was pushing me towards the shore. I could see a line of huge breakers ahead of me, crashing over a reef and into a bay. This gave me another fright, but I must have been on the crest of the wave and it carried me over the reef and into the bay and much smoother waters. Coming towards me from the shore was what looked like a native dugout canoe with two men in it. Both of them were wearing some kind of conical hats and I immediately thought they were Japs. I got my .45 out and tried to shoot at them, but luckily the gun wouldn't fire. They were GIs and they towed me to shore.

We had to wait at the landing strip for two B-24s and two B-25s to crash land on the strip before we could cross it. They took me to their first aid station and made temporary repairs to my face. I had torn off the bridge of my nose, had a large cut on my forehead and over my eyebrows, and my front teeth had been driven through my lip. They told me the strip was at Yami Point, north of Saidor. The next day they sent me by LST to Saidor and then by plane to an Army hospital in Sydney, Australia. They kept me there for four months for plastic surgery and R&R, and then it was back to the squadron, now on Biak Island, in August.

[Six other 475th FG pilots weren't as fortunate as Lt. Wire that day; they were all missing in action and eventually declared killed in action. One other pilot survived after bailing out of his P-38. Altogether, the 5th Air Force lost 31 aircraft on April 16, 1944—including two Lightnings from another group—and 32 airmen, all of which were evidently weather related. Hence the infamous name, "Black Sunday."]

LINDBERGH'S PACIFIC AIR VICTORY
John Stanaway

There are several versions of the incident in which Charles Lindbergh reportedly shot down a Japanese Army Air Force Ki-51 "Sonia" reconnaissance aircraft. This one was gleaned from his own writings as well as several eyewitnesses. [Lindbergh "advised" and flew P-38s with the 475th Fighter Group from June to August 1944.]

The 433rd Fighter Squadron took off around 7:40 on the morning of July 28, 1944, from its base at Mokmer Strip on Biak Island, off the coast of northwest New Guinea. Its task was to escort some B-25 bombers to enemy airfields on several small islands off the south coast of the larger island of Ceram, southwest of New Guinea. Major Warren Lewis, the squadron's C.O., was flying as Possum Red One— the 433rd's radio call sign—at the head of seventeen P-38s. 475th FG commander Colonel Charles MacDonald led the second flight as Possum Blue One, and Charles Lindbergh led his second element as Possum Blue Three with Lt. Ed Miller as his wingman.

As they rendezvoused with the B-25s, which were also based on Biak, the latter had to abort the mission due to the heavy cloud cover at their altitude. One of the P-38s had already aborted when both of its engines failed. Lt. Herb Cochran, Possum Red Three, had to ditch in the sea near Biak—and paddled his dinghy all the way home! He later denied emphatically that the bombers jettisoned their loads over his head, in spite of a widely circulated but spurious story that made the rounds after the war.

MacDonald decides to continue the mission as a freelance fighter sweep, with just Blue and Yellow Flights. These eight P-38s patrol at about 13,000 feet over the south coast of Ceram, without seeing any enemy aircraft. Lindbergh notes that the Japanese don't seem to have any intention of opposing Possum Squadron in the air on this mission.

Suddenly, the radio comes alive with the sounds of battle. It becomes apparent that some P-38s of Captive (9th Fighter) Squadron of the 49th FG are engaged with enemy aircraft. Possum Blue Flight descends below the clouds to find black puffs of antiaircraft fire above the Amahai airstrip and Captive Squadron in combat with an enemy plane its pilots have incorrectly identified as a "Val," the infamous Japanese Naval Air Force dive bomber.

Captain Saburo Shimada, commander of the JAAF's 73rd Independent Chutai (Squadron), and another pilot of the same unit were returning from an unsuccessful search for a missing comrade when they ran afoul of the 9th FS, which quickly shot down the wingman. Shimada was obviously a particularly skilled pilot, however, and his Ki-51 was very maneuverable. Although a 9th Squadron pilot

95

Charles Lindbergh entering the cockpit of Dick Bong's personal aircraft, P-38J-15 serial #42-104380, prior to a mission in the summer of 1944. Bong, who was on leave in the States at the time, had been officially credited with 27 victories when he left, as shown on his plane, but another was confirmed shortly thereafter. (Stanaway)

claimed to have damaged it, the Sonia was still airborne after nearly half an hour—and the Captive P-38s virtually out of ammunition—when Colonel MacDonald arrived on the scene with his flight.

It may have been that the Ki-51 pilot was too involved with Captive Squadron to notice the four fresh P-38s attacking from above. MacDonald orders auxiliary tanks dropped and attacks the enemy plane. His initial attack draws smoke from the Sonia, which evades further damage by making a sharp opposite bank.

The Captive pilots can do little more than circle above with empty ammo cans and watch in frustration while the Possum P-38s box in the enemy airplane for attack. It seems to them that their 475th FG rivals are deliberately forcing the Japanese aircraft into Lindbergh's sights, to give him a set-up chance at an aerial victory. From Lindbergh's point of view, the Sonia has made desperate maneuvers to evade the guns of many P-38s and then faces him in a head-on pass.

Lindbergh quickly calculates the time it will take before the two planes collide. He has already pressed the Lightning's gun triggers, and 20mm cannon shells and .50-caliber bullets converge on the frontal silhouette of the enemy aircraft as it grimly steadies onto a direct collision course. The closure rate is about 500 miles per hour, and Lindbergh can see the little cooling fins on the enemy's engine cylinders before he veers from his course.

There is a violent shudder as the two airplanes pass. Lindbergh estimates that less than ten feet of air separated the two metal bodies from a catastrophic meeting. He climbs steeply to the left before he changes his mind and reverses to the right in respect for the antiaircraft fire from the Amahai strip. A quick visual sweep reveals some other P-38s and his opponent of a moment before, heading down in a spin toward the sea.

The P-38s are from Captive Squadron. Lindbergh finds his wingman, but none of the other Possum aircraft. By radio, Possum Blue One advises that they are above the clouds. Lindbergh comes up through the thin layer only to lose his wingman—and finds no other aircraft! Later, he is able to reestablish radio contact and arrange to meet Possum Squadron at the rendezvous point.

The P-38s landed back at Mokmer a few minutes before 4:00 in the afternoon. The forty-two-year-old Lindbergh had been in the air for at least eight hours. He had capped his combat experience with a certain kill—even though for a number of political and technical reasons he would never be officially credited with it. He amended his diary entry for the day with a note of confirmation:

"Lieutenant [Joseph E.] Miller, my wingman, reported seeing the tracers of the Jap plane shooting at me. I was so concentrated on my own firing that I did not see the flashes of his guns. Miller said the plane rolled over out of control right after he passed me. Apparently my bullets had either severed the controls or killed the pilot."

CHAPTER FOUR

CHINA-BURMA-INDIA THEATER OF OPERATIONS

LIGHTNINGS IN THE CHINA-BURMA-INDIA THEATER

10th AIR FORCE (India-Burma)

The 10th Air Force became operational in India in March 1942 and oversaw USAAF units in China as well as India and Burma during the following year.

The first Lightning unit to see action in this theater was the 9th Photo Reconnaissance Squadron, flying the F-4 recon version of the P-38, which became operational in December 1942. (It later received improved F-5 models.) The 9th PRS provided the 10th AF with extremely valuable photo recon service, particularly during the Burma Campaign, right up to the end of the war. It was assigned to the newly arrived 8th Photo Recon Group in March 1944, with which it was joined by another F-5 unit, the 40th PRS, in September of that year.

The 459th "Twin Dragon" Fighter Squadron was activated in September 1943. Its first major assignments were bomber escort missions to Rangoon, but it began offensive fighter sweeps over Burma in late December. During the spring of 1944 the 459th FS was the scourge of the Japanese Army Air Force in Burma. Although nominally assigned to the P-40-equipped 80th FG, the squadron was at that time attached operationally to the RAF's 224 Group. It was credited with destroying over 60 enemy aircraft in the air (and many more on the ground) from March 11 to June 6 of that year. Its top scorer, with ten confirmed air victories, was Capt. Walter F. Duke, who was killed in action on the latter date.

The 33rd Fighter Group, then equipped with P-47s, was transferred from China (14th AF) to India in September 1944. Its 58th FS converted to P-38s in November 1944 and its other two squadrons, the 59th and 60th, did so in early 1945. The 459th FS was reassigned to the 33rd Group in May of that year.

14th AIR FORCE (China)

The first operational Lightning unit in China was the same as that in India—the 9th PRS. At that time the highest USAAF authority there was the China Air Task Force, a subsidiary of the 10th AF that became the 14th AF in March 1943. The 9th PRS had a detached flight at Kunming and Kweilin from November 1942 to July 1943.

The latter month was a significant one for Lightnings in China. A new photo recon squadron, the 21st, arrived there from the States, replacing the 9th PRS detachment, which returned to India. The 21st PRS established its own detached flights in various parts of China, enabling it to obtain photo coverage of virtually any corner of that huge country with its F-5s, as well as to make photo recon flights over Formosa (Taiwan) and the Japanese mainland.

Also arriving in China in July was the 14th AF's first and only P-38 fighter squadron, the 449th. It had been organized in North Africa as "Squadron X" before receiving a numerical designation and was comprised of both newly trained P-38 pilots from the fighter training center in Casablanca and volunteer veteran pilots and ground crewmen from the P-38 groups in that theater. The squadron's pilots flew their planes from Africa to China, via India, and had already scored its first victories there by the end of the month.

The 449th performed well in China and, among other accomplishments, scored 73 air victories. Its more prominent and successful pilots included Major Rex Barber, whose first combat tour had been on Guadalcanal in the South Pacific. Barber was already famous as a fighter ace and the pilot who helped shoot down Admiral Yamamoto. Lt. Col. George McMillan was the squadron's highest scoring pilot, with a total of 8.5 air victories scored almost equally with the A.V.G. "Flying Tigers" and the 449th. (McMillan was killed in action on June 24, 1944.)

The last Lightning combat unit to arrive in China was the 35th PRS, which became operational with its F-5s there in September 1944.

Chapter Four photo: A 14th Air Force F-5 over China. (Phil Schaff)

THE TWIN DRAGON SQUADRON
Steve Blake

One of the most interesting and successful P-38 units of World War II was also among the least publicized. This was mainly because the 10th Air Force's 459th Fighter Squadron fought in one of the USAAF's most obscure combat theaters, India/Burma.

The 459th was constituted on August 2, 1943, in Karachi, India (now Pakistan), one of the few USAAF units activated outside the U.S. Its personnel were transferees from the Mediterranean Theater and from two other 10th AF units—the 80th Fighter Group (P-40s) and the 311th Fighter-Bomber Group (P-51As and A-36s). The squadron was equipped with P-38Hs and assigned (nominally) to the 80th Group. In fact, it operated for the most part as an independent squadron, the only one in the 10th AF then flying P-38s.

During October, while the squadron was still being organized, several of its officers were enjoying a typical fighter pilot bull session when the need for a squadron insignia was raised. After considerable discussion, the emblem of a two-headed dragon was adopted. Soon the design began appearing on squadron jackets and, starting in early 1944, on the engine nacelles and booms of some of its Lightnings. Thus was born the "Twin Dragon Squadron."

The 459th's first operational base was Kurmitola, just east of Calcutta, to which it moved on November 5, 1943. Its first successes were scored on November 16, during a bomber escort to the Japanese base at Meiktila, Burma, when three Oscar fighters were claimed destroyed and two more as damaged. It then flew a series of bomber escort missions to Rangoon from November 25 to December 1, during which two enemy aircraft were claimed for the loss of two P-38s and their pilots. On December 26 the Twin Dragons attacked the Anisakan airdrome and destroyed four enemy aircraft on the ground.

In mid-February 1944, the 459th received additional gunnery training from the Royal Air Force and on March 4 it moved to Chittagong, south of Kurmitola, where it was attached to the RAF's 224 Group. During the next three months the Twin Dragon Squadron became the scourge of the Japanese Army Air Force in Burma.

The unit's first really big action—and its most successful mission of the war—took place on March 11. Led by its C.O., Capt. Verl Luehring, twelve P-38s attacked the Japanese airfield at Aungban just as a large group of Oscars was taking off to intercept them. These were picked off, one by one, and then the field was strafed, resulting in claims for thirteen destroyed and five probably destroyed in the air. Seven were destroyed and two damaged on the ground. Capt. Maxwell Glenn, Capt. Willard Webb and Lt. Walter Duke each claimed two aerial kills.

Between March 11 and May 26, 1944, the Twin Dragon pilots claimed 61 enemy aircraft destroyed in the air and 67 on the ground. Five of its pilots became aces: Lt. Hampton Boggs on April 2, Capt. Duke on April 25, Major Webb on May 14, and Capt. Glenn and Lt. Aaron Bearden on May 15.

The tragic climax to this amazing run came on June 6, when the 459th tangled with Oscars of the JAAF's 64th Sentai (Group) over Heho and claimed to have shot down three of them. However, Capt. Duke and Lt. Burdett Goodrich were MIA, never to be seen again. Ironically, Goodrich had destroyed an Oscar earlier in the action to become the squadron's sixth and last ace.

Japanese records obtained after the war indicate that three other Oscars were destroyed by Duke before he went down, which are not included in his official score. One of them was flown by Lt. Goichi Sumino, a 27-victory ace, who was also killed in action. Capt. Duke was the Twin Dragons' most successful pilot; he was credited with ten aerial victories and eight and a half destroyed on the ground, plus many probable and damaged claims.

Major Willard J. Webb's P-38J, 459th FS. Webb's victories included five destroyed in the air and three on the ground. Ground crew—S/ Sgt. J.H. Burns (crew chief) and Cpl. C.L. Spear (armorer). (USAF)

Thereafter, enemy aircraft became scarce, and the 459th concentrated on ground attack, becoming in the process a premier bridge busting unit. Its last aerial victory was scored on February 11, 1945, by Capt. Boggs, which was his ninth.

The squadron moved to Rumkha, India, on February 1 and then to Dudhkundi on May 11, where it became part of the 33rd Fighter Group. The 33rd's other three squadrons had recently converted from P-47s to P-38s, making it the only Lightning group in the 10th AF. After the war's end, the 459th FS moved to the U.S. in October and was inactivated at Camp Kilmer, New Jersey, the following month.

The 459th's total credits in the air came to 82 destroyed, 14 probably destroyed and 49 damaged, plus nearly that many on the ground. It is doubtful that any of the Japanese who encountered it would ever forget the Twin Dragon Squadron, should they have been lucky enough to survive the encounter!

FLYING TIGER AND LIGHTNING PILOT
Steve Blake

In 1941 Frank Schiel, Jr. was a USAAC test pilot at Eglin Field, Florida, when he was recruited for the Chinese Air Force's American Volunteer Group (A.V.G.), which was to become famous as the "Flying Tigers." He subsequently served as vice squadron leader with the group's 2nd "Panda Bears" Squadron. Although Schiel was very successful in air combat, destroying four Japanese planes in the air and another three on the ground by strafing, he was even better known in the A.V.G. for the reconnaissance missions he flew in a special stripped-down P-40 that had been fitted with an aerial camera.

Frank Schiel was one of the few Flying Tigers who joined the USAAF in China and stayed on as a member of the new 23rd Fighter Group, which replaced the A.V.G. Schiel, now a 25-year-old major, was assigned to command the group's 74th Fighter Squadron. In addition to his normal duties, he continued to fly photo recon missions in a converted Republic P-43 Lancer.

On November 26, 1942, there took place what turned out to be a life-changing event for Major Schiel. That day, three Lockheed F-4A recon Lightnings of the 9th Photo Reconnaissance Squadron arrived at Kunming, the 74th's base, for temporary duty there. The first bona fide modern Allied reconnaissance planes in China, they had a top speed of 400 mph, a very long range, four K-17 aerial cameras and an autopilot.

Schiel was, of course, fascinated and immediately checked himself out in this wonderful new aircraft. On December 1st he flew his first mission in it, to Thailand, and by the 5th had two more under his belt. On that date he and the F-4 flight commander, Major Dale Swarz, flew a photo recon mission all the way to the island of Formosa (now Taiwan). After refueling at another Chinese base on the way back and then taking off again for Kunming, the two pilots became separated in bad weather. Swarz eventually landed at yet another airfield, but nothing was heard from or of Major Schiel. Thirteen days later his remains were discovered in the wreckage of his Lightning, which had crashed into a mountain not far from Kunming and burst into flames.

106

ESCAPE FROM THE JAPANESE
Mary Lou Neale

Former football great and present day sports commentator Tom Harmon, who "bailed out twice and never hit the ground," credits "those big Allison engines on either side of the cockpit" with his survival during the Great Conflict. But it was his own stamina and courage which aided that survival after he lost his plane in a lopsided five -to-one dogfight with Zeros. Even in the offhand, pared-down version that he tells with characteristic modesty, it is quite a story.

"As a member of the first P-38 squadron (449th) in China, we flew high cover, close cover, long-range strikes, skip bombing and dive bombing. Our mission on October 30, 1943, was to destroy a smelter plant on the Yangtze River. The Japanese apparently had a few spies around. There could be no other answer to why the squadron of eight ran into some forty Zeros. It was comparable to running into an exposed beehive.

It was a hell of a fight, but while chasing one of the Zeros and trying to knock him off the tail of one of our planes, I had my plane in a steep climb firing everything I had before I realized my mistake. I had killed my airspeed, and the next thing I knew bullets were rattling against my armor plate. Then WHAM! There was an explosion in the cockpit as a Zero hit the gas primer between my legs.

The cockpit was suddenly full of flames. I tried to stamp the fire out with my hands, but with no success. I then noticed I was in a vertical dive. I released my safety belt, popped the canopy and boom—I was out. I pulled the ripcord at once and the chute opened. I saw a lake beneath me. I also saw two Zeros circling me. I remembered hearing about pilots before me who had been machine-gunned in their chutes, so I decided to play dead. I slumped in the chute and the Zeros headed back to their base.

I landed in the lake, rose to the surface under the chute and saw several sampans coming out. I was picked up by one man who motioned me to get into his boat. As I climbed in I got the shock of my life, for on the wall of the boat's hut was a broken mirror." The horrible site Harmon saw was the skin of his face hanging down on his chest "like a limp dishrag. The skin had been burned off, and I guess the landing in the water caused it to peel off like a banana," he recalled.

The boatman gave Harmon a coolie hat, white shirt and black pants so he was dressed exactly like all the boatmen in the flotilla. As they went toward the Japanese shore, the boatmen began jumping from sampan to sampan so that "anyone watching would have a hell of a time telling who was who and on what boat I landed." That well-rehearsed tactic gave his rescuers time to spirit him away to a

Lt. Harmon and his assigned P-38G-10, "Little Butch II." "Butch" was Harmon's nickname for his girlfriend (and later, his wife), movie actress Elyse Knox. (Harmon)

farm house.

It was there that the old Chinaman, Wong, appeared. "I would have been lost without him. The Chinese guerrilla soldiers were hard to reason with and impossible to understand. But with Wong (who spoke English) telling them what I wanted, I was able to keep some measure of control over the group that I came to label 'Harmon's Army.'"

When the Japanese came to the farm house he was obliged to lie down, hidden in the bushes for many hours despite the pain of his burns. "I had no intention of being captured if I could avoid it." The rescue team was composed of about 25 men who carried the crude stretcher. Harmon's legs were so badly burned he could not walk. After a few days, his 200-pound frame was found to be too heavy for the small men, so eight larger Chinese men were sent down from "up north."

There were many narrow escapes along the way, but the guerrillas finally deposited Harmon back at an American air base. Everyone was amazed to see this grimy, big guy dressed as a Chinese coolie—someone whom they had long thought dead. "All I wanted was to get back to the 449th, but there was something I had to do first." That something, of course, was to try to reward his friend and savior, Wong. "When I asked him what he wanted, Wong quietly said, 'I am happy you are back home.' Then he paused and almost timidly continued, 'All I would like is some American cigarettes. Do you think that could be possible?' I said, 'You damn betcha!'"

Harmon got the biggest box of cigarettes in the PX, containing 50 cartons. Then he found a wheelbarrow. "I piled Wong's cigarettes into the wheelbarrow and tried to thank him from the bottom of my heart for saving my life. Wong has probably passed on from this life, but I hope while he lived he remembered the P-38 pilot who was fished out of the lake that day."

I am sure he never forgot Harmon—and Harmon is absolutely sure he will never forget Mr. Wong.

PHOTO RECONNAISSANCE IN CHINA
Second Lieutenant Daniel Jackson, USAF

The value of aerial photo reconnaissance to the American air war in World War II is undisputed. However, few are aware that photo recon aircraft operating with Major General Claire Chennault's 14th Air Force in China provided the lynchpin of his offensive intelligence organization, and contributed to the greater war effort against Japan through missions to Formosa (Taiwan), the Philippines and even Japan itself. Chennault's photo recon aircraft provided three services without which the 14th AF would have proved impotent in any offensive role: target reconnaissance, mapping and post-raid analysis.

21st PRS pilot Winfree Sordelett flew one of the longest photo recon missions of the war, from China to Japan, in early 1944. (Arthur Griggs)

While commanding the American Volunteer Group, Chennault realized that he would need some sort of offensive intelligence in order to take the fight to the enemy, so he had one of the group's P-40s modified into an observation plane, including the mounting of a camera in its baggage compartment. This lone P-40 photo ship served through 1942, even after the A.V.G. passed into history on July 4th to be succeeded by the USAAF's China Air Task Force, also commanded by General Chennault.

As more offensive missions were mounted, the need for more and better photo reconnaissance aircraft became acute. Without photo intelligence on possible targets, Chennault's meager resources could not be used in an efficient manner to strike at the most lucrative targets. Additionally, attacking pilots had little idea of the location of their targets with respect to the surrounding area. To rectify this, several F-4 Lightning photo recon aircraft were sent to the theater. Major Frank Schiel, an A.V.G. veteran, flew one of these planes. Unfortunately, Schiel died in December 1942 when his F-4 crashed into a mountain in bad weather [see *Flying Tiger and Lightning Pilot* story].

The events of 1942 showed Chennault that he needed more reconnaissance planes and with them crews specially trained in photo recon. Though a theater the size of China would normally require a photo reconnaissance group, the logistical problems in China would not make it possible, so Chennault requested one squadron. The 21st Photo Reconnaissance Squadron, nicknamed the "China Falcons," arrived in China during the summer of 1943. To make this squadron capable of covering the four million square miles necessary, Chennault divided it into four independent flights. Each flight possessed anywhere from one to five aircraft and two to seven pilots along with maintenance crews, photo interpreters and camera repair specialists. Each would operate out of a different airfield and be responsible for a specific geographic area. Headquarters Flight was based at Kunming and was responsible for Burma and Indochina. "A" Flight flew out of Chengtu and was responsible for northeastern China (including Manchuria). "B" Flight was based at Kweilin and was responsible for Hong Kong and central China. "C" Flight was based farthest east, at Suichwan, and was responsible for eastern China and the outlying islands.

It did not take long for the China Falcons to prove their worth. Continuous reconnaissance (subject to weather) began immediately. On November 24, 1943, an F-5 Lightning from Suichwan photographed over 100 Japanese aircraft at Shinchiku Airdrome on the island of Formosa. The next day, B-25s and long-range fighters attacked the field and destroyed 14 enemy aircraft in the air and 43 on the ground.

It was not uncommon for Chennault to act this quickly on intelligence provided by his photo recon aircraft. Usually photographs were developed within a few hours of the plane having landed. Photo interpreters would then analyze them for potential targets. More often than not, the results of the interpretation were radioed to headquarters, though high priority photos could be flown to Kunming. The victory at Formosa ensured that Chennault would immediately order attacks on any significant concentrations of enemy planes discovered by the reconnaissance aircraft.

Photo intelligence gathered by the 21st PRS did not just benefit the tactical air forces in China, it also benefited the strategic air forces (B-29s) based at Chengtu in mid-1944, U.S. Navy submarines conducting anti-shipping operations off the China coast and other Allied forces in the Pacific. Recon Lightnings at Chengtu provided photographic intelligence on Japanese industry in Manchuria for the B-29 raids there, and in early 1944 Winfree Sordelett flew his F-5 from Suichwan to Nagasaki and Sasebo in southern Japan on an eleven-hour-and-forty-minute mission. Sordelett was so stiff from being crammed into the cockpit for so long that he had to be lifted out when he returned from the mission. He was awarded the Distinguished Flying Cross for his achievement.

Ed Penick, commander of "C" Flight at Suichwan, remembered performing sea sweeps over the Straits of Formosa during which he would mark Japanese ship positions and headings on a grid and use specially marked binoculars to estimate their speed. Naval intelligence personnel at Suichwan would radio this information to submarines in the straits that would use it to track and sink the enemy vessels. The China Falcons' reconnaissance of Formosa would later aid the U.S. Navy and the B-29s in their raids on the island, and reconnaissance of the Philippines would provide valuable information in advance of MacArthur's landings.

Key to achieving success in the realm of photo reconnaissance was the ability to evade or defeat Japanese defenses. The F-5 could fly at 35,000 feet, well above the useful altitude of Japanese fighters. The Lightning was also much faster. Penick remembered a particular mission to Formosa during which a Japanese fighter scrambled to meet him. After photographing his objective, Penick dropped his

A 14th Air Force F-5 over China. Note the camera compartment bulges on its nose. (Phil Schaff)

21st PRS "C" Flight command-er Ed Penick, with the F-5 he flew over Formosa following the famous Thanksgiving Day 1943 raid to assess the dam-age. (Penick)

external fuel tanks and sped for home. The enemy fighter could not climb high enough to reach Penick's F-5 and was not fast enough to keep pace; whenever the enemy pilot would lift his nose to fire, his fighter would slow down and Penick, cross-controlling to avoid being hit, would speed out of range. The Japanese pilot would then drop his nose to gain speed and re-peat the process. This hap-pened for some time until he finally gave up and returned home. Normally, the Japanese would not even bother respond-ing to a lone recon aircraft.

Penick flew many missions to Formosa because his unit was in-volved in mapping the island. Mapping was an important role of the photo reconnaissance units in China because few detailed maps exist-ed at the beginning of the war. It was not an uncommon occurrence for a flight crew to die because they ran out of gas, lost without a map. Trimetregon photography—three six-inch focal lens cameras which photographed a fifteen-mile-wide strip—provided 14th Air Force map makers with enough information to map in detail a theater that previously was not mapped at all. The Lightnings would fly a specific pattern over an assigned area, methodically photographing China until everything was covered.

In late 1944, the 35th Photo Reconnaissance Squadron arrived in China to help the overtaxed 21st. Sterling Barrow, a pilot with the new unit, remembered flying damage assessment missions in addi-tion to the mapping and target recon missions. Often an F-5 or a B-25 mounting an aerial camera would be dispatched after a mission to assess damage done to the target. In the heat of combat, crews' claims were often exaggerated, whether in regard to enemy aircraft destroyed while strafing or bombing or bridges and other infrastruc-ture destroyed. To provide accurate results photo reconnaissance was employed. Chennault dispatched as many assessment missions as any other type of reconnaissance in his attempt to accurately determine how best to defeat the Japanese. Barrow remembered some missions where a recon aircraft was required to take photos before, during and after a mission.

Of his photo reconnaissance units Chennault said, "There was not more striking demonstration of the China-based air force's capabilities." From the early days of the A.V.G., photo recon undisputedly enabled the 14th Air Force to carry the offensive to the Japanese and benefited the larger war against Japan. Chennault's photo recon airmen were the first Americans over Formosa, the first over Japan after the Doolittle Raid and the first over the Philippines after the fall of Corregidor. Photo recon also proved its worth in providing detailed maps of China and assessing the aftermath of offensive missions on Japanese targets.

These brave pilots, aerial photographers, photo interpreters, map makers and ground crewmen filled a role no less important to the war than any combat soldier or fighter pilot, and in fact enabled bomber and fighter pilots to do their job. Unfortunately, their contribution remains largely forgotten today, though their legacy lives on in the record of impressive missions they enabled during World War II.

The official caption for this USAF photo is: "Crew chief aids the pilot of a Lockheed F-5A of the 21st Photographic Reconnaissance Squadron as he adjusts his crash-straps prior to take-off from China on a mission." Unfortunately, the men are not identified.

A LONG RECON FLIGHT TO THE PI AND BACK
John M. McNicholas

Nearly 50 years after the fact, John McNicholas, a veteran of the 14th Air Force's 21st Photo Reconnaissance squadron, recalled his most memorable mission, from China to the Philippines and back on May 12, 1944—reportedly the only pilot to make that trip. His photos were used for General MacArthur's reinvasion plans.

"Lt. Colonel John Foster, Commanding Officer of the 21st, brought in a new F-5 for this mission. It was the first uncamouflaged Lightning in China, and it shone like a new dime.

I flew the F-5 from Kweilin to Suichwan the day before the flight. That night, the Japanese bombed Suichwan. The ground crewmen had improvised a makeshift antiaircraft weapon, which consisted of two .50-calibers mounted to swivel on a post with a bent pipe to lean back on. They hit one of the Betty bombers and it exploded in flames over the field. The next morning, when I went to the line for preflight, there was a Japanese cap and burned pieces of uniform around my plane.

I flew at 10,000 feet over the South China Sea, making a course correction off the Pratas Islands. I climbed to 30,000 feet and turned on the Tri Met cameras. My course took me down the east side of Lingayen Gulf. I turned on my target cameras and photographed Clark Field, the Manila area, Manila Bay, Cavite and Corregidor and headed for home. My head was on a swivel the entire flight but I saw nothing at my altitude. Later, photo interpreters told me there were many planes below me, especially near Clark Field.

I made my landfall right over Swatow at 10,000 feet. There was an enemy airfield in the vicinity but I never saw any other planes. I could not raise Suichwan as I neared it. When I turned to enter the pattern, I saw a burning P-40 by the runway and knew that they were under attack.

I pulled up and headed south to an emergency strip that was no more than a cart track through a field. I nursed it in with the nose pumping up and down as I braked to a stop. A dilapidated Chinese tanker truck showed up, and we hand pumped enough gas, through chamois skins, to get me home. At that time, a fellow pilot circled over us and said that Suichwan was all clear. So I headed home after more than nine hours of sitting on the life raft cylinder, which was placed in the most unsuitable spot. I could barely walk when I finally got out.

I think I know why I was the only pilot to make that flight. I heard that General MacArthur put out an order that no more planes from China were to go near the Philippines. I guess he didn't want the Japanese alerted."

John McNicholas (21st PRS, 14th AF) shares his F-5's cockpit with his dog, "Prang," at Kunming. He bought the dog in London when serving with the RCAF. Prang actually flew home with him to the States and then to China and home again after his final tour. McNicholas is convinced the men of the 14th AF will remember his dog more than him. (McNicholas)

BOTH ENGINES DEAD
Paul Mann

Simultaneous failure of both engines in a P-38 is admittedly a very rare occurrence, but not impossible. It is infinitely worse than losing just one engine. After losing one engine, and when the ship is under control, it is still flying, with plenty of time to locate the trouble, or at least to continue to fly home on the good engine—a very public spectacle. When you lose both engines you have a slight idea of the cause and usually little or no time to seek a cure. It could be that the lack of common knowledge of double engine failures is due to the fact that they *always* end in a crash, a forced landing or a successful solution of the problem. None of these outcomes is liable to warrant much publicity for the double engine failure or help to determine its cause.

Double engine failure happened to me while I was a pilot with the 9th Photo Recon Squadron stationed at Paradoba, India, in June of 1945. I was flying a food supply mission out of Dum Dum Airfield near Calcutta. My war-weary F-5E had the cameras removed and I flew it weekly to haul supplementary rations for the squadron mess—fresh eggs, oranges, etc. The preflight and run-up for my return flight showed everything in order, so off I went. The camera compartment was loaded with groceries and a case of Scotch that I was lucky enough to procure from one of my Calcutta suppliers. As soon as I cleared the traffic pattern I switched my fuel selector valves to Outer Wing Tank. I could see the fuel from those tanks siphoning overboard, and this would burn it rather than have it wasted.

My next order of business was to light a cigarette, relax and head for home, a flight of about half an hour duration. I was some 1,500 feet in the air, right over the middle of Calcutta, when it happened: Both engines quit without warning—not a cough, not a pop, not a sputter. Nothing! They just quit running as if someone had switched them off. The first order of business in such a situation is to pick out a spot for a forced landing, but where? There were buildings everywhere except the park, and it was full of huge trees and paved with people. Not an option!

Calcutta is 60 or so miles inland on the Hoogley River, which is large enough to accommodate ocean-going steamships all the way to the city. So that's my choice for an open space to land in. I establish my forced landing pattern, hopefully to end up near the riverbank. Even if I survive the crash, my swimming leaves much to be desired. Also, I'm concerned about salvaging my Scotch from shallow water.

Now back to the business of flying. My altitude is running lower with every passing second, and if anything is to be done, it has to be done immediately. A quick check of the cockpit doesn't reveal any problem, so for lack of anything better to do I switch fuel tanks. Not for any good reason, except that in an extreme emergency "Do something even if it's wrong" seems a better plan than sitting there like a twit or a bump on a pickle and letting the disaster just happen without a fight. Fortunately for me, that was exactly the right thing to do. Both props were windmilling (feathering Curtiss Electric propellers without electricity cannot happen), so the engines fired right up, at an altitude of only ten feet or so above the river, but below the riverbank (I had to look up to see the tops of the masts on the sailboats parked nearby!). Had I chosen a ground landing site I would already be history.

After climbing out of that predicament, a closer check of the instruments showed one altimeter charging on the peg—120 amps, as I recall. After turning that generator off, the other one showed the same thing, so it had to be shut down as well to prevent further damage, fire and who knows what. The ship is now without electricity. The spark plugs don't require it to keep the engines running, as they are powered by magnetos. Since we will be better off at home than in Calcutta, and the distance not much farther, that's where I headed. Flying without instruments, radio or warning lights, but running smoothly, we struck out for home. After landing I told the crew chief of the problem I'd had so he could get to work on it. While I was in Squadron Ops closing my flight plan he sent for me. We looked in the cockpit and he pointed out the problem. Here is the unlikely chain of events that caused the difficulty that was so nearly disastrous on that trip:

A five-cent spring broke inside the starter switch. It was supposed to return the switch to neutral upon being released after the engine started. Broken, the switch couldn't turn the starter off. The engine starter motor was running all during taxiing, warm-up and takeoff. Since it was some ten feet away, the starter couldn't be heard running over the engine noise. The starter motor uses a lot of electricity and is only designed to run for brief periods. After running for so long it burned out and shorted out the whole electrical system. Unfortunately for me, it waited until after I had switched fuel tanks. It is common practice to switch to the outer wing tanks as soon after takeoff as practical. When the outer wing tanks are full of fuel, some of it can be seen siphoning out of the filler caps. The reason for the switch is to burn that fuel and lower the level in the tanks rather than have it spill overboard. When the fuel selector valve is set to Outer Wing Tank, it shuts off all the main tanks and opens an electric valve that feeds fuel directly into the engine from that outer wing tank. When the electrical system shorted out it closed the electric outer wing fuel valves. I was out of gas immediately and on *both* engines.

Luckily, when I switched the fuel selectors back to the main tanks, the engines were still turning and they fired right up, saving my day, my ship, my Scotch—and more than likely my scrawny neck!

Paul Mann in the cockpit of the "war-weary" 9th PRS F-5E-2 (serial #43-28600) that he nearly crashed into the Hoogley River in Calcutta. Its regularly assigned pilot was Lt. John Whitley. Note the mission markings (103 camera silhouettes) on its nose behind the camera compartment. (Mann)

A THAI SCORE—THE USAAF VS. THE THAI AIR FORCE
Steve Blake

The 449th Fighter Squadron flew an especially interesting and eventful mission on November 11, 1944. One of the participants, Joe Fodor, recalled it many years later:

"Nine P-51s from the 25th FS and eight P-38s from the 449th FS took off from Yunnanyi, China, for targets in Thailand. The '38 pilots were: Flight #1: Lt. Dale D. Desper, Lt. Frederick A Roll, Jr., Lt. Leonard W. Flomer and Lt. Charles J. Robinson. Flight #2: Lt. Richard D. Conway, Lt. Grover W. Stubbee, Lt. Robert H. Jones and Lt. Joseph N. Fodor. Shortly after takeoff Lt. Robinson had to abort and return to Yunnanyi due to engine failure.

The remaining sixteen airplanes continued the flight to their first target area, Chiang Mai. The P-51s dropped down from our high-altitude position to sweep the enemy airfield at Lampang on strafing runs. The P-38s stayed high for top cover. At that point Desper's flight encountered a single 'Nate' fighter, which was destroyed by the entire flight—all three pilots striking the enemy aircraft, which exploded in mid-air. During this action nine more Nates jumped the P-38 flight at medium altitude. The '38s engaged the enemy fighters while the '51s stayed at low altitude, strafing the airfield. Lt. Conway lost an engine after scoring a probable and had to head for home on single engine. He landed at Szemaoi in friendly territory and then returned to Yunnanyi safely. Lt. Flomer's plane was also damaged in the ensuing air battle, causing a fire in the right internal wing tip fuel tank. The fire did extinguish itself and Lt. Desper left the dogfight to escort him to Yunnanyi."

By the time the fight was over, the P-38 pilots had scored four other victories: Lt. Stubbee, one destroyed; Lt. Jones, one destroyed and one probable; and Lt. Fodor, one probable. The P-51 pilots claimed to have shot down two more Nates, making a total of six destroyed and three probables in this action.

It was unusual to encounter Nates (Nakajima Ki-27s) at that point in the war, as they were by then quite obsolete. The nimble little Ki-27 had been very successful for the Japanese Army Air Force in numerous air battles with the Chinese and Russian Air Forces in the late '30s and had seen a fair amount of action early in WWII, especially in China. But by 1944 it was no match for the much faster and heavily armed Allied fighters, such as the P-38 and the P-51. (The Nate had fixed landing gear, and its maximum speed at altitude was just under 300 mph. It was powered by a 700-hp radial engine driving a two-blade propeller, and its armament consisted of just two fuselage-mounted 7.7mm machine guns.)

The Nates encountered that day were not, however, serving with

120

the JAAF. They belonged to the Royal Thai Air Force (RTAF). The Japanese supplied their "puppet" government in Thailand with quite a bit of military equipment, including a few Ki-27s and some Ki-21 "Sally" bombers—and later some more modern Ki-43 "Oscar" fighters. The RTAF's main task was bombing and ground-attack in support of the Thai army, which was assigned to engage Chinese forces in the north, protecting the Japanese flank.

It has been determined from RTAF records that during the action on November 11, 1944, at least five Nates were, in fact, shot down or severely damaged, and one pilot, Chief Warrant Officer Nat Sunthorn, was killed. Pilot Officer Kamrop Bleangkam claimed a P-38 before he had to crash land his Ki-27. (This was undoubtedly one of the two P-38s that were damaged during the dogfight.)

Joe Fodor assures us that he "can positively confirm that all seven P-38 pilots returned to Yunannyi after the air battle, plus the eighth that returned to base prior to the engagement. Thai Pilot Officer Bleangkam was absolutely wrong in claiming a P-38 was destroyed in that encounter. There is, however, another possibility that may shed some light on the issue. One of the P-51 pilots, a Lt. Minco, radioed during the melee that he had a Nate cornered in a remote canyon area and would be claiming a victory soon. That was his last transmission. To my knowledge he was not heard from again nor did he return to Yunannyi. As far as I know the other eight P-51s did return safely to base."

Lt. Joe Fodor probably destroyed a Thai Ki-27 in the 449th Squadron's big fight on November 11, 1944. (Fodor via Dan Jackson)

A HAIRY CHRISTMAS
Keith Mahon

[The following is the author's reply to a request from a young boy for a "war story."]

So you're ten years old! To me that always seemed to be sort of a magic age for some reason or another. I remember a lot of things I was involved in at that age. For example, I built my first model airplane, which I designed myself. It didn't fly, but I had fun and learned a little bit about aerodynamics—and it was at that time I made up my mind to learn to fly full-size airplanes someday.

I had a cousin a year older than I, and he was just as crazy about airplanes as I was. When we had enough money saved we would buy a certain paperback in serial format called "G-8 and His Battle Aces." The setting was always an airfield close to the "front lines" in France during World War I. G-8 was always getting himself into trouble of some kind, like having to land behind German lines, getting captured and going through all sorts of scary experiences to get home again. And boy, there wasn't a German fighter ace in the air that could shoot down 'ole G-8 and his S.P.A.D. The year was 1932, and the world was just beginning to smolder into what was to become another war bigger than what my hero was involved in. Not in my wildest imagination did I ever think that eleven years later I would be fighting Japanese "Zeros" in the sky over China, flying P-38s, and using some of the same flight tactics as my old storybook idol.

It was Christmas Day 1944. But before I get into the mission itself I need to give you a little background that adds to the drama a bit. During that time in China, because of the territory occupied by the Japanese, the only way anything could be brought into the country was by airplane. All the fuel, bombs and ammunition, medical supplies—everything had to be flown in. What we ate was what was available at the time, which depended in part on the growing season. The details of our diet are not important. What really mattered was that Christmas dinner, as you and I know, just wasn't possible without some clever planning.

A couple of months earlier four of us were sent to Calcutta, India, to ferry back new P-38s. This airplane had the ability to carry tremendous loads attached to the bomb shackles, including two fuel tanks that would hold 310 gallons each. That much external fuel was not needed on the trip, so we modified one tank on each airplane with a detachable door, so that we could fill the tank completely with canned food that we got at a huge Army supply center in Calcutta. We had enough Christmas (and other) food goodies for the entire squadron to really celebrate. The turkey was canned, but turkey nonetheless—and not the usual pork and rice.

122

So, O.K., it's now Christmas morning. No missions were scheduled, and the weather was so bad we didn't even have anyone standing alert at their aircraft in the event of an air raid. About mid-
morning a message came in to send five airplanes on a mission to
"beat up" a certain Japanese airfield on Hainan Island, which extends
down into the South China Sea. It was my turn as mission leader,
and I was irate because of several things, not the least of which was
the thought of missing Christmas dinner. From a practical standpoint
there was the question of being qualified for such a mission. We
were a day fighter squadron and had neither the equipment nor the
pilot qualifications to operate in conditions involving flying in bad
weather or at night. These were the types of missions the four-
engine bombers flew routinely. Also, it would take precious time to
prepare the airplanes, which involved changing the external loads
and loading ammunition appropriate for this mission. The best I
could calculate was that if everything went smoothly we would arrive
at the target just before nightfall.

I contacted a friend at 14th Air Force Headquarters who worked
with us a lot and asked him to try to persuade *someone* to postpone
this crazy mission until at least the next morning. He was aware of
the situation. He said that General Chennault, Commander of the
14th Air Force—the number one "Tiger" himself—laid that mission on
to show the Japanese that we were capable of and willing to strike
one of their strategic bases on a long mission with a very small force,
on one of the holiest of our holidays. So, I picked four volunteers,
briefed them on the mission, and we finally got airborne.

We had to start out at about 500 feet of altitude because of the
weather, but about an hour out we found a thin place in the clouds
that enabled us to climb. Our en route altitude was generally 18,000
feet because we had a fairly good idea of wind conditions that would
affect our flight. By the time we reached altitude, the cloud condition
below was solid overcast again, which meant that we had to rely
strictly on clock and compass for navigation. About half way to the
target, around the time we should have been crossing the French In-
do-China (Vietnam) coastline, one of the pilots pulled up beside me
to signal that one of his engines had started to overheat. The condition was visible, because there was a thin, wispy white trail of engine
coolant from a pressure relief valve. It was squadron policy in such
situations to send another plane back with the cripple (they both got
home alright). We did all this by hand signals so we could maintain
our strict radio silence. I didn't like being down to only three, but we
chugged along.

As the clock was winding down to target time I began to make out
an irregularity in the cloud layer ahead of us. I guessed right that we
were nearing the island and that the cloud buildup was probably

Captain Mahon and his P-38 named "The Eula D II" after his mother. It displays victory symbols for eleven of the twelve enemy aircraft he was credited with destroying—five in the air and seven on the ground. (Mahon)

caused by the temperature difference between the ocean and the land mass. We were soon flying directly across the island but couldn't see it yet, then the cloud condition became broken and we could see water below. I had some scary thoughts as to where we might *not* be. I started a slow circle and saw the outline of the island below. WOW! What a relief; at least we weren't lost out over the South China Sea somewhere. It was just like the parting of the Red Sea for Moses. We looked down and the clouds had parted. I maintained radio silence; let's not give them a freebie in case they didn't know already that we were there. I gave the signal and we slowed up, dropped our external fuel tanks, put down our dive brakes, and headed down.

I spotted a landmark that consisted of a very small dock facility with a rail line which ran directly to the airfield we were after. Piece of cake—just follow the "yellow brick road." We came in under the thin cloud cover at about 450 miles per hour. The cloud ceiling was about 700 feet, and the visibility was pretty good. No need for radio silence now, so I told the guys to stay loose and be particularly alert for any other aircraft in the air (it's someone's good fortune that there were not). As I remember, it was about 25 miles to the target and we would be there in about four minutes. Flying that long at level flight was costing us precious airspeed, so we set the engines for combat and bored on in. I instructed as to what maneuver we would follow upon completing the first pass and tried to say something funny to break the tension.

Now, we were probably over the target no more than eight minutes at the very most. That's long enough to fire all your ammunition, do all the damage you're going to do and not get shot down by ground fire. When everyone gets home and is being critiqued individually as to what happened he has a chance to learn what each of the others did. The first thing I remember was seeing tracer bullets coming our way as we neared the airfield boundary. No large shells were bursting around us (yet), so it was not too distracting. I chose a radar unit dead ahead and fired into it. I could see good strikes all over it so it didn't require any more attention. As I was preparing to fire at the radar, I noticed that I was right over two fighter aircraft parked beside the runway. When I came back around one of the others had beaten me to them. They were both on fire, but I now had a good view into a large aircraft hangar in which there were several more airplanes. I directed that we concentrate our firepower through the open hangar doors. You can imagine what damage could be done with all the .50-caliber armor-piercing incendiaries and our 20mm cannon's high-explosive incendiaries bouncing and zigzagging around and exploding inside that hangar. WOW—it was a dream target! We probably made four passes.

By now we had attracted the attention of a large gunboat in the harbor nearby. I had not noticed it before. It started belching out anti-aircraft shells—I mean the exploding kind. I had strafed airfields before and had been able to fly inside the burst range of the anti-aircraft fire so that it would have taken a direct hit to get me rather than an exploding shell (shrapnel). But those guys had stuff bursting all around us, and then they started firing WP (white phosphorous) at close range. It was time to go home!

I instructed the guys to head west, get as low to the ground as possible until we got out of range, then, on my signal, to zoom up through the thin overcast one at a time, and we would assemble on top. I made a partial turn so I could take a quick look back and try to get an assessment of the damage. The radar unit was burning merrily, so were three aircraft along the runway, and the hangar was a roaring inferno. Mission accomplished! When I turned back in the cockpit I was headed straight for a haystack! There was not time to think; I just reacted by yanking back on the wheel. I went through just the top of it with my propeller tips, not enough to cause any damage. The guys behind me said it happened so suddenly no one had time to yell, but there sure was a big hay storm! I told them later what they were thinking—that the fool was too close to the ground to be looking anywhere but straight ahead.

O.K., now we were on top, climbing back to altitude and at the same time assessing what damage we had sustained. We looked each other over carefully to be sure no one was losing fluids of any kind—fuel, oil or engine coolant. We were alright in that respect. We all had holes shot in the airframe here and there, but our controls were responsive, so we knew the flight cables were good enough not to cause worry. My big worry then was how to get these brave men home, in the dead of night and without any navigational equipment. At our altitude the sun was disappearing rapidly out of a clear sky, and I remember thinking that on the ground it was already night time. And it would still be at least three hours before we could possibly get home.

We had a low frequency radio band that was not always dependable. I fiddled with it, trying to raise a friendly voice and give a position report, but didn't have any luck. I could hear voices, but nothing seemed to be directed my way. We chatted a little back and forth among us as a morale booster, but no one felt like telling a funny joke or any such thing. When I calculated that we should be about 30 minutes out, the sky condition beneath us was becoming clear, and we could see the dim lights from an occasional village. What I was now hoping for was to see the flashing beacon from an air base, and I assigned a sector for each of us to scan, instead of everyone staring straight ahead. Soon the pilot on my right said that he thought he saw a flash ahead and to our right. I started a turn in that direction and sure enough, there was another.

We rolled our wings level in that direction and flew on, but we didn't see any more flashes and I soon realized that we were flying over a very large lake. There was enough reflection from starlight to make it out. BINGO! I knew where we were—near a large airfield used by the Air Transport Command. We were about 30 miles from home, but it would have been insane to pass up this chance to land. We turned toward the shoreline where we knew the field to be, and I called the control tower for landing instructions. After a pause we were told to go to Kunming (our base), because they did not have facilities to accommodate combat aircraft crews. I declared our situation to be an emergency and requested that they turn the runway lights on so we could land. They refused on the grounds that they were under a "red alert," expecting a bombing raid. They said that the Chinese air raid net had been plotting heavy engine noise progressing toward that air base for over an hour, and it was about 40 minutes out. I accepted that in good faith, because I knew that no ground tracker could have heard us overhead at 18,000 feet.

That was also the reason they had turned off the rotating beacon. But 40 minutes! I could land and be in bed in a few minutes! Well, I'm not going to tell you how the dialog went for about five minutes between me and the tower officer, but I made a threat that he could not ignore. So he turned on the lights long enough for the other two to land, then turned them off when I was about halfway down on final approach. My two buddies had parked together because they had the advantage of better lighting. I parked close by, and after some whistling and yelling, we were joined again. I still wanted a piece of that tower bunch, so that's where I headed. When we arrived I found that the tower officer that night was a major. I was a captain so didn't have much clout, especially on his turf.

One lucky thing happened though. A good friend of ours who was our former flight surgeon came into the tower. He had heard the un-mistakable sound of P-38s and expected to see friendly faces. He was a major also, and when he sensed the antagonism he took me by the arm and ushered us out, then took us to his tent and scram-bled some eggs for us over a Coleman stove. Christmas dinner, at last! The heavy engine noise did not result in a bombing after all. They went back the other way.

We got home the next day and gave our reports, and everything became normal again. Each of us was awarded the Air Medal. It was my 59th mission. I flew 28 more before coming home.

One thing that bugged my crew chief from that time on was how I managed to bring back hay straw stuck to the front of my oil and coolant radiators. He was never satisfied with the truth. I should have told him that it was a secret between me and 'ole G-8.

[Keith Mahon, an Oklahoman, was 22 years old at this time. He had won his wings with Class 43-F at Williams Field, Arizona. In Decem-ber 1943 he was assigned to the 449th Fighter Squadron in China and served with it until May of 1945, by which time he had earned three Distinguished Flying Crosses and four Air Medals. The 449th was the only P-38 squadron in China (14th Air Force) and was at-tached to the 51st Fighter Group. Mahon was one of the squadron's aces, which status he achieved over Hainan Island on January 5, 1945, when he shot down three Japanese Army Air Force Oscar fight-ers to bring his total of air victories to five. He retired from the USAF as a Lt. Colonel in 1970.]

CHAPTER FIVE

MEDITERRANEAN
THEATER
OF
OPERATIONS

LIGHTNINGS IN THE
MEDITERRANEAN THEATER OF OPERATIONS

The first P-38s arrived in North Africa a few days after the Allied invasion of Vichy French-controlled Morocco and Algeria on November 8, 1942—as soon as airfields and basic facilities were available there. The pilots of the 1st and 14th Fighter Groups flew their planes in from England and began combat operations almost immediately.

It was tough going for the P-38 pilots of the new 12th Air Force those first few weeks. They were fighting a difficult foe; some of the opposing Luftwaffe fighter pilots had several years' combat experience and had scored dozens of aerial victories, plus the Americans were often outnumbered. Fortunately, they were reinforced with another P-38 group, the 82nd, in late December. As their experience level rose and their tactics improved, they were gradually able to hold their own—and better—in their fights with the Luftwaffe and the Regia Aeronautica, and their scores increased accordingly.

Due to being short one squadron and to heavy losses, the 14th FG was withdrawn from combat at the end of January 1943 to reform. It was assigned another squadron and re-entered the fray shortly after the surrender of the Axis forces in North Africa in mid-May.

The only other Lightning unit involved in the North African campaign was the 3rd Photographic Group, which arrived from England in December 1942 and subsequently did yeoman photo recon work with its F-4s and (later) F-5s. (Until March 1943 the 3rd PG was commanded by the President's son, Colonel Elliott Roosevelt, who went on to become C.O. of the 90th Reconnaissance Wing, which oversaw all the USAAF photo recon units in the MTO.)

Once all of North Africa was in Allied hands, their air forces—including the USAAF's Lightning units—focused their attention on the strategic Axis-held islands between it and Italy, especially Pantelleria, Sardinia and Sicily, all of which were captured that summer. The P-38 was particularly well suited to those long over-water missions, with its superior range and "extra" motor that enabled many of its pilots to return home on a single engine.

Even as the invasion of Sicily proceeded to its inevitable conclusion in July and August 1943, plans were made for landings on the Italian mainland in early September. In preparation for the latter, a series of missions were flown there to reduce the strength of the Axis air forces and their ability to interfere with the invasion forces, and to destroy strategic facilities and enemy war materiel. The P-38, the only Allied day fighter with the range to fly round trip from North Africa to Italy, was a major participant. A particularly outstanding mission took place on August 25th, when all three P-38 groups flew a low-level strafe of airfields in the Foggia area, destroying dozens of

A 3rd Recon Group F-4 over North Africa in early 1943. (USAF)

Axis aircraft. It resulted in Distinguished Unit Citations for the 1st and 82nd Groups.

There was also a series of bomber escort missions to the mainland, especially the Naples area, which often stirred up hornet's nests of enemy fighters. The most memorable were on August 30th and September 2nd, involving the 1st and 82nd Fighter Groups, respectively. They resulted in two of the biggest dogfights ever seen in the MTO and heavy losses to the fighters on both sides, but little or no damage to the American bombers. Both units received another DUC for these missions.

Two other USAAF units in the MTO received a few P-38s temporarily in mid-1943. The 81st and 347th Fighter Groups were at that time assigned to air defense duty in North Africa, but their Bell P-39s were not up to the task of intercepting enemy bombers, which the Lightning certainly was. The 347th scored ten kills with its P-38s and the 81st, one.

The invasion of Italy commenced on September 8th, and as it progressed, Allied air units began moving to newly captured airfields there, putting them much closer to European targets to the north, east and west. This made possible the activation of the new, strategic 15th Air Force commanded by General Jimmy Doolittle on No-

132

vember 1st. The three P-38 groups were transferred to the 15th, mainly to escort its four-engine bombers to targets in Southern and Eastern Europe.

The 15th AF's Lightning units were the 1st Fighter Group (27th, 71st and 94th Fighter Squadrons), the 14th Fighter Group (37th, 48th and 49th Fighter Squadrons), the 82nd Fighter Group (95th, 96th and 97th Fighter Squadrons), and the 5th Photo Recon Group,

Then-8th Air Force C.O. General Jimmy Doolittle is about to take to the air in a P-38H in England, March 1944. (USAF)

which had arrived in-theater in September 1943 and was comprised of the 15th and 23rd (and later the 32nd and 37th) Photo Recon Squadrons. Another F-5 unit, the 16th Photo Recon Squadron, served at "higher headquarters in the MTO."

This left the re-designated 3rd Photo Recon Group as the only remaining 12th AF Lightning unit. Its squadrons were then the 5th and 12th Photo Recon, although the 23rd PRS was later transferred to it from the 5th PRG. The 3rd Group's primary missions were low-level tactical assignments in support of the ground troops, while the 5th Group mostly performed long-range, high-altitude strategic photo reconnaissance.

It should be noted that even though the 15th AF's Lightning units would henceforth be flying the majority of their missions to European countries, they were still officially part of the Mediterranean Allied Air Forces (MAAF), based as they were in the distinctly Mediterranean country of Italy, to the northern part of which many 15th AF missions were also flown. For example, all the kills scored by its fighter pilots anywhere over Europe were officially categorized as MTO victories.

Another, rather unusual, P-38 unit was the 154th Weather Recon-naissance Squadron, which was assigned to 15th AF Headquarters in Bari, Italy. Its main job was to send out one or two (armed) Light-nings to check and report back on the weather over the tentatively scheduled targets for the 15th's bombers, greatly assisting in the task of deciding which, if any, could or should be bombed that day.

One of the most famous (or infamous) P-38 missions of WWII was the dive bombing of the oil refineries at Ploesti, Romania, on June 10, 1944. The 82nd FG did the bombing while the 1st FG provided cover. Considerable damage was done, but at the cost of twenty-four P-38s to enemy fighters and the wall of flak surrounding the refineries. The 82nd was awarded another DUC for that one.

During the spring and early summer of 1944 the 15th AF's P-38 and P-51 units decimated the Axis air forces in Southern and Eastern Europe, and although they would continue to fly many bomber escort missions during the last nine months of the war, enemy fighter oppo-sition was minimal and sporadic. Thus, the Lightning pilots began flying more ground attack missions, often on the way home after the conclusion of their escort duties. Trains were particularly lucrative and vital targets, and they destroyed hundreds of them.

In no other theater was the Lightning more successful than in the MTO during its two and a half years of service there. For example, the Mediterranean P-38 pilots were credited with destroying 1,425 Axis aircraft in the air, second only to the much larger Pacific Thea-ter.

MISSION IMPOSSIBLE
Kenneth W. Herrick

At first, flights by P-38s were relatively short—a couple of hours or so, but the introduction of belly tanks changed that. I recall making a round trip from Foggia, Italy, to Berlin that took about eight hours. In a cramped cockpit that a six-footer must slouch to keep from hitting his head on the canopy, that is a *long* time.

It was very cold at altitude, too, with the temperature decreasing three degrees for every 1,000 feet of altitude. When it was 60 degrees on the ground at Foggia, it was *minus* 45 degrees at 35,000 feet.

One of the complications of long flights was that "nature's call" was no longer easy to postpone. Hence, a relief tube was now part of every P-38. The relief tube consisted of a little funnel attached to a rubber hose with a diameter about that of a pencil. The funnel snapped into a bracket under the front of the pilot's seat, and the hose exited at some lower extremity of the pilot's compartment.

The theory was that in case he needed to relieve himself, the pilot could reach down, snap the funnel out of its bracket and do so, with the fluid running down the thin rubber hose out into the "wild blue yonder."

Because of the intense cold, pilots dressed as warmly as possible. Generally, this meant cotton shorts, then woolen long johns, followed by woolen G.I. pants and shirt. Next came a "blue bunny" electric flying suit made of thick, coarse wool and, finally, a cotton flight jump suit. The latter had big knee pockets which we filled with an escape kit and various favorite articles such as candy bars, apples, etc.

Strapped around all of this bulk, most of us carried a .45 pistol in a shoulder holster and a big Bowie knife. On our feet we wore cotton socks, felt electric slippers, heavy knee-high woolen socks and G.I. boots. We stuffed all this into *very* large rubber, fleece-lined flying boots. Our hands were encased in silk gloves over which were leather, fleece-lined gloves. We topped this all off with a helmet, goggles and an oxygen mask. Fully dressed, we looked more like a herd of penguins waddling toward the edge of an iceberg than a group of fighter pilots going out to their planes.

And so, into the air for what often seemed like an endless journey. In due course, if the postponable became unpostponable, step one was to unbuckle the two heavy chute straps that went between your legs and then fastened with big, heavy metal clips to other straps on top of your hips. Then you started digging through all those layers of clothing—unzipping, unbuttoning, unzipping, unbuttoning. Bear in mind that while all this unbuttoning was going on you were trying to keep your plane in formation. This meant you needed a hand for the wheel and a hand for the throttles. The design engineer for the relief tube evidently thought P-38 pilots had four hands, because that's what you really needed to fly and relieve yourself at the same time.

If you managed to dig through all those layers of clothing without running into another plane, your problems were still far from over. A law of physics states that heat causes expansion and cold begets contraction. This law applies double at 35,000 feet. In fact, it all reminded me of that picture of a robin stretching a reluctant worm from a grass lawn the first day of spring.

For those super pilots able to overcome all the aforementioned obstacles to relieving oneself at 35,000 feet, two obstacles remained. Invariably, the relief tube, because of its cramped position under the seat, would have a kink or two in it. Or, the tube would freeze the fluid solid as it began flowing through it. Thus, after a few seconds, the funnel would begin to fill up. As disbelief and panic registered on his face, he would realize the full meaning of the expression "my cup runneth over."

Ever aware of that, suddenly, from out of the blinding sun, could come the wily Hun to end his career literally in mid-stream, the pilot needed a quick solution to his full funnel. There, only inches from his hands, were the tops of his big rubber, fleece-lined flying boots stuffed with all those layers of *absorbent* clothing. War *is* cruel.

[Ken served with the 96th Squadron of the 82nd Fighter Group in Italy 1944-45.]

A HEROIC RESCUE
Steve Blake

On August 4, 1944, the 82nd Fighter Group, based at Foggia, Italy, received a particularly hazardous assignment. It was a "shuttle" mission to Russia, a number of which, code-named FRANTIC, were flown by the 8th Air Force in England and the 15th Air Force in Italy that summer. After completing a mission over Axis Europe, the American planes would land in Russia, from which they would fly others, returning to their home bases at the end of the last one.

This mission, FRANTIC 4, was to strafe enemy airfields and other ground targets in Romania en route to Poltava in the Ukraine, its temporary Russian base. As the 82nd attacked some trains and trucks near Ploesti, antiaircraft fire knocked out the left engine of the P-38 flown by 96th Squadron flight leader Dick Willsie. It was Willsie's 59th mission and turned out to be his most exciting.

Although now on one engine, First Lieutenant Willsie joined in strafing a nearby airfield, where his good engine was also hit by flak. "I noticed coolant streaming from my right engine cooler located aft of the boom. This meant I only had a few minutes left, at best. I then made a call and reported my plight, and that I was going down." A response came from one of his squadron mates, 20-year-old Flight Officer Dick Andrews of Portland, Oregon, whose 10th mission this was: "Pick a good field and I will come in after you." Willsie, whose hometown was Long Beach, California, recalled later that:

"I had to get down quickly if I wanted to have any control of the landing. I forgot about everything else and concentrated on putting the plane down. Suddenly, my windshield cracked from another hit. I felt a sting on my head and then a warm trickle down my forehead. I saw a place to land, and two quick turns and a sideslip put me in position over some trees and down. As I slid over the last obstacle and touched down, I placed my head against the rubber padding on the gun sight—and before the plane skidded to a stop, my nose felt like Joe Louis had broken it with several of his left jabs and right hooks! I put my hand up to my face and it came back with thick blood all over it. I felt sick. But I could still move, and move I did! I jumped out on the left wing.

I could hear planes overhead and saw some P-38s and Me 109s dogfighting. I also saw men in the distance and trucks not far off. I heard rifle fire and the whine of bullets. I headed down the left wing, which was flat against the ground, and turned to run for the cover of the nearby trees. At this time I saw Andrews' plane with its landing gear down. Spellbound, I dropped down and watched it. I thought, 'My God, he *is* coming in to pick me up!' The field was soft and had obviously been planted recently, as there was stubble about an inch

Willsie and Andrews posed themselves in the cockpit of a P-38 at Poltava the day after their August 4, 1944, adventure but couldn't quite fit both of them in fully as they had when it was so vital that they do so. Note the dressing on Lt. Willsie's wounded forehead and Lt. Andrews' American flag armband identifying him as "friendly" to our Russian allies. (Andrews)

high. I had on sheepskin flying boots—not the best running gear, but I ran anyway, for what seemed like the length of a football field, toward his plane. When he finally stopped, he started to taxi in my direction, but someone called on the radio and said to stay there, because I was coming to him."

Andrews had watched Willsie land, "then I made a 180-degree turn, putting my gear and flaps down. Seeing I was too close to the field, I picked my gear up, made a 270-degree turn and started my approach, putting my gear back down when I saw I could make the field. I landed with the furrows, making sure to make a smooth landing. I stopped 100 feet from a cornfield, pulled my flaps up and set them in takeoff position. Leaving the engines running at 1800 rpm, I locked the brakes."

While this was going on, other 82nd FG pilots were battling the Me 109s and strafing the enemy troops that were trying to kill or capture the two temporarily grounded fliers. Willsie remembered well what happened next:

138

"When I got to Dick's P-38 he was standing on the wing. He had dropped the fold-down ladder and thrown his chute away. Although out of breath, I managed a big smile. He grabbed my hand and pulled me up on the wing. He said, 'You fly,' and we both jumped into the cockpit with a miracle of precision. I sat as far forward as I could, with him behind me, not really on his lap and he not really on my back. His right leg had to be placed over my right shoulder because the control column on a P-38 comes up from the right side of the cockpit. His left leg was down under my left arm. My hind end was on the front part of the bucket seat.

We pulled the canopy closed. He put up the right window and I put up the left one. This all occurred within seconds. I then pushed the propeller control to low pitch, pulled back on the controls to keep the nose up, and eased the throttles forward. I felt the nose wheel dig into the soft earth of the plowed meadow when I let go of the brakes. I couldn't get the control wheel back any farther, so I cranked in full trim—nose up. It did come up, and we started rolling. There were trees ahead of us, so I put down the flaps to combat position, which helped us lift off. Now I had to play the climb just enough to clear the trees—not too much or we would mush right into them. We did clear those trees, but I sure was glad they weren't ten feet taller."

They were, miraculously, in the air and on their way again. There followed an extremely uncomfortable two-and-a-half-hour flight to Poltava in a *very* cramped cockpit, with a bleeding pilot (Andrews swabbed Willsie's cuts with iodine). Dick Andrews remembered that "We kept our spirits up by joking about it and kidding each other. We landed at the Russian base ahead of the other planes, due to Willsie's expert piloting. Those crew chiefs really flipped out when they saw both of us climbing out of that P-38"

When they returned to Foggia two days later, the two Lightning pilots were treated like celebrities. When they landed they were greeted by several VIPs, including Generals Nathan Twining, Commanding Officer of the 15th Air Force, and Dean Strother, the 306th Fighter Wing's Commanding Officer. As Andrews stepped out of his plane he was greeted by General Twining, who gave him a spot promotion to second lieutenant and awarded him the Silver Star. A few days later he received a special commendation from General Ira Eaker, Commanding Officer, U.S. Strategic Air Forces in Europe (8th and 15th Air Forces).

Both men completed their combat tours, Willsie having flown 82 missions, 32 over the requirement. He was soon promoted to command the 96th Fighter Squadron, with the eventual rank of major.

Dick Andrews chats with General Twining (on the left) after his return to Foggia on August 6th. (Andrews)

"MY BABY": ONE LIGHTNING'S STORY
Steve Blake

On November 4, 1942, a brand-new P-38F-15, serial #43-2181, began a cross-country flight from the Lockheed factory in Burbank, California, to the East Coast. At its destination it was disassembled, crated and shipped to Liverpool, England, where it was then reassembled. A pilot from the 78th Fighter Group flew this Lightning to North Africa in February 1943, turning it over to a service group at Casablanca. After flight testing there, 43-2181 was flown later that month to Telergma, Algeria. At Telergma it was assigned to the 82nd Fighter Group's 95th Fighter Squadron—and specifically to Lt. Wilbur S. "Will" Hattendorf, of Evanston, Illinois.

Will and his brother and fellow pilot, Richard "Biff" Hattendorf, had been reassigned to the 82nd FG In Southern California the previous summer from the 55th FG in Washington State. They sailed to Britain with the rest of the 82nd's personnel on the *Queen Mary* in late September. Three months later the 82nd FG's pilots flew their P-38s to North Africa—and into combat.

As a new member of the 95th FS, 43-2181 was assigned the code letters "AY," which were painted in white on her outer coolant radiator

Will Hattendorf (on the left), a mutual friend from another unit and brother Biff Hattendorf in North Africa, early 1943. (Hattendorf)

housings. "A" stood for the 95th and "Y" indicated that particular aircraft within the squadron. She also received a name, *My Baby*, in honor of Will's wife, Betty. The squadron artist painted a picture of Betty on its nose above the name, from a small photograph.

My Baby was soon in the thick of the North African air war. On March 22, 1943, the 82nd escorted B-26s on an anti-shipping sweep. When the bombers attacked a convoy just off Bizerte, Tunisia, a large number of enemy fighters intervened, and a savage dogfight ensued. The 95th and 97th Squadrons claimed nine Me 109s destroyed, three probables and two damaged for the loss of three P-38s and their pilots in this action.

Will Hattendorf and *My Baby* probably destroyed one of the Messerschmitts, using up all their ammo in the process. Hattendorf then spotted another Lightning, bullet-riddled and with one engine shot out, under attack by a pair of Me 109s. He made bluff passes at them for several minutes, all the while calling for assistance. Responding to his cries was his brother Biff, who had already shot down one 109. Together, they managed to drive off these other two. Needless to say, the pilot of the shot-up P-38 was profuse in expressing his gratitude to the Hattendorf brothers after they had all returned to base.

On April 5, while escorting B-25s to Bo Rizzo Airdrome in Sicily, *My Baby* carried Will safely through a 30-minute dogfight, during which they shot down another Me 109. Six days later, Lt. Hattendorf and AY participated in the squadron's biggest and most successful air battle yet. During a fighter sweep, a large formation of enemy transport planes (Ju 52s), escorted by single- and twin-engine fighters, was spotted off the Gulf of Tunis. While some of the P-38s went after the transports, others (including *My Baby*) took on the escort. She and Will quickly dispatched a Ju 88 and an Me 110. In all, twenty transports and seven enemy fighters were claimed destroyed by the 95th.

Although Hattendorf was her principal pilot, he was by no means the only one to fly *My Baby*. On April 28, his squadron mate Lt. James R. Gant of Fort Worth, Texas, shot down an Italian fighter with her during a sea sweep off Sicily.

Years later, Will recalled that after he had flown about half his required 50 missions, his crew chief, Sgt. Vern Taylor, found out that two new and more powerful Allison engines had become available; they had just been off-loaded from a freighter in Algiers. "We requested them for AY," Hattendorf said, "got them, and with help from other crews, the engines were exchanged. After test flights and adjustments, AY went back to work—and boy did she move!"

My Baby continued to fly regularly right up to the time Hattendorf completed his tour in early August 1943. She had 60 missions to her

Lt. Hattendorf and his crew chief with "My Baby." At that point, late in Will's tour, she had shot down five enemy planes and flown eleven dive-bombing missions. (Hattendorf)

credit by that time, 38 with Will at the controls. He had claimed three enemy planes destroyed and a probable while flying her, and damaged two more with other squadron P-38s. Other pilots had scored two additional "kills" with *My Baby*, making her an "ace" air-craft. Her only "wound" was a flak hole in the left engine nacelle, incurred while dive bombing Pantelleria Island.

Will was supposed to fly *My Baby* home for a bond tour (a distinct honor)—destination Miami, via Ascension Island and Brazil. He suc-cessfully tested over-sized, long-range ferry tanks—two of them at 300 gallons each—on her several times. For some reason the flight was cancelled, however, and Hattendorf returned home by ship in-stead.

AY *was*, however, flown back to the States, a month later. Lt. Clarence O. "Tuffy" Johnson, a tour-expired 96th Squadron pilot, left North Africa with her on September 26, 1943. Unfortunately, *My Ba-by's* subsequent history is not known, but her fate was undoubtedly quite different than those of most of her North African contemporar-ies.

143

RENEGADE LIGHTNING
Steve Blake

During World War II the Axis captured hundreds of Allied aircraft that were either intact or repairable. A few were actually utilized by them in an operational capacity; the official records of the USAAF contain many accounts of hostile encounters with American military aircraft that were evidently being flown by enemy pilots. The following, carefully researched, story relates the only known incident in which an American fighter plane, flown by an enemy pilot, shot down an American bomber. Sad to say, the culprit was a P-38!

On June 12, 1943, a USAAF P-38G landed at Capoterra Airfield in Sardinia, the Regia Aeronautica thereby acquiring an example of the most advanced Allied fighter in the Mediterranean Theater—in excellent condition. Italian sources indicate that this Lightning was en route from Gibraltar to Malta when its reportedly inexperienced American pilot became lost and landed in Sardinia, nearly out of fuel. His name and unit and his aircraft's serial number have unfortunately not been determined.

The following day Colonello Angelo Tondi, commander of the Regia Aeronautica's Test and Research Center at Guidonia, a few miles northeast of Rome, arrived at Capoterra to take charge of this extremely valuable acquisition. Tondi was Italy's most famous test pilot and held several flight records. Before his arrival, personnel of an Italian fighter squadron based at Capoterra had repainted the P-38 in R.A. markings.

Colonel Tondi and his flight mechanic—who had somehow squeezed himself into the rear of the cockpit—were soon on their way to Guidonia in the Lightning. En route, they encountered some Luftwaffe Me 109s, which nearly opened fire before their pilots spotted its Italian markings. Shortly thereafter, Tondi discovered that the P-38's compass was off 30 degrees, which helps to explain how its American pilot had become lost.

During the next two months the Lightning was studied carefully by Italian aeronautical engineers and test flown by Colonel Tondi. Also during this time, Tondi formed a plan to use it in combat against the American heavy bombers that were now bombing the Italian mainland regularly. This was evidently approved, because just before noon on August 11, 1943, he took off in the P-38 to intercept USAAF B-17s approaching the coast of Italy just south of Rome.

The Flying Fortresses in question belonged to the 301st Bomb Group, which was based at Oudna, Tunisia. Their target was Terni, a few miles north of Guidonia. Not surprisingly, Tondi was able to approach the B-17s without being fired upon, his Lightning's familiar silhouette identifying it to the American crewmen as a "friendly" fighter. Some of the bomber gunners later reported first spotting the P-38 as it fired on an "Me 109." The latter was, in fact, a Macchi 205 single-engine fighter flown by another Italian test pilot, who joined in the attack on the B-17s. We can be sure that Tondi *wasn't* firing at the Macchi!

Colonel Tondi's attack was directed at a flight from the 419th Bomb Squadron, and he shot at several of the Fortresses in turn. His most effective pass was on B-17F serial #42-30307, piloted by 1st Lt. Albert J. Fensel. Staff Sergeant Jerald E. Tate, a tail gunner in one of the other bombers under attack by the P-38, later described what happened:

"When the P-38 was first seen we were about two or three minutes from the coast and it was reported from eight o'clock upper. He came around to five o'clock and was reported to be friendly Air Craft. He wiggled his wings and started in slowly to the formation. He came in to approximately 300 yards and opened fire. Our waist gunner shot at him and he turned toward seven o'clock and I gave him a burst. He went on to ten o'clock and attacked, whereupon our waist gunner and ball turret gunner fired at him. He then went around to two o'clock and made an attack on A/C 42-30307. He hit this plane and it peeled off, passed our tail, and seemed to go out of control...the plane went into a spin...and just before the plane hit the water it straightened out into a dive and hit the water nose first. In

The captured P-38 after it had been repainted in Italian Air Force markings at Capoterra. (Ferdinando D'Amico)

all I saw six chutes open. The P-38 then made another attack on us, and followed this by an attack on the plane on our right."

Several of the American gunners commented in their reports on the professionalism of the enemy pilot, his tactics—mostly head-on attacks and holding fire until within several hundred yards—having proved most effective. Although numerous witnesses (including the Macchi pilot) saw six chutes open, only three of the nine crew members of 42-30307 survived. The bombardier, navigator and tail gunner were picked up from their life rafts by a Catalina flying boat two days later, on August 13.

Needless to say, there was a great deal of anxiety among the 12th Air Force's bomber and P-38 groups after word of this incident spread. The bomber units were warned to be on the lookout for a lone Lightning. P-38 pilots received instructions *not* to try to join up with bomber formations should they become separated from their own.

However, this was both the renegade Lightning's first and last combat mission. Although it had been hit by some of the bomber gunners, the damage was not serious. The highly corrosive Italian aviation fuel, however, had ruined the P-38's fuel tanks. Thus, this Axis/Allied fighter never flew again.

FUGITIVE LIGHTNING
Ferdinando D'Amico with Steve Blake

Although the central event of this almost unbelievable story took place in Italy on October 13, 1944, it really began eleven days earlier in Karachi, India, when novice USAAF P-38 pilot 2nd Lt. Martin J. Monti was posted AWOL.

Monti was of Italian descent and had visited his ancestral homeland before the war. He later said that he had gotten tired of sitting around in a replacement depot and, therefore, hitched rides on transport aircraft to "join his buddies" (other P-38 pilots with whom he had trained) in Italy.

Arriving in Foggia, Lt. Monti reportedly approached the C.O. of the 82nd Fighter Group, with which some of his "buddies" were serving, and requested a transfer, but was turned down. Shortly thereafter, at Pomigliano Airfield near Naples, home of the 354th Air Service Squadron, he spotted a brand-new F-5E (serial #44-23725). Supposedly succumbing to a desire "to see what the front line looked like," he managed to finagle a clearance to flight test the Lockheed's engines. Monti took off shortly after noon—and wasn't heard of again until seven months later!

He met up with American soldiers in Milan on May 13, 1945, claiming to be an escaped prisoner of war from the 82nd FG who had been shot down on his first mission. Lt. Monti was debriefed, but was arrested a few days later.

At his court martial in August, the charges were desertion and wrongful misappropriation of an aircraft "of the value of more than $50." In his defense, Monti testified that he had been hit by flak, lost an engine and bailed out near Milan. He claimed that he was held prisoner in Italy and then Germany for four months, and that he then escaped with the intention of heading for Switzerland but ended up in Milan in April, awaiting American troops.

Prosecution witnesses testified that the F-5E had not been officially released, and a former comrade of Monti's told how he had opined that the peoples of Italy, Germany and the United States had been misled into war by propaganda. He had talked of getting to Italy and then flying to Switzerland and parachuting into internment there after giving suitable "distress signals." This witness concluded that, "In my opinion [he] was merely trying to get out of fighting. I do not believe that he would sell out to the Germans, but was so queer and strange that he might well do this."

The court martial found Monti guilty of being absent without leave rather than desertion, and of stealing the F-5. He was sentenced in 1946 to dismissal from the service and fifteen years confinement. Harsh as the sentence was, it would likely have been more so had the

This illustration of the stolen F-5E in Luftwaffe markings was made by Italian aviation artist Gabriele Valentini.

court heard evidence of what *really* happened at Milan on that Friday the 13th, according to an official Luftwaffe report: "Air situation, 13 October. 1500 hours: landing of a Lightning on Milan/Linate Airfield. Pilot (American) taken prisoner. Aircraft undamaged (unarmed reconnaissance model with built-in camera)."

A few days after its capture (presentation!), the F-5 was flown to Villafranca Airfield, east of Milan, by which time it had been sprayed yellow on its undersides to identify it as Axis-operated and had been given German markings. On October 25, it was flown to Germany, where it was incorporated into a special Luftwaffe unit equipped with captured Allied aircraft for testing and for demonstration flights. U.S. troops recaptured 44-23725 at Schwangau, Germany, in May 1945.

As to Martin Monti, he was pardoned within a year on condition that he rejoin the Army, this time as an enlisted man. However, it was soon learned that he had collaborated with the Germans to a much larger degree than had been realized—to the extent of becoming an officer in the SS, so strong were his fascist beliefs. He was rearrested in 1948 and re-tried, for treason this time, found guilty and sentenced to 25 years in Leavenworth Penitentiary. He was paroled in 1960.

KEEP YOUR HEAD OUT
Colonel Donald A. Luttrell, USAF (Retired)

On June 14, 1944, I was a combat pilot flying P-38s in the 49th Fighter Squadron, 14th Fighter Group of the 15th Air Force in Italy and feeling pretty good about myself. I had completed four combat missions and was scheduled to fly my fifth, had achieved one victory, and had graduated to "Tail End Charlie" in the formation lineup. I was beginning to feel like a seasoned veteran and starting to think I was a hot pilot. Big mistake! You don't get to feeling hot until just before you die.

At the briefing that morning we learned that the 14th Group was flagged to provide fighter cover for the 55th Bomb Wing as it bombed the oil refinery complex at Pétfürdő, Hungary. All aspects of the briefing—weather, flak, enemy fighters, etc.—were routine and indicated nothing unusual. All three squadrons were off a little before nine o'clock and set course for the rendezvous point with the bombers. One of the pilots in the 49th had been suffering from diarrhea for the past few days, and about halfway across the Adriatic he had an accident with which he felt he could not cope sitting in that cockpit for the next four hours, so turned around and went back to the showers. This left fifteen 49th Squadron aircraft to continue on.

Rendezvous with the bombers was made on schedule and our three squadrons positioned themselves above the bomber stream, making lazy turns back and forth across the route of flight to maintain position. Our bombers were the last in the stream, and as we approached the target we found a column of smoke rising to above 25,000 feet from the attention the refinery had received from the bombers further up the chain.

Standard procedure was to escort the bombers to the initial point and as they turned on the bomb run to the target we would swing wide and go around to meet them on the other side, the thinking being that the enemy fighters didn't follow the bombers through the flak so there was no reason for us to do so. For reasons I never learned, the 37th and 48th Squadrons went around the smoke column to the east. The 49th went around to the west. When we were halfway around the arc taking us to the other side we were probably 50 miles from the other two squadrons, with a big column of smoke between us.

Now came the second big mistake. The bombing was very good and we could see the bombs exploding in the tank farm at the refinery. Guys started making comments on this over the radio, and fifteen pairs of eyes were on the target below instead of looking around as we should have been doing.

Then a voice came on the radio: "51s high at ten o'clock," followed immediately by "51s hell, those are 109s!" All heads snapped to the left, and there they were. Later estimates fell somewhere between 50 and 75, but they looked like a thousand. Talk about activity in the cockpit: drop tanks, switch gas selectors, mixtures to rich, rpm's high and throttles forward—all in a hard left turn.

This was a textbook example of hours of boredom interspersed with moments of sheer panic. In seconds the situation had turned into a John Wayne movie, with airplanes twisting and turning, shooting and being shot at, and voices crackling over the radio. Someone called for the other two squadrons to help us, but they might as well have been in the Pacific, so we had these guys all to ourselves. Being outnumbered 75 to 15 is bad, but one bright spot in a very dark picture is that they can't all shoot at you at once.

In a short time the 49th had split into two groups, each doing a Lufbery circle, one clockwise and one counterclockwise. I was in a turn to the right when my element leader, Clyde Jones, did a wingover and turned out to the left. I followed him. When we had turned about 90 degrees his aircraft suddenly turned into a ball of fire. The Me 109 that got him had obviously dived down from above, as he had a speed advantage over us. He pulled up over Clyde and began to climb away. I rolled level and gave him a three-second burst. A wing dropped, and I gave him another, two-second, burst. A ball of smoke came out and he fell down and away, trailing smoke all the way.

I began a turn to the left to return to the squadron when out in front of my upraised wing I saw a 109 diving down about 90 degrees to my flight path, firing at me. The 109 had armament in both wings and the nose, and when it fired it looked as if the whole front of the airplane was afire—a riveting sight if it is firing at you! I reefed in on the control column as hard as I could, and that probably saved my life, as it is very difficult to follow an airplane through a spin.

When I recovered from the spin the 109 was nowhere in sight, but I was sitting out there all alone and the sky was full of enemy aircraft. I could still see the melee going on high at ten o'clock, so I headed back toward my friends. Lou Benne was leading the squadron that day, and it appeared he had gone down when the 109s first tore through us, so for a time no one was in charge. [Houston] "Moose" Musgrove was leading Blue Flight, and he called out that the next time he came around he was going to break out and climb into the sun, and for all of us to follow him. He did, and we did.

As we came out of the Lufbery the 109s broke away and were gone. The nine aircraft we had left formed a loose formation and headed for home. We learned later that another '38, flown by Swanson Shortt, had dived into the oil smoke to get away from three 109s. He set course for home and put on war emergency power in-

150

side the smoke cloud, so when he popped out, by the time they saw him they couldn't catch him. He landed with numerous holes in his airplane, including from a dozen-plus cannon shells, but the self-sealing tanks worked. Most of the other aircraft had varying degrees of battle damage. I was unscathed.

Back on the ground we learned that we had lost five planes and pilots. We submitted thirteen claims. We found out later that all five shot-down pilots survived, although one (Jones) was so badly burned that when he pulled his helmet off, part of one ear remained inside.

Thirteen to five is an O.K. score when you're playing baseball, but when you have lost a third of your force and five guys you ate breakfast with that morning aren't there to eat supper, you don't feel like winners. In addition, all of us knew we had been remiss in not looking around. I learned a lesson from this mission. I flew 53 more, but never again did I fall into that trap. Anytime I was over enemy territory my head was on a constant swivel!

[Don Lutrell's Me 109 was credited to him as destroyed. The 49th

This photo of Lt. Luttrell in the cockpit of his P-38 was taken at Triolo in January 1945 for publication in his hometown newspaper. (Luttrell)

Squadron was credited with fifteen destroyed, two probables and two damaged, including claims made later by returning POWs. Its primary opponents on June 14 were pilots of the elite 101st "Puma" Fighter Group of the Royal Hungarian Air Force, who claimed to have shot down eight P-38s in that action (some Luftwaffe fighters were also involved). The author completed his combat tour in December 1944.]

"MILK RUN" TURNED SOUR
H. B. Hatch

During the summer of 1944, almost all our missions were high-altitude missions escorting the "heavies" of the 15th Air Force. We had a few strafing missions and one forgettable dive-bombing mission, but most of the time we were high above the ground. With the '51s pulling fighter sweeps ahead of the bombing force, we went many times without any contact with the enemy forces at all. It got to be pretty dull after a while. A little excitement at the time would have been welcome.

It was on the way home from one of the "milk runs" [on September 2] that I got me and my whole squadron in a mess of trouble. I was leading the 71st Fighter Squadron that day—not for the first time—and as usual we let down from oxygen level so those of us who smoked could take off the mask and light up. We were cruising along somewhere over Yugoslavia when one of our group called and said, "Red Leader, look at the little train down there at about 10 o'clock." I looked and there it was—in a fairly wide valley between two mountain ridges. It was just too good to resist, and the urge for a little action was even harder to resist.

I hit the radio button and said, "O.K. Cragmore [71st Squadron], drop belly tanks and follow me down in train." I peeled off and headed down. I chose to make the pass from west to east because there was more room between the hills and the track on the west side of the valley. Art Hoodechek was the relatively new boy flying my wing as number two.

Everything looked lovely as I leveled off to make my run, and then all hell broke loose. The sides of those four cars dropped off and exposed multiple-mount, 40mm Bofors guns, two to a car. And the flak started flying. I hit the radio and yelled, "Break it off, Cragmore, break it off!"

It was too late for me to stop my pass, so I opened fire, blew the engine up and tried to spray the Bofors, but it was too late for "Hoody." They nailed him dead center, and I watched him in my rear view mirror pull straight up about 1,000 to 1,200 feet, stall out, roll over and crash. I saw no 'chute, nor did any of the others, and I was one sick squadron leader.

I had heard of those "Q" trains but had never seen one before. Not only had I lost a pilot and plane, but I had disobeyed an order. We had been expressly forbidden to go strafing when we were on escort missions. I was not looking forward to explaining Hoody's loss when I got back to the field.

I caught hell, which I deserved, but also got a C+ from the intelligence officer for the info on the "Q" train, justifying their previous

Lt. Herbert B. "Stub" Hatch, Jr. flew a few other missions that weren't milk runs. Here he points to the results of one of them painted on the nose of his P-38, "Mon Amy." During the infamous Ploesti dive-bombing mission on June 10, 1944, Stub shot down five Axis fighters, for which he was awarded the DSC. (USAF)

warnings. It was the first actual sighting of one of them.

Life goes on. I finished my tour and returned to the States, my wife and my son. It was the practice in those days to give returning pilots a couple of weeks at home and then have them report to an R&R center for further rest and some physical and mental evaluation. For those of us on the West Coast, the center was the Del Mar Club in Santa Monica, California, one of the plush resorts prior to the war. Wives were welcome and Amy went with me.

We had been there four or five days and were sitting in the dining room having lunch when a ghost walked up the three stairs and entered the dining room. Amy says I turned white as a sheet, jumped up and yelled clear across the room—"Hoody!" Sure enough, it was Hoodechek, alive and in perfect health. We had old home week for about an hour and this is his story:

When he got hit his airplane caught fire immediately, and his only chance was to try to bail out. He pulled straight up, as I had seen, and when the plane started to stall, he popped the canopy and went over the side. He said his 'chute opened, the plane hit the ground and he hit the ground in just about that order.

He hit pretty hard, but didn't break anything. His first reaction was to get the hell out of the area as fast as he could. He started running east toward the nearest hills. There was no pursuit, and he just kept going.

You do funny things under circumstances like that. After a few minutes running he became aware he still had his bright orange Mae West on and decided he had to get rid of it fast. So, since he was running through a field of pumpkins, he tore the vest off, wrapped it around a pumpkin and took off again. The vest blended in beautifully with the pumpkins!

He kept going east and up into the mountains and forest without having seen a soul until late that afternoon, when he came around a bend and bumped into what he said was the meanest looking SOB he'd ever seen, complete with a submachine gun and a nasty look.

He stopped in his tracks, raised his hands over his head and froze. He spoke to this character using the phrase we had been taught to use: "Americanski Piloto." Nothing happened. The guy didn't speak or move, just kept that gun pointed at Hoody's belly. He tried again with the same results.

Hoody then had a bright idea. He'd show the guy his wings. He dropped his right hand, reached for the zipper on his flight suit and pulled it down a little to show his wings. At this point the guy let go a burst from his machine gun into the ground at Hoody's feet.

Hoody said it took a little while for him to come down out of the tree, but the gunner made him slowly undo his flight suit and took the .45 Hoody had forgotten he was carrying. Still with no words, he was waived up the trail and set out with this mean looking guy behind him.

To make a long story a little shorter, Hoody had been picked up by one of Tito's partisans and that night was taken to a camp where he found several other American aircrew members who had been shot down and rescued by the partisans. The group spent some time in that camp and were then taken down to a field where a C-47 came in, loaded them up and took them back to Italy.

I've seen Hoody several times at the 1st Fighter Group reunions. He never seemed to hold it against me for getting him shot down. And I can tell you, he was a welcome, unexpected sight in that dining room!

SPIN INSTRUCTIONS, PLEASE!
Ed Baquet

I was fresh from the States with thirty-seven hours and fifteen minutes experience in the P-38. I was assigned to the 14th Fighter Group (49th Fighter Squadron) and on my first combat mission—to cover the bombers over their target, Blechhammer, Germany.

Our squadron of sixteen aircraft quickly formed up, with me nervously glued to my flight leader's wing. I soon realized that I had missed part of the briefing somewhere. No one told me that radio jamming was part of this war game. The headset was chanting, "Go-ring, Go-ring." Herman Goering was sending his entire Luftwaffe after me! That was bad enough, but my present discomfort wasn't due to fear of the enemy but to shivers from the cold. Obviously I was not dressed properly for this type of operation. We were crisscrossing over the bombers at 32,000 feet, an altitude I had never before experienced—and no cockpit heat. My hands and feet were killing me.

All of a sudden my leader made a hard break to the right. I did my best to stay with him, but my turn was too tight and my bird snapped over into a spin. Maybe it was the cold or the shades of Goering's best out there somewhere, but this did not feel exactly like a BT-13 spin. I white-knuckled the wheel to turn against the spin and was jarred by a considerable noise coming from the nose of my aircraft. In my panic I was squeezing the gun trigger and spraying all of Germany with my .50-calibers!

The spin stopped, but the dive continued. Each time I tried to pull out, the P-38 stalled. As we oscillated through the air, the plane and I had one thing in common—we were both confused. The high speed and thin air flowing over the elevators would not produce the needed response.

According to the books, I was applying the low-altitude recovery technique in this high-altitude, low-density air. But book learning was not uppermost in my mind at this time. After two more attempts I decided it was time to bail out. But, going straight down with that giant boom looming behind me, that did not look like an inviting prospect. I decided to give the recovery one more try. The bird responded at this lower altitude. I was flying again!

But where was everybody? My head was spinning like a top, looking for enemy fighters or friendly anything. My oxygen gauge read zero. I would pass out for sure or the "Jerries" were going to get me. Then to my amazed relief I spotted another P-38 off to my left. God, thank you! I'm saved! I flew over and latched on to him. Another surprise: Guess who? It was my flight leader. We descended over the Adriatic Sea and landed at our home base.

My crew chief greeted me, all smiles as he looked at the smoke around the gun ports. "Hey, Lieutenant—looks like you saw action on your first mission!" I looked back at him and said, "Yeah, Sarge. I sure did."

[The title of this story came from that of a cartoon by the late USAF artist Bob Stevens.

Edwin C. Baquet graduated with Class 43-K at Luke Field in December 1943. He flew a six-month, fifty-mission combat tour with the 49th FS in Italy, which he completed in December 1944. Among his other accomplishments, he destroyed three enemy aircraft on the ground plus probably two Fw 190s in the air. After returning to the States, he flew the USAAF's new jet fighters there until the end of the war. Ed stayed in the service and flew 55 night bombing missions with B-26s during the Korean War. He was then assigned to a ferrying squadron and led the first group of sixteen F-86F single-engine jet fighters across the North Atlantic for delivery to Germany.

Baquet retired from the USAF after twenty-three years as a lieutenant colonel and then entered the Civil Service as Ground Safety Director with the 15th Air Force, retiring from that duty after another twenty years. Most recently he was an officer of the P-38 National Association.]

December 27, 1944: Lt. Baquet completes his 50th and final combat mission. (Baquet)

THE JET STREAM INCIDENT
Jack Cooper

On an overcast morning in the spring of 1945, my 15th Photo Recon Squadron mate Orrie Engle and I took off minutes apart in a couple of F-5s, on separate photo missions from our base at Bari, in eastern Italy. Our targets were due north across the Adriatic in Austria, Czechoslovakia and Hungary. Typically, they were railroad marshaling yards and airfields.

In time we broke out a mile and a half apart, above a cloud layer that must have been 15,000 to 20,000 feet thick. After we had settled down at 25,000 feet on almost parallel courses, I heard Orrie key up and say, "Convent Six, look behind you." So I checked my rear view mirror, and there, right at my altitude and directly behind me by a quarter of a mile, was a single antiaircraft burst! Talk about conserving ammo! I wonder how close they came?

Gradually we lost sight of each other and went our separate ways. After several hours I figured by dead reckoning to be over my first target, which was obscured. Knowing the ground elevation below me, I descended, hoping to break into the clear for some photos. Eventually I dropped out of the soup and set about orienting myself. Not a thing even remotely matched my charts, nor did I recognize any roads, rivers, villages or railroads—nothing was familiar.

Puzzled, I kept scanning the area. Then, suddenly I spotted two Soviet fighters racing toward me, a couple of miles away. They didn't look one bit friendly to me, so I gave up, turned back toward home and started climbing up through the clouds. I felt confident that I could outdistance my pursuers should they decide to follow me, as we P-38 jocks had been told repeatedly that our aircraft, in shallow dive or climb, could leave any enemy fighter behind.

Sure enough, several minutes after I came out on top I spotted them in my mirror, clawing their way into the thin, clear air. They saw me, I guess, but gave up the chase. I steered for my base for about an hour and figured I'd be able to raise our homing station, "Big Fence," for a reliable fix to Bari. Nothing. Unbelievable!

I stayed on my heading, calling Big Fence every 20-30 minutes. Soon I dropped both external tanks, having sucked them dry, and realized that I needed to worry about the diminishing fuel in my mains. Boy, I had to know where I was—*immediately*. I still hadn't gotten close enough to raise Big Fence, but my dead reckoning told me that I might be nearing the west coast of Italy, a clear case of overshoot. Figuring that was possible, I decided the best plan was to go a little farther, then let down over the water, double back, find a fill-up and return to base. Simple. But where was Big Fence?

I started my letdown through the undercast—down, down, down

Lt. Jack Cooper in the cockpit of a 15th PRS F-5 in early 1945. (Cooper)

to about 3,000 feet, where suddenly my eager eyes spotted a hole in the clouds as they whizzed by. Hoping it was a good, *big* hole, I slammed the F-5 on its side and headed back, gyros tumbling. In seconds the airspeed needle sank to 0. I mean zero! Wow, I'm headed straight up and stalling! My reaction was to shove the wheel and throttles to the stops. But nothing felt at all right, and I still had no airspeed indicated.

Then a little light went on right over my head—ice! I switched on the pitot tube deicer, and before I could whimper, the needle shot up from 0 to 100, 200, 300, 400 mph, and I broke out of the clouds, pointing straight down! I was maybe 1,000 feet from the ground, so I throttled back and pulled up with a little room to spare.

Looking west, I saw what had to be the Tyrrhenian Sea and the west coast of Italy, right where it should be. But why was I there? Once again I called Big Fence, and this time they came back. "Give me a steer to the closest field; I'm wringing out my tanks as we speak," I cried. Big Fence: "Steer 270, there's a base right on the coast." Me: "I may have to ditch." Big Fence: "Drop us a line."

Well, I had learned one thing: I had dropped out of the clouds on the west coast of Yugoslavia and not where I had thought. I could have been killed!

During those 75 miles I allowed my Allisons only the merest vapors of the little 100 octane that was left. I called for a straight-in approach as soon as I identified the strip and touched down with a giant sigh. Refueling the tanks took exactly the amount they held. I probably couldn't have flown another ten seconds. This didn't start out to be an especially long mission—what happened?

After refueling I took off and headed south for Bari, giving Convent 10 (Engle) a call for the heck of it. I was overjoyed when he answered. He said he'd landed for fuel about 30 minutes inland and would look for me. In a couple of minutes he was beside me, along with a lone P-51 he'd met along the way. We three flew a loose formation south over the Adriatic, and eventually Orrie and I peeled off and landed at Bari.

During interrogation I learned that a 100-mph jet stream from the west at 25,000 feet (just our altitude!) had been reported after we took off on our missions. For every hour we flew, we were blown 100 miles eastward and off course. For much of the mission I was out of range of Big Fence and quite lost, but didn't know it.

That jet stream accounted for all that wild disorientation, plus the lack of communication. Orrie and I had plenty of dumb luck just when we needed it.

CZECHS HONOR AMERICAN P-38 PILOT
Steve Blake

April 11, 1945, began as a typical day for the 15th Air Force's 14th Fighter Group, based at Triolo, Italy. Its mission was certainly not unusual: strafing railway targets in areas of the eastern portion of Hitler's now not-so-great Reich. The targets were still— temporarily—under German control.

The group split up into squadrons in the target area, and the squadrons into sections. One of the 37th Fighter Squadron sections, comprised of only five P-38s of "C" and "D" Flights instead of the usual eight, was led by 1st Lt. Robert W. Whitehead. While "working" on the railroads south of Prague in Czechoslovakia late that morning, Whitehead's section claimed thirteen locomotives and a "goods wagon" destroyed and others damaged.

After attacking a shunting station near Písek shortly after 10:30, the P-38s reformed at 2,000 feet and headed southwest, for home. A few minutes later, over the village of Srubec, the American pilots encountered some Fw 190s that were returning from a mission to their airfield at Planá, near the city of Ceské Budejovice.

The ensuing aerial duel was brief, but deadly. Lt. Harry Morris, Lt. Whitehead's wingman, shot down one of the Focke-Wulfs, but Whitehead's P-38 (an L-5 model, serial #44-25720) was also hit and crashed, carrying its pilot to his death. (The Luftwaffe pilot, who managed to bail out, visited the Lightning's crash site several hours later to "pay tribute" to the American flier.)

Charles Turner was a member of "C" Flight that day. He remembers:

"At the time the incident occurred we were climbing up to regroup after strafing a train. At this point there were only four P-38s remaining [in our section]. The flak was very heavy and we took a lot of damage. My guns overheated, and I was down to a few last rounds of ammunition.

As I climbed, I saw an airplane landing in the distance and was about to call that they were approaching an airfield when a garbled radio call came through and I made out the words 'Focke-Wulf 190.'

I immediately turned around in time to see a smoking Fw, its pilot ejecting, his parachute opening and a P-38 spiraling toward the ground. This was Lt. Whitehead's plane.

Leslie Knapp was flying as wingman in 'D' Flight. Knapp and I had made several runs on a target when Knapp's P-38 was damaged by a train car explosion. Whitehead and Morris were top cover on this run. Knapp and I were rising to join them when the Fw 190 flew under us."

Lt. Whitehead's remains were buried in the cemetery at Trebotovice in a dignified ceremony presided over by local officials. They were exhumed three months later and returned to the U.S. His mother was present for the exhumation and was made a gift of her son's leather flight helmet by a witness to the crash who had removed it from his head. Local residents have continued to maintain the gravesite though no remains are there. A sexton is currently assigned that responsibility.

In addition, a memorial to Lt. Whitehead was unveiled near the site of his crash on September 28, 1945, which was attended by a U.S. military delegation. Over the years, the memorial fell into disrepair. The then-communist government of Czechoslovakia was not inclined to honor an American hero!

However, the situation changed drastically with the collapse of the Iron Curtain in 1989. A group of local historians began planning to restore the memorial. A new monument was unveiled on September 28, 1990, the 45th anniversary of the original ceremony.

Thus, the memory of an American pilot who fought and died for world peace and freedom is being perpetuated by an extremely dedicated group of people in far-off Bohemia, which is now part of the Czech Republic.

Left: New memorial to Lt. Robert Whitehead near the site of his fatal crash in April 1945. At right is the headstone at Whitehead's grave. (Karel Donát)

CREW CHIEF DAZE
Fred Montgomery

The following are portions of a letter the author wrote to his mother on November 23, 1944, while he was serving as a P-38 crew chief with the 96th Fighter Squadron, 82nd Fighter Group in Italy.

"You say you want to know what my average day is like, Mom? Well, yesterday the whistle blew at 4:45 a.m., and I fell out in the mud and pitch dark to preflight my ship.

When you've got one engine turning up 2,300 rpm's and pulling 30 inches manifold pressure, you're holding the brakes so hard your spine is putting dents in the armor plate in back of you. Before you check your mags you have to run her up to 2,600 or 2,700 to clear out the plugs. By the time you've checked one engine, your legs are so tired that you have to set the parking brakes and let her idle while you rest up for the other one.

If both engines check out O.K. then you're plenty happy, but if one cuts out, that's life's darkest moment. You either start tearing the cowling off, holding the flashlight in your mouth and praying your Flight Chief will come along in the jeep and go fetch you some plugs, or you go on a mad dash from one neighbor to another in search of some.

By now a dirty grey light is beginning to filter over the hills. You jump back in, having changed 12 plugs, and run up the sick engine again. Hooray, she's O.K. this time! You hit the mud again, slap on the cowling, grab two rags, one wet with gas and the other with water, and a chamois, climb back up and clean out the mud from the cockpit floor and wipe the instruments, windshield, canopy, side windows and mirror—and check the oil in both engines' hydraulic reservoir and the gas tanks.

That finishes topside, so you slide down again, prime the nose strut shimmy dampener, drain the supercharger balance lines, make out your daily form, give the whole ship a visual and remove covers from the pitot and relief tubes. (You only forget this once!) Time for the pilots to arrive and your assistant to take over.

You are free to shuffle through an acre of muck to your shack to grab the M-1 mess gear and get your powdered eggs, oatmeal, bread and jam and good old G.I. coffee. Then it's time for school—an Allison/Lockheed refresher course—from 8 a.m. to 11:30.

School is out in time for you to grab early chow and return to the line to relieve your 'boy.' It's a hard and fast rule that there must be a man 'on the line' while each plane is flying in case of an early return.

When your worry-bird comes home, the pilot signs the form and tells you what's wrong with her today. You run her up and check

One of the 96th Squadron P-38s Fred Montgomery was assigned to work on was a G-10, serial #42-13209, named "African Wolf" - at that time as assistant crew chief. S/Sgt. Montgomery, on the left, was photographed with crew chief T/Sgt. "Big Jim" Baker, pilot Lt. Larry Shepard and Sgt. Royal Lamb, the plane's armorer. (Montgomery)

mags and general operation. This is the afterflight check and not as extensive as the morning preflight.

Next, if she checks out O.K., you begin your hour-long Daily Inspection. Then you wash down the landing gear, doors and boom, clean the mud out of the wheel wells, hang belly tanks for tomorrow's mission, enter flight time, cumulative time on aircraft and engines, gas and oil consumption, mechanical work done, etc., on your daily form. After you've gassed up, locked surface controls, closed and covered the cockpit and the relief and pitot tubes, it's chow time.

But you're not through yet. You stop by the Engineering shack and transfer pertinent data to your permanent maintenance record. Then to the Operations office to turn in the daily form. You check to see if there are any new T.O.s [technical orders] or AF memos which you must read and initial.

By now chow is nearly over and it's almost dark and colder than a gold digger's passion, so you head for the heavenly, lumpy old sack of straw, your Beautyrest. You'd like a couple of belts before you turn in, but this is no place for a hangover, so you hit the sack.

But comes 11:30 p.m. and a not-too-gentle rousing from dreamland. There is to be a surprise bombing party tomorrow and you must therefore go out and drop those belly tanks you struggled to hang a few hours ago. You pull on your sheepskins, grab your flashlight and take off. You remove your empty belly tanks and give the armorers a hand in bombing-up the ship. And so to bed again until the whistle blows reveille around four and the routine starts all over again.

Occasionally, that Eighth Wonder, the New Pilot, arrives on the scene. With a sick smile and murder in your heart, you slap her back together for his First Training Mission. Then a last-minute climb back up to the cockpit to tell him his left engine is flooded and will probably start if he'll turn off the damn booster pump. He almost blows you off the wing when it does.

On his return, after you've listened to all the things he found wrong with the ship, all of which you told him in the briefing, patted him on the back and sent him on his way, secure in his knowledge that he's the hottest jockey in the USAAF, then you've just time to run up, clean up, pull a quick daily, make out your forms, etc.— providing, of course, that you don't have to change a nose strut as a result of his trick landing.

And so you log another entry in your book entitled 'Crew Chief Daze.'"

THE MAKING OF AN ACE
Robert Carlton

The 49th Fighter Squadron of the 14th Fighter Group had been operating in North Africa for a little over a week, escorting medium bombers and performing other tactical missions as directed by higher headquarters. On November 24, 1942, a mission was laid on the squadron to fly a reconnaissance and fighter sweep over the enemy airfields at Gabes and Sfax on the coast of Tunisia. Lt. Virgil Lusk, Lt. James Butler and I were selected to take this mission. I was designated to lead the flight.

The flight to Gabes was uneventful, except that we ran into a sandstorm and had to climb to 10,000 feet to get on top of the layer of dust. As we approached Gabes the weather was clear, and we descended to ground level as we approached the airfield. We observed that there was a Ju 52 transport parked on the field and as I was in the lead I had a good shot at it. It went up in flames after I fired at it. I then pulled up and the three of us made another pass across the airfield. There was a small tank parked near the Ju 52, and I made a pass at it, firing into its tracks, hoping that it would damage the tank. After this pass we pulled up and headed for Sfax.

A short time after leaving Gabes, Lt. Lusk called me on the radio and said my P-38's right engine was smoking. I looked at it and saw that white coolant vapor was flowing out of it. So I shut the engine down, feathered the engine and turned the flight over to Lusk. We proceeded on up the coast toward Sfax, and after a short time we observed a flight of nine Ju 52s coming our way at the same altitude we were flying. Lt. Lusk told me to stand by and that he and Lt. Butler would check them. I was concerned that they might have a fighter escort, so I stayed off to one side.

Lusk and Butler proceeded to attack them, and the longer they attacked them the more I wanted to get involved. However, I didn't, and soon they had shot all nine of the transports down. Lt. Lusk had shot down five of them and Lt. Butler four. All of the C-47 transport aircraft we had in North Africa had removable plugs in their windows so that the troops could remove them and fire out the side of the aircraft, if necessary. I suppose the Ju 52s had the same type of plugs, for after Lusk attacked the last one he flew alongside of it to look it over and was promptly fired on by someone in the aircraft, which damaged his left engine.

When we all got back together, Lusk had feathered his left engine and I gave up on going any farther toward Sfax and instead headed for our base at Youks-les-Bains in Algeria. Arriving over the field, Lusk and I peeled off in different directions, and we all then landed safely. Upon inspecting my aircraft we found that I had received just one bullet hole in its engine, but that bullet had hit a coolant line, which caused me to lose all of my coolant.

Debriefing our mission, we were able to account for ten Ju 52s destroyed—one for me on the ground, four for Lt. Butler and five for Lt. Lusk, making him an ace. Not bad for one mission!

Postscript: Jim Butler was killed in action four days later when he was shot down by an Me 109. Then-Captain Virgil Lusk was killed in a midair collision in a P-38 after returning to the U.S., near San Diego on March 9, 1943.

Left to right: 49th FS P-38 pilots Bob Carlton, Virgil Lusk and Jim Butler at Hamilton Field, San Francisco, California in early 1942. (Carlton)

THE BEANTOWN BOY
Gary W. Metz

When the tower operator at the Bedford Army Air Base saw a P-38L with its left engine feathered at 0950 on July 19, 1945, he immediately contacted the pilot to see whether an emergency landing was required. Flying at 1,000 feet over the field, the pilot replied in the negative. He added that he was "only practicing."

At the controls of the Lightning was Captain Daniel Kennedy, whose Medford, Massachusetts, home was less than ten miles to the east. Kennedy had some experience flying a P-38 with less than optimum engine performance. More than once he had nursed a damaged ship back from a combat mission in North Africa. He had also been credited with five confirmed aerial victories—three of them in one day, making him an ace. Today, with the war in Europe over and the war in the Pacific winding down, he was just up for a leisurely practice flight. He was making himself comfortable with the flight characteristics of the P-38L as opposed to the older F and G models he had flown overseas.

Before enlisting, Daniel Kennedy (who had no middle name) had graduated from Medford High and worked as a copy boy and reporter for the *Boston Traveler* newspaper. With military service looming, he began to study for the aviation cadet examinations. He took them but failed trigonometry. Not one to give up, he sold his car, hired a tutor and spent all his spare time studying. He passed on his next attempt. On January 29, 1942, he began his pilot training at Camden Field in South Carolina. He received his wings on August 5 at Spence Field, Georgia.

January 13, 1943, found the young pilot assigned to fly the twin-engine P-38 Lightning with the 27th Fighter Squadron, 1st Fighter Group. The 1st FG was then stationed at Biskra, Algeria. Biskra was, and is, an oasis town on the northern edge of the Sahara Desert. Windswept and inhospitable, it had a still-functioning aqueduct built by the Romans. The pilots were housed in the Transatlantic Hotel. While very modern by Algerian standards, the hotel lacked heat. Their diet consisted mainly of tangerines, oranges and dates.

Three days after arriving Second Lieutenant Kennedy destroyed his first plane. Unfortunately it was one of our own. While on a test flight he forgot to lower his landing gear, causing the total destruction of the personal ship of Lt. Marcus Linn. He flew his first combat mission on January 27. The next day, while escorting B-17s over Sfax, Tunisia, he lost an engine but managed to coax his plane home and land safely.

Mid-February found the 1st FG moved about 100 miles northwest to a base near Chateau-Dun-due-Rhumel just in time to have two of

The colorfully underdressed Daniel Kennedy poses with one of his tent mates, Virgil Radcliffe, in front of their abode at Chateau-Dundue-Rhumel. (Frank McIntosh)

its squadrons participate in strafing missions during the German Kasserine offensive. The new location provided a slightly better climate, colder but with less blowing sand. The unit had gone from "sandstorms to snowstorms," as it was stated in the 27th FS Daily Reports. Housing was less permanent, with the pilots sleeping in five -man pyramidal tents. Kennedy shared his tent with Lts. Stuart Bennett, Harry Dowd, John MacKay and Virgil Radcliffe. This move put them closer to the shipping and ports that were targeted by the bombers they escorted. The long-range P-38s were now flying missions as far north as Sardinia and as far east as Sicily.

As a replacement pilot, Lt. Kennedy was not assigned his own ship until February 25. On that day he took possession of HV-L—HV being the identification letters of the 27th FS and L being the individual plane marking. He painted the name *The BEANTOWN BOYS* on its nose to identify the aircraft as his.

On February 28 Kennedy was credited with damaging an Italian Macchi 200 fighter while on an escort mission over Cagliari, Sardinia. On March 7 he was again taxed with the chore of flying a damaged ship back to base. While on an escort mission over Sousse Harbor, Tunisia, his plane's left rudder and both static balances were shot away. Cannon shells perforated the gondola no more than eighteen inches from his body. He released the canopy to bail out, but as the plane slowed he realized he could keep it stable. Later, after returning to base, another pilot from his squadron admitted to being the one who had shot up Kennedy's P-38! The following day, while escorting bombers on an anti-shipping raid north of Bizerte, Tunisia, Kennedy scored his first confirmed victory, an Fw 190. The squadron Daily Reports gave this account of the massive dogfight:

"One of the enemy approaching from the left pulled away when he saw his course would take him into the field of fire of an attacking P-38. Second Lieutenant Daniel Kennedy followed him as he turned. The enemy executed a slow half roll which, unfortunately for him, allowed the Lieutenant to draw a perfect bead on the plane. Direct machine gun fire from 200 yards tore sections off the enemy aircraft and he went into a steep dive from which he did not recover."

The squadron as a whole claimed eight victories in that air battle, with the 1st FG claiming a total of seventeen. Kennedy did not escape unscathed. On the return, his left engine began pounding and smoking. Forced to feather the engine, he once again made it back on the remaining motor at speeds down to 105 mph.

Mechanical problems plagued the squadron as the wear and tear on its P-38s began to become apparent. On an April 10 mission fourteen Lightnings departed, with eight—including Lt. Kennedy's—returning early with various mechanical malfunctions.

Further victories eluded Kennedy over the next few weeks. The Axis forces were driven out of Tunisia, and the P-38s used their long-range abilities to escort the bombers to targets farther out into the Mediterranean. The 1st FG also began to use its Lightnings as dive bombers. It was while returning from one of these dive bombing forays, near Palermo, Sicily, that Lt. Kennedy lost his best friend in the squadron. On May 25, sixteen P-38s participated in the dive bombing of an Axis airdrome. Eleven 1,000-pounders were dropped, with one P-38 being unable to release its bomb. Twenty minutes into the return, the squadron was jumped by a mixed bag of Me 109s and Fw 190s. After shooting down an Me 109, Stuart Bennett was attacked by a 190. He did not respond to warnings of the attack—his radio had malfunctioned on previous missions—and his damaged P-38 was seen crashing into the sea. Bennett and Kennedy had arrived together at the 27th and may have entered the service together. They were both from the same area of Massachusetts and both were promoted to first lieutenant the day Bennett was shot down.

On May 31 Kennedy chalked up his second confirmed victory. Thirteen P-38s of the 27th FS acting as fighter-bombers attacked a transformer station near Guspini, Sardinia. Approximately five minutes after the bomb run they were jumped by eight Me 109s. In the ensuing melee Lts. Kennedy and Herb McQuown each bagged one of their attackers, with Lts. George Smith and John McKay getting credit for damaging two more. Lt. George Elkin's P-38 crashed into a mountain and exploded with an unreleased bomb. Lt. Eldred Loder's ship was seen to crash into the sea.

On June 9, after leading a dive bombing mission to the island of Pantelleria, Lt. Kennedy found himself involved in another dogfight. Me 109s jumped his flight and Kennedy pulled up to nail one as it flew over him. After nearly stalling out in the climb, his ship fell off on one wing. As he recovered he found himself behind four other 109s. He opened fire, destroying two and damaging another. His wingman, Lt. Bob Britz, shot down the remaining Messerschmitt. With his ace status confirmed, Kennedy finished his combat tour three days later.

He did have one more *non*-combat mission to fly. On June 19, three P-38s flown by Capt. Jim Pate, Capt. Elza Shahan and Lt. Kennedy escorted an Avro York transport carrying the King of England from a base near Tunis, Tunisia, to Tripoli, Libya. His North African flying days now at an end, he left that continent on July 4, 1943— Independence Day—to return to the United States.

On returning home Kennedy was involved in publicity and morale work in connection with the aviation cadet training program. Over the next two years he was promoted to captain and married Catherine Henley of Bridgeport, Connecticut. He was then stationed at Bedford AAB.

It was of course from this base that he had taken off on the morning of July 19. After his short conversation with the Bedford tower, Capt. Kennedy's P-38 turned west until it reached a point about eight miles from the field. The plane circled slowly to the right and then proceeded on for a mile or two. As it banked slowly to the left, it suddenly flipped over on its back and dove into a nearby golf course. The plane hit the ground at about a forty-degree angle, burying the engine assemblies three feet into the earth, with the rest of the aircraft bouncing to a stop 35 feet farther on. Fire broke out immediately. The twenty-five-year-old captain was killed instantly. At first investigators were at a loss as to the cause of the crash. The initial report stated:

"There is no evidence of willful violations of flying regulations. From the facts and close personal knowledge of the pilot, the Accident Board is unable to determine or assume that he was buzzing. The Accident Board is unable to determine what caused the loss of control which resulted in the inverted crash."

A second report issued on August 15 made the following statements:

"a. On or about 15 March 1945, the pilot of the aircraft, Captain Daniel Kennedy, stated to Captain Earl P. Miller that it apparently made no difference if the aileron boost were turned on in flight, that he had done it several times in a P-38L with no effect.

b. Within 24 hours before the accident Captain Kennedy discussed the aileron boost system with Sgt. Charles R. Chase, his former crew chief overseas, now assigned to the Bedford base. At this time, Captain Kennedy inquired why the aileron boost should not be turned on during flight and seemed unacquainted with the fact that if so turned on the system might cause sudden full aileron application.

c. T.O. 01-75-L Pilots Operating Instructions does not cover this situation or give warning of the danger involved.

d. It is known that the aileron boost having once been turned off, if turned on again during flight with the control wheel not perfectly aligned, a sudden surge of hydraulic power (1,100 lbs. per sq. in.) will cause the aileron control to be applied in the direction the wheel is turned.

e. In view of the above evidence, the Aircraft Accident Committee believes that the loss of control which resulted in the inverted crash was caused by the pilot turning on the aileron boost valve after completion of practice feathering. The aileron application which would have resulted if the plane was starting a left turn, as witnesses reported, would have been violent enough to cause loss of control and affect a half-roll to the left."

The aileron boost system had not been on earlier models of the P-38 that Kennedy had flown in North Africa. Apparently his lack of familiarity with the system had caused his death. Low cloud cover over the area was the reason for the plane being at 1,000 feet. Had he been above 5,000 feet it is possible he would have had time to recover.

Captain Kennedy was laid to rest in the West Medford Cemetery. He was the holder of the Distinguished Flying Cross, fourteen Air Medals and other honors.

Lt. Kennedy paints the last of three new swastikas on his P-38, "The BEANTOWN BOYS," the nose of which also displays two colorful figures depicting historical Boston characters. This was right after the June 9, 1943, action in which he became an ace. (Metz)

WHERE DID *HE* COME FROM?
William C. Cable

In early 1945 I was a 20-year-old second lieutenant assigned to the 12th Air Force's 23rd Photo Reconnaissance Squadron and stationed at Sesto, Italy. Sesto was a small town about ten miles north of Florence and about 30 miles south of the lines, so most of our missions were between an hour and a half and three hours in duration. On this day I was en route to a target northeast of Villach, Austria, and was flying an F-5B painted a baby blue. Why the USAAF painted some recon aircraft light blue is beyond me, as all it accomplished, in my view, was to let enemy fighter pilots know that here was easy pickings with very little chance of injury to themselves.

The weather this day was clear, and I could see the Alps on my left, with Yugoslavia and the Adriatic Sea on my right and the smoke from Vienna about 150 miles ahead. I was cruising at about 25,000 feet, between contrail levels, and as I turned my head to the left there was another aircraft just off my left wing, about 100 yards away and going in the opposite direction, southwest bound. Our closing speed must have been 700 mph, but he seemed to pass by very slowly. I could see that it was a Spitfire—it had the British roundel painted on the side of the aircraft—and that the pilot's head was turned toward me. I wonder if he was as shocked as I was. This guy was where a friendly Spitfire shouldn't be. He was more than 200 miles from the nearest British base in Italy, and the Spitfire's legs were not that long.

I started a left turn and began looking around wildly to see if there was anybody else in the area, but I couldn't see anyone other than the Spitfire and me. That made me feel a little better. I saw that he also had turned left—fortunately for me, because now I was not going to have to go through him to get home. His turn also warned me that this guy was definitely not a friendly. I had been briefed that the enemy was using captured Allied aircraft but had never talked to anyone who had seen one. I figured I had just been introduced.

As the left turn continued I was getting my aircraft ready to go when the time came. Fortunately, I was not carrying drop tanks, so my aircraft was clean. My plan was that when the Spitfire headed north and I was headed south, I was going to execute the famous recon maneuver called "Run Like the Devil." We were about a half a mile apart and holding the turns. When over the F-5's nose I could see the town of Fiume and the Adriatic Sea beyond, I rolled out of my turn, put the nose on the horizon and went to war emergency power. I knew the Spitfire had better acceleration than I did, but he had to get turned around, so I thought it would all even out and he would be too far back to shoot.

I was wrong! In the rear view mirror I could see him roll out of his turn and lift his nose—and then his wings light up. I hunkered down behind the armor plate and waited to take some damage. I didn't feel any hits and didn't see any rounds go by. A few seconds later he must have realized that I was drawing away from him, as he stopped shooting, broke off and turned southwest again. I went straight home, thanking God and the crew chief that the Allisons stayed with me even with the massive overdose of manifold pressure I had applied.

A couple of days later, Captain Masterson, our intelligence officer, told me he had received a report that about 30 minutes after the Spitfire left me a Spit had encountered some 15th Air Force Mustangs southwest of Udine and was shot down.

The most disturbing part of the whole episode for me was my not seeing the other aircraft until he was far too close. For any airman in a combat situation the idea is to see the enemy first. For the recon pilot it is even more vital because you can't fight your way out. You have to run, and a head start is really nice to have. I still don't know where he came from or why I didn't see him until it was almost too late. Training and planning and topnotch equipment are essential, but a liberal dash of just plain good luck sure helps!

Bill Cable as a young photo recon pilot in Italy in 1944. (Cable)

174

ADVENTURES OF A LOCKHEED TECH REP
Richard "Stumpy" Hollinger

When I got to Italy at "Bella Napoli" (which wasn't so "bella" when I got there), they gave me a "Duck" (a jeep with a boat body) and told me to report to the 82nd Fighter Group outside of Foggia. The Duck had less than 400 miles on it when I got it and about 15,000 when I left.

I arrived at the 82nd and was billeted in a tent with Ed Stanley, a 90-day-wonder rep for the Allison engine (General Motors) and Capt. Roy Barlow, Group Ordnance Officer. Not long after that I helped three master sergeants build a shack about 14' x 28' and occupied one corner of it.

After a few weeks, Lt. Col. Bill Litton, the Group C.O., called me up to his office. He asked me questions about P-38 operations and maintenance. Most of them were answered, but a few I told him I wasn't sure about but would get back to him with the answers. I was with him about two hours, and he asked me if I knew the reason for the questioning. I said, "Sure, you want to know if I know what I'm doing, or if I'm some Humpty Dumpty." He said, "Right. And now I want you to write a lecture outline covering most of what we've discussed and give it to all the pilots." I worked out a lecture to cover all the technical problems that might be encountered in the air and what to do about them—also a lot of "don'ts" to keep them out of trouble and get them back on the ground. I was careful not to praise the airplane or Lockheed. They all knew how good the P-38 was.

One result of the lecture was that we never lost another pilot or plane in a single-engine landing, nor did we have a loss from getting into compressibility during a dive. I lectured them one morning on the compressibility factor and how to recover from it. When they got into it they had no control of the airplane until they got down to about 11-12,000 feet, depending on the air density at the time, and should have had complete control again at around 5-6,000 feet. That afternoon I was at one of the revetments talking to a ground crew when a young lieutenant came up to me and said, "Stumpy, that works just like you said—I just tried it!" I know that did something for my credibility.

I had to go to Bari one day to see some people at the 15th Air Force HQ. Lt. Bill Burgess of the 96th Squadron was off the mission that day and wanted to go along. I drove my Duck over to pick up Bill while the mission was taking off. We got in the Duck and then decided we had better make a "pit stop" before we left. We then started for Bari. As we were approaching the gate we heard a loud report or blast. The planes were going on a bombing mission with RDX bombs. These bombs, while only 500 pounds, had devastating

Lockheed tech rep Richard "Stumpy" Hollinger and his "Duck" amphibious vehicle. (Hollinger)

power. One of the planes going over the fence at scarcely 100 feet in altitude had an engine "sneeze." The pilot jettisoned his bombs on "safe," but one of them went off anyway and made a large crater just short of the road to the city of Foggia. One following P-38 was badly damaged by the explosion, but the pilot came around and landed safely. The plane taking off next to him was also damaged but flew the mission. I stopped the Duck, and Bill and I made some calculations and decided that but for the pit stop we probably would have been close enough to where the bomb hit to have been casualties!

Vernon "Dixie" Walker was a big young man, and by his nickname you know he was from the South. He was a nice looking chap and very enthusiastic about his job, which was chief of a P-38 ground crew who had the airplane shipshape and ready to go after the Krauts at any time.

We had a bad storm one night, during which our tower was blown down. A day or two later when the airplanes were returning from a mission, Dixie's P-38—flown by Lt. Ernest Benkoski—was having trouble extending its landing gear. We had all the radio gear on the ground and I was talking to Benny, trying to help him get the gear down. I turned around, and in back of me was Dixie, with a very large wrench in his right hand. He tapped me lightly on the chest and said, "Stumpy (pause), if you don't get that gear down ahm gonna kill ya." He was very stern and unsmiling. Obviously, we did get the gear down, because I'm still here!

One of our planes coming from Foggia into Poltava, Russia, during a "shuttle" mission had some battle damage and the pilot bellied in on a farm, but we didn't know where. Major Joel Wolfe, our Group Maintenance and Materiel Officer, a Russian major and I set out to find this wounded P-38. We drove all over the area—even climbed a well derrick—to no avail. There was a big G.I. trailer waiting for us back at Poltava. I saw a Russian boy near the trailer, and I had a hunch that kid might know where the plane was. I had a silver ID bracelet with a little P-38 soldered on it. I pointed to the P-38 on my bracelet, with my hand sliding on the ground like a plane landing. Well, that little guy's eyes lit up, and he said "Da! Da!" and pointed. We put him in the cab of our truck and he took us right to the plane.

I got a call one day that 15th AF HQ wanted me down at Bari again. Col. C. T. "Curly" Edwinson, the 82nd's new C.O., said he'd take me there in the group's B-25. We had the engines running and the day's mission was returning, so we taxied out and got out of there before the guys flying the mission started to land. I had a headset on but Curly didn't. I was tuned to Gocart tower and soon Deputy Group C.O. Lt. Colonel Joe Dickman called Gocart (the group's radio call sign) and said he couldn't get his P-38's right gear down and that he was on the emergency hydraulic system. The operator in the tower told him to continue pumping. We were approaching Bari and the colonel told me to get landing instructions, but I said, "Let's orbit around here to see if Joe Dickman gets his gear down." Curly then put on his headset and listened—and then asked if I knew what the trouble was. I said, "Yes, I know what's wrong." So he told me to call Joe and tell him what to do. I did call Joe and did tell him what to do, and he acknowledged.

I told Joe to climb up to 9,000 feet and call back, which he soon did. I then told him the up-lock pin was still engaged and for him to pump the hand pump until he could feel the pressure relieve, then pull the nose up, then push the yoke over to put negative G's on the plane—and not to get too violent because I didn't want him to "red out." I asked him to call me back when he'd caused the negative G's. He soon called back, and I told him to look out and see if the right gear doors were open, which was the case. Then he was to pump until he got a down-and-locked indication and fly by the tower so the operator could see that all three landing gear were at the same angle. He made a normal landing.

Stumpy Hollinger poses with Lt. Dick Andrews (on the left) and Lt. Dick Willsie at Poltava the day after their now-famous Romanian rescue incident on August 4, 1944. (Andrews)

CHAPTER SIX

EUROPEAN
THEATER
OF
OPERATIONS

LIGHTNINGS IN THE EUROPEAN THEATER OF OPERATIONS

8th AIR FORCE (ENGLAND)

Interestingly, the first Lockheed Lightnings in Europe did not belong to the USAAF but had been purchased for the Royal Air Force. These were unique export models designated 322-Bs. The RAF's interest in the P-38, one of the most advanced fighter designs in the world at that time, is understandable. But after evaluating three Model 322-Bs in England in early 1942, the RAF canceled its order for the rest of them, as it found the aircraft to have inadequate performance for service in the European Theater. This is understandable, as the RAF had ordered these aircraft without turbo superchargers and with right-hand-rotation (that is to say, non-counter-rotating) propellers! These changes negated much of the P-38's acclaimed performance, as regards to both handling and high-altitude performance. (The USAAF absorbed most of the 322-Bs that had already been built and utilized them primarily for flight training.)

The first USAAF Lightnings in England were the P-38s of the 1st and 14th Fighter Groups, which flew them across the Atlantic from early July to early August 1942 as part of an operation called BOLE-RO, in which small groups of Lightnings were "escorted" by B-17s for navigation. One of these flights went awry when six P-38s and two Flying Fortresses were forced down on the Greenland icecap due to bad weather on July 15. Exactly fifty years later one of those P-38Fs was recovered from the ice and eventually restored and now flies regularly at airshows with the name *Glacier Girl*.

The 1st and 14th Groups trained in England with the new 8th Air Force for the next few months and flew a few "milk-run" missions over France and the Low Countries to gain some (very limited) combat experience. While there, their P-38s were modified for service with the new 12th Air Force in Northwest Africa, to which both units were transferred shortly after the Allied invasion in early November 1942.

En route to England, the 1st FG's 27th FS had been ordered to remain in Iceland for a month, and on August 14, 1942, 2nd Lt. Elza Shahan shared a four-engine Fw 200 "Kondor" with a P-39 pilot, thereby scoring the first P-38 victory in the ETO. The 14th FG also lost one of *its* squadrons—in its case permanently—when the 50th FS was reassigned to the 342nd Composite Group in Iceland to beef up its air defense. While there, in mid-1943 the squadron's pilots shot down a Ju 88 and an Fw 200.

In October 1942 another P-38 group, the 82nd, arrived in North-

181

ern Ireland, also to train for service in North Africa, but unlike its predecessors it was not operational until it moved to the MTO in late December. The 78th Fighter Group, yet another Lightning unit, arrived in England about the time the 82nd left, but before *it* could become operational it was decided that most of its pilots and P-38s were needed more urgently in North Africa, to where they were sent in February to reinforce the other Lightning groups there. (The 78th re-equipped with P-47s, acquired new junior pilots and entered combat with the 8th AF in April.)

It was in January 1943 that a new type of Lightning arrived in England—the F-5s of the 13th Photographic Reconnaissance Squadron. This unit flew the first Lightning photo recon mission in the ETO on March 28, 1943. The 13th was joined by the 14th PRS in May and the 22 PRS in June, all of them becoming part of the new 7th Photo Recon Group at Mount Farm in July. (Yet another F-5 squadron, the 27th, was assigned to it in November of that year.) These were the 8th AF's only photo recon units, and they did excellent—mostly long-range, high-altitude, strategic-work for it until the end of the war in Europe.

P-38 fighters became operational with the 8th AF again during the fall of 1943, this time semi-permanently. With their comparatively long range, they were badly needed to escort the 8th's four-engine bombers to their distant targets in Germany and occupied Europe. The first to arrive was the 20th Fighter Group (made up of the 55th, 77th and 79th Fighter Squadrons), in August, at Kings Cliffe, followed by the 55th FG (38th, 338th and 343rd Squadrons) the following month, at Nuthampstead (from which it moved to Wormingford in April 1944). Ironically, although it arrived later than the 20th, the 55th was the first to fly a combat mission, on October 15. 20th FG pilots began flying missions while TDY with the 55th on November 3 and did not fly their own first full-group mission until December 28.

These two Lightning units had a tough time of it during that winter of 1943-44, one of the worst on record. Their P-38s, especially the early H models with which they entered combat, were ill suited to the high altitudes and the cold, wet Northern European weather. Cockpit heating was inadequate, and numerous mechanical problems manifested themselves, resulting in lots of aborts and non-combat related operational losses, not to mention those too often highly experienced Luftwaffe pilots. Although claims for enemy aircraft were not high, they did provide the best defense they could for the B-17s and B-24s. At least they were usually not misidentified by the bomber gunners as Me 109s or Fw 190s as was all too often the case with P-51s and P-47s.

The 20th and 55th were joined by a third P-38 group, the 364th, whose base was Honington, in February. Comprised of the 383rd,

182

These P-38Js of the 38th Squadron, 55th Fighter Group are airborne from England in the spring of 1944. (USAF)

384th and 385th Fighter Squadrons, it flew its first mission on March 2. Coincidentally, the following day the 55th FG made WWII aviation history when some of its P-38s became the first Allied fighters to fly over the capital of the German Reich (its pilots were subsequently known in some quarters as the "Berlin Buzz Boys").

Their situation was much better by the spring of 1944. The older P-38Hs had been replaced by much-improved J models, their mainte-nance and their pilots' tactics and aircraft management skills had also improved, and the warmer weather made a big difference. Also, the Lightnings began operating at lower altitudes more often as fighter-bombers and strafers, at which they proved to be very effective. The pilots especially enjoyed targeting locomotives, and the 20th FG's in particular became famous as "train-busters."

It was also in the spring of 1944 that a very unusual Lightning appeared in the skies over Europe. The "Droop Snoot" was a P-38 that had been modified by having its gun compartment replaced with a Plexiglas nose, a Norden bombsight and a seat for a bombardier. The plan was for a Droop Snoot to lead other P-38s (and sometimes P-47s) on level-bombing runs over important targets, the latter drop-ping their bombs on the order of the bombardier in the Droop Snoot. The attackers then had the speed to escape the flak and the P-38 and P-47s the armament to protect themselves and the Droop Snoot from enemy fighters. The first such mission was flown by the 20th and 55th Groups on April 10. Each 8th and 9th Air Force P-38 group (and, for a time, the former's P-47-equipped 56th FG) were provided with at least one Droop Snoot.

The final P-38 unit to be assigned to the 8th AF was the 479th FG (434th, 435th and 436th Squadrons). It arrived at its new base at Wattisham on May 15 and, amazingly, flew its first combat mission just ten days later.

Unfortunately, by this time it had already been decided that all the 8th's P-38s and P-47s would be replaced by P-51s. Thus, the 20th, 55th and 364th Groups flew their first P-51 missions and their last P-38 missions between July 20 and July 27. (Several would typically be flown with both types until the transition was complete.) The 479th FG took a bit longer to make the transition; its first joint P-38/P-51 mission was on September 12 and its 436th FS flew VIII Fighter Command's last P-38 mission on October 3. (Many of the 8th's P-38s, including Droop Snoots, were passed along to the 9th Air Force on the Continent and the 15th Air Force in Italy.)

The 8th Air Force's P-38 pilots had been only modestly successful shooting down enemy planes during that year, having been credited with just 282 victories, but they did do a lot of valuable bomber-escort and fighter-bomber work. Five of them achieved the status of ace (five or more air victories), the highest-scoring of whom was Capt. Jim Morris of the 20th FG with 6 1/3 kills.

The Lightning was also utilized in England for some "special ops." For example, a couple of P-38s were loaned to the RAF's famous 100 Group for a while to test its capabilities as a low-level night fighter/intruder, although it was eventually decided that it held no real advantages over the types already being used for those purposes. Four modified Droop Snoots and their American crews (from the 7th PRG and the 8th AF's 36th Bomb Squadron) were also TDY with 100 Group for special "ELINT" (Electronic Intelligence) duties, monitoring and interfering with enemy air defense communications. Too, a highly modified P-38L with a huge, bulbous nose containing an operator's compartment and H2X ("Mickey") radar equipment for blind bombing and navigation flew some experimental missions with the 8th's 654th Bomb Squadron (25th Bomb Group) in January and February 1945.

At least two other Droop Snoot Lightnings were TDY with the Royal Air Force as of the summer of 1944, and they both displayed RAF roundels. One of them was reportedly flown by Wing Commander Guy Gibson, leader of the RAF's famous "Dam Buster" mission and a recipient of the Victoria Cross, on an unauthorized daylight reconnaissance to the Netherlands in August 1944.

9TH AIR FORCE
(ENGLAND AND THE EUROPEAN CONTINENT)

The 9th Air Force was transferred from North Africa to England in October 1943. Its new task was to provide tactical support for the ground troops in France and beyond, after the invasion that was to commence in about six months. In the meantime, its soon-to-be fighter-bomber groups would spend much of their time escorting the 8th Air Force's bombers to strategic targets in *Festung Europa*.

Three P-38 fighter groups were assigned to the reorganized 9th AF: the 370th (comprised of the 401st, 402nd and 485th Squadrons), in February, 1944, the 474th (428th, 429th and 430th Squadrons), in March, and the 367th (392nd, 393rd and 394th Squadrons), in April. They were based at Andover, Warmwell and Stony Cross, respectively, although the 367th moved to Ibsley a couple of weeks before departing for France in late July. The 370th also moved to France in July, and the 474th in August. From then until VE Day they did yeoman fighter-bomber work while moving constantly from one base to another in that country, Belgium and, finally, Germany.

The 9th AF also received five F-5 photo reconnaissance squadrons, the 30th, 31st, 33rd, 34th and 39th. The first four arrived in England from March to May 1944 and moved, along with the 9th's fighter groups, to France in July and August. The 39th PRS arrived in France from the U.S. in January 1945. These units were shuffled around among no less than five reconnaissance groups—the 10th PR, the 67th PR, the 69th Tactical Recon, the 363rd Tac Recon and the Provisional Recon. The four original squadrons flew some particularly important and hazardous low-level missions (as most of theirs were) photographing the German defenses along the Normandy beaches just before D-Day.

August 25, 1944, the day Paris was liberated, was one of the greatest in the history of the 9th Air Force. Its 367th FG earned the first of its two Distinguished Unit Citations that day, for both its ground attack work and for the results of a huge fight with Luftwaffe fighters. The Germans were in full-scale retreat from France, on the ground and in the air, and there were some ferocious encounters between 9th AF fighters and Luftwaffe units that were escaping eastward while also attempting to protect their comrades on the ground who were trying to do the same.

After a huge battle with Fw 190s that bounced them while they were attacking airfields at Clastres, Peronne and Rosieres around 1:00 p.m., the 367th's pilots claimed twenty-five destroyed (including, incredibly, five by Capt. Laurence Blumer of the 393rd Squadron), one probably destroyed and seventeen damaged. The 367th lost seven P-38s, one from the 392nd Squadron and the rest

185

from its hard-hit 394th, two of whose pilots were killed (the other MIA pilots were either taken prisoner or evaded capture with the help of the French underground).

Not long after the 367th's big air action, the 474th Fighter Group had a similar experience in that same general area north and east of Paris, also while attacking enemy airfields. Its aerial claims totaled 21-3-15 for the loss of eleven P-38s.

As with the 8th AF, it had been decided that the 9th would eliminate P-38s from its inventory, in favor of P-47s and P-51s. The 367th FG made its switch to Thunderbolts in February 1945 and the 370th to Mustangs the following month. The 474th somehow got a reprieve and ended up being the only P-38 (as opposed to F-5) unit in the ETO (8th and 9th Air Forces) on VE Day. Second Lieutenant Kenneth Swift of the 429th FS scored the group's last air victory that day, May 8, at 2005 hours, when he shot down a Siebel Si 204 light transport near Rodach, Germany. This was also the last victory by a P-38—and the last USAAF victory, period—in the European and Mediterranean Theaters.

Although the main job of the 9th AF's P-38 fighter-bomber groups was not aerial combat and most of that in which they did engage was defensive in nature, these three units managed to shoot down 214 enemy aircraft—96 by the 474th, 77 by the 367th and 41 by the 370th. Three of their pilots qualified as aces: Laurence Blumer of the 367th FG, with six kills, and Lieutenants Lenton Kirkland and Bob Milliken of the 474th, with five each.

Captain Larry Blumer of the 367th Fighter Group poses with his P-38J-25 "SCRAP-IRON IV" (serial #44-23590) in late 1944. He was assigned this plane not long after the big fight on August 25 in which he shot down five Fw 190s. (USAF)

186

THE P-38'S ESOTERIC RAF SOJOURN
Steve Blake

One of the Lightning's most obscure and unusual assignments during World War II took place in England when a half-dozen 8th Air Force P-38s and their crews were detached for service with the Royal Air Force's famous 100 Group.

The task of 100 Group, whose motto was "Confound and Destroy," was to render ineffective the Germans' air defenses, especially against the RAF's night bombing campaign. It included special bomber squadrons equipped with sophisticated electronics that interfered with the enemy's radar and radio transmissions.

Their official job description was "radio countermeasures" (RCM). 100 Group also had night fighter/intruder squadrons whose main task was to destroy Luftwaffe night fighters, in the air and on the ground. Strangely enough, USAAF aircraft also performed both these roles with the RAF.

In late March of 1944, a small 8th AF detachment was assigned to Little Snoring in Norfolk, the home of several of 100 Group's Mosquito night fighter squadrons. This detachment, equipped with two P-51s and two P-38s, experimented briefly with night intruder missions over occupied Europe, but it was soon decided that the American fighters were not suitable for this work. (In fact, other American P-38 pilots did fly successful low-level night intruder missions in other theaters.)

In the late summer of that year, four P-38J "Droop Snoots" of the 7th Photo Reconnaissance Group were modified for "electronic intelligence" (ELINT) work. These Lightnings carried special electronic equipment to monitor the enemy's radar defenses. They were to map them by locating and recording the source of the radar beams.

From late August 1944 to March 1945, these aircraft were attached, on a rotational basis, to 100 Group's 192 Squadron at Foulsham, which is also in Norfolk. One of the ELINT missions with the RAF, which were flown in daylight, resulted in the loss of a Droop Snoot and its crew.

On October 26, the P-38J-20 (serial #44-23515) piloted by Captain Fred Brink of the 7th PRG's 13th Photo Reconnaissance Squadron and carrying electronic equipment operator/observer 2nd Lieutenant Frank Kunze, crashed into the North Sea after both engines failed during a mission to the coast of Holland. Both men were killed. (Kunze and his fellow operators were TDY from the 36th Bomb Squadron, which also performed electronic countermeasure duties.)

Was there any task in aerial warfare the P-38/F-5 could not or did not perform?

ELINT pilot Lt. Ellis B. "Bruce" Edwards of the 22nd PRS poses with one of the four ELINT P-38s, serial #44-23156, a J-15 model. Note the all-metal nose that replaced the original Plexiglas version. (Peggy Edwards via Peter Randall)

AN AMERICAN "P-38 KAMIKAZE" WHO SURVIVED
Tom McGuire

On April 5, 1944, its C.O., Lt. Col. Harold J. Rau, led the 8th Air Force's 20th Fighter Group on an airfield strafing mission to the Salzwedel area west of Berlin. While so engaged, the P-38 (J-10 serial #42-67753) of Rau's wingman, 1st Lt. Jack J. Yelton of the 55th Fighter Squadron, was hit by flak. Yelton later reported what happened:

"Both windows were broken and the cockpit was a mass of pulp and glass from shattered instruments—no compass, no nothing. Both engines were streaming oil and prop 'juice,' but the thing was still running. I had some cuts on my face and neck and there was a lot of blood, but nothing serious.

My problem was which way to go as long as the engines kept running. Without a compass, I had no idea which way. It seems I had hit among a maze of German airfields. Within the next four or five minutes, I shot down two aircraft which were low and obviously in the traffic pattern. The first was an Fw 200 with wheels down at 500 feet. I got it broadside from stem to stern. The thing exploded. Two minutes later I saw an Fw 190. I crawled within 2,000 feet of him before he noticed me. He pulled a dumb maneuver, beginning a gentle, straight climb. I crept on his tail, keeping the trigger down. At about 900 feet, he caught fire. I saw the pilot climbing over the side.

A few seconds later, both my engines—both, not one—started to quit! The props were windmilling. I didn't have enough altitude to bail out. I decided to crash-land on a German strip, intending to make a nice, but rough, belly landing with no injuries to myself. As I came in, dead stick, I must have gone crazy, for I pulled the act which I shall always regret.

It was a wide runway. I started in. I noticed two Me 110s sitting in a very tight position on the right side, getting ready for a formation takeoff, about 500 feet from the runway. I must have gone completely batty, because I kicked right rudder and aimed straight at them. The last thing I remember was looking into both cockpits and then—wham! The whole world exploded.

The crash and explosion must have been simultaneous. The next thing I knew, I was lying on the runway a few hundred feet from the burning wreckage with a few rosy-cheeked Hitler Youth kicking me in the ribs!"

Yelton was lucky to survive, because he was thrown out of the cockpit, landed some distance away and broke both his shoulders. His injuries were aggravated by no medical attention being given to him for 15 days. Jack was repatriated to England due to their severity and he returned to the U.S. in February 1945.

Col. Harold Rau, who led the April 5, 1944, mission on which Lt. Yelton was lost (temporarily) in such a spectacular manner, was photographed with his famous P-38 "Gentle Annie" (a J-10, serial #42-68165), his ground crew and his dog Honey at the 20th FG's airfield at Kings Cliffe. (USAF)

GARLAND YORK: "THE OMAHA KID"

"To Garland York, the youngest of the pilots in the squadron, went the plaudits of all. As the D-Day invasion unfolded it became common knowledge that he had photographed the exact section of the Normandy beaches that the American forces landed on. He had photographed all of 'Omaha' and most of 'Utah.' Like similar low-level missions, Garland had pinpointed the beach barriers, teller mines attached to imbedded posts underwater and other coastal defenses in minute detail, as well as scattering his share of German soldiers working along the beach. He was in and out with his great photography before the Germans had time to shake off their surprise and grab their weapons." (Colonel W. Donn Hayes, former C.O. of the 9th Air Force's 34th Photo Reconnaissance Squadron.)

"Dicing" was the name of the game and Garland Alvin York was one of the best. (He was named after his cousin, WWI Medal of Honor winner Alvin York.) The term did *not* originate with Lt. Louis Lanker, as reported in *WWII Magazine*, although he was the first pilot on such a mission over Normandy. It was a British slang term for an extremely dangerous feat, i.e. throwing the dice against death— "dicey."

This form of suicidal flying demanded superior nerves, flying skill and alertness. There was not a moment to relax when flying on the deck, and no means of defense. It had been established that photographic material from higher altitudes did not supply the fine details necessary for information on the enemy's defenses. After Lt. Lanker's successful run, several more were scheduled.

On May 19, 1944, a second series of dicing missions were flown, three of which were by Lt. Donald Thompson, Lt. Rufus Woody and Lt. Garland York, of the 30th, 31st and 34th PR Squadrons, respectively. As Woody reported, "We were all scheduled to fly at the same time, for surprise and to keep the enemy from alerting other areas."

It was important to fly at the lowest of low tides. That meant they had to be planned for a certain phase of the moon. Weather delayed them for a couple of days, so there was time to "think and worry," said Woody. "We were getting very edgy. Finally we were told that the weather was breaking and cautioned against low fog. We took off after 4:30 p.m. Al York and I flew in formation to mid-Channel and then he turned right to make his landfall on the Cherbourg Peninsula. We were barely above the waves." All of them photographed their assigned areas successfully and returned to land within minutes of each other.

Over the Normandy beaches the missions were flown at an average altitude of 25 feet. The pilot would push his throttles all the way forward, set the cameras at "runaway" speed and head over the beaches at approximately 375 mph. With the nose camera and the oblique cameras filming simultaneously with overlapping coverage, the target area could be obtained in one pass. Many of the F-5s had a bare metal finish, as the paint had been removed to lighten the aircraft, and seams were filled and polished to help increase their speed.

Besides the obvious hazards of the dicing missions, there was another cause of fatalities in the photo recon squadrons. "Four of our original eighteen pilots were lost while

This excellent drawing of then-Captain Garland "Al" York is uncredited.

we were flying missions at altitudes of 30,000 feet and above," reported Colonel Hayes.

York himself was an anoxia near-mishap. He was fortunate to have Lt. Wallace Bosworth with him when he became affected by the lack of oxygen. The inadequacy of the early life-supporting systems at extreme altitudes had contributed to several deaths, so Bosworth was alerted to the problem. He noticed that York was flying erratically, and when contacted by radio he responded incoherently. Bosworth managed to talk York down to a lower altitude immediately, and although York was still disoriented and giving erroneous reports (on two altitude checks he gave a reading of 10,000 feet higher than his actual one) Bosworth guided him to a safe landing.

Garland York has probably never counted the times he has "beaten the odds," not only while flying but on other occasions. A very sobering event had taken place earlier. Through the squadron members' energy and enthusiasm, they were ready for orders overseas early, replacing the 32nd PRS. They were sent to England, while the 32nd took their originally designated spot in the "Med" (Mediterranean Theater). All the flying personnel and the bulk of the enlisted corps of the 32nd were on one troop ship, which also carried a heavy load of explosives. They were torpedoed by U-boats and all lives were lost.

This 34th PRS F-5, a B-1 model, serial #42-68229—in "bare metal finish" and with the names "Mary" and "Bret" and newly painted D-Day stripes—was photographed on June 10, 1944. S9 was the aircraft code for the squadron. (USAF)

A SHORT WAR AND A LONG BATTLE
Mary Lou Neale

Lt. Bert Shepard, P-38 pilot. (Shepard)

This is not so much about the short bursts of valor associated with the P-38 fighter pilots as it is about courage and determination over the long run as demonstrated by a remarkable man, Bert Shepard, who served with the 38th Fighter Squadron, 55th Fighter Group of the 8th Air Force in England in World War II. On his 34th mission, May 21, 1944, First Lieutenant Shepard was shot down:

"I was going in to strafe an airfield at treetop level doing about 390 mph when my right foot was shot off. I called my group leader and told him I had a leg shot off and would call back later. In the meantime I must have been hit in the chin with flak and was knocked out, for the next thing I remember I was about to hit the ground at a slight angle. I horsed back on the wheel [but] couldn't pull out in time and crashed wide open [south of Warlow, Germany].

I remember nothing [more] until I woke up in a hospital in Ludwiglust, Germany. My right leg had been amputated eleven inches below the knee and a two-inch square of bone had been removed from above my right eye. The German guard explained that my P-38 crashed and burned, throwing me many yards forward, end-over-end.

I think this crash is amazing when you realize that if I did not have the leg shot off and the gun sight caving in my head, I could have walked away from [it]. Incidentally, I was wearing a shoulder harness, and I always had the nose trimmed high when I was flying at low level in case I had a loss of power."

In this case, "The war is over for you, soldier" did not apply to POW Shepard. His long battle was just beginning.

Prior to enlistment in 1942, Shepard had played professional baseball in the minor leagues, and his ambition was to play in the big leagues. According to his fellow prisoners, his will was indomitable. "He told me that he would be playing ball again, and I said, 'Sure you

194

December 1944: Shepard (front row, third from left) joins fellow POWs incarcerated together in a camp at Anaberg, Germany—Stalag IX-C. (Shepard)

will' and felt sick inside myself for the disappointment I thought Shep was going to face," wrote columnist Wright Bryan, who had been with him in Stalag IX-C.

But Shepard, even in the POW camp, wasted no time. He was outfitted with a crude artificial leg made by Canadian POW Dan Errey and immediately began practicing by going through hitting and pitching motions. After eight months, in February 1945 he was returned to the United States via a prisoner exchange.

Shepard arrived at Walter Reed Hospital on February 25, got a new leg there on March 10 and signed as a player/coach with the Washington Senators on March 30. He pitched against the Boston Red Sox and the Brooklyn Dodgers and also barnstormed with the American League All-Stars. He was the only man to actually play major league baseball with an artificial limb.

From a news clipping:

"On the night of July 10 against the Dodgers in a war fund game, Bert Shepard showed 'em! He pitched his first big league game and came off flushed with triumph. His body tingled wonderfully as teammates slapped his back.

'Looks like I'll have to put him on the active player list,' said manager Ossi Bleuge.

Shepard toiled four innings in his first mound appearance to get credit for the win. He held Brooklyn to five singles. Bert turned over a 3 to 2 lead to relief pitcher Roger Wolff."

In a later report, dated August 4, 1945, the headline read: "Bert

Shepard Makes Major League Debut Before 13,000 Fans At Washington Stadium." The article stated that "The 5'11" 185-pound southpaw walked from the bullpen to the mound with only a slight trace of a limp. Shepard thrilled the fans as he struck out George Metkovich to end the inning. The fans gave him a standing ovation as he walked to the dugout. Bert finished the game pitching five and one-third innings, giving up three hits, one run and striking out two batters."

After the baseball season was over, the Surgeon General called Shepard back into uniform to make a tour of amputation centers, for which he received a special commendation. He also toured various children's hospitals and rehabilitation centers. Employment for the handicapped was his major concern then and has been to this day.

His own employment record substantiates his belief that a physical handicap need not be a major detriment. He worked as a safety engineer for Hughes Aircraft, various insurance companies and Fluor Construction—including a year in Saudi Arabia and one in Venezuela—continuously until 1982.

Somehow he also found time not only to design and fabricate a natural-motion ankle for the artificial leg, but to be the National Amputee Golf Champion in 1968 and 1971. And he has not slowed down yet.

Today he speaks of his desire to assist amputees in gaining better prostheses and of his wish to travel back to Germany to locate and thank the hospital personnel who saved his life. "I know they would be happy and surprised," he says, "to see how well that broken, bloody body they saved has so completely recovered." And he speaks of a dream "to rent a P-38 and put on a show for the four children and seven grandchildren."

John Wayne, move over; Bert Shepard has been demonstrating "true grit" for years and years.

[Bert R. Shepard passed away on June 16, 2008, at the age of 88. He graduated with Pilot Class 43-H at Williams Field, Arizona.]

REUNION IN FRANCE
Steve Blake

On May 13, 1997, Norbert Greuet and Bill DuBose meet again— for the first time. Fifty-three years earlier, Norbert had seen Bill (then Lieutenant DuBose, USAAF) parachute to earth after exiting his burning P-38. Their meeting was the happy result of a 30-plus-year search by Norbert for the American pilot.

The mission for the 8th Air Force's 55th Fighter Group on June 17, 1944, was to the Picardy region of northern France. Its task: to dive bomb a railroad bridge across the Somme River near Perrone and the railway station in nearby Chaulnes. The Allied invasion of France had been underway for nearly two weeks, and these were small but important links in the system delivering supplies to German forces in Normandy.

Forty-eight Lightnings took off from the group's base at Wormingford, England, a little after 1 p.m. One of them was flown by 20-year-old 2nd Lt. William C. DuBose, Jr. of the 38th Fighter Squadron. Although the 55th was the most experienced P-38 group in the ETO, Lt. DuBose had very *little* combat experience, having joined it just three weeks earlier. Years later he described what happened as the 38th Squadron neared its target:

"When our turn came, my flight leader, Capt. Don Penn, and I dove down and flew along the river toward the bridge. We could see French people atop the high banks, waving and cheering us on.

As we lined up on the bridge, one of the bombs from the previous P-38 went off in the water far short of the bridge, and I could not help flying through the splash. Don released one bomb instead of two, so I quickly changed my trigger switch so I would also only release one bomb. My thought at that moment was that we were to make a second run. Then all hell broke loose.

German flak positions on both sides of the tracks opened up on me. They couldn't miss. Shells flew through my wings and nacelles. Instantly, I triggered my guns and dropped the bomb, but it was too late. My plane was on fire, and Don was screaming for me to bail out. [Despite fatal damage to his P-38, Lt. DuBose dropped his bomb on the Chaulnes railway station and strafed a train there!]

I pulled up, jettisoned the canopy, unhooked my seat belt and decided to go out over the top, because smoke was pouring into the cockpit. After I pushed myself up into the slipstream, I was pinned against the back of the canopy, hanging half-in and half-out of the plane. I couldn't move and just dangled there for a few seconds until my plane turned over into the dead engine and started down. A few seconds later I was pulled free. I saw the tail whip by and I pulled the rip cord. My parachute opened with an explosion, and I saw my

P-38 pilot Lt. William C. DuBose, Jr. (DuBose)

plane burning on the ground."

Lt. DuBose came down west of the target, between Chaulnes and the village of Lihons, about 100 yards from where his plane crashed. He landed awkwardly, breaking and dislocating one ankle and spraining the other. DuBose miraculously avoided detection by hiding in a hedgerow. Late the next day he was found by members of the French resistance. Thus began a three-month odyssey, evading capture behind enemy lines.

Sixteen-year-old Norbert Greuet saw what happened to Bill DuBose from near his home in Lihon, about a half mile away. He later heard that the pilot had been rescued by the underground. Norbert still remembers vividly the other P-38s circling the crash site after bombing the bridge and the railway station, and that Lt. DuBose landed right next to an AA gun emplacement the Germans had abandoned the day before!

In early September DuBose and eight other evaders were finally liberated by the British First Army in the city of Lens, where they had been hidden by a French family. He was hospitalized near London for a month and returned to the U.S. in November. Soon thereafter he was back home in California.

Norbert retained his curiosity about the downed P-38 after the war. He moved away from Lihon in 1955 but returned often to visit his parents. He sometimes went to the crash site and he tried to find out more about the pilot, without success.

Finally, in 1995, Norbert Greuet contacted the P-38 National Association and was referred to its Historian, Steve Blake. He could not remember the exact date of the Lightning's crash but subsequently was informed of that and other basic details—including the pilot's name and unit—by a French historian. Blake then referred Norbert to P-38 Association member Bob Littlefield, a 55th FG pilot who had written a book—*KIAs, MIAs, POWs & Evaders of the 55th Fighter Group in WWII*—that contains a detailed account of Lt. DuBose's last mission and his experiences as an evader. Littlefield put Norbert in touch with Bill DuBose, with whom he began a correspondence.

Bill and Norbert immediately began planning Bill's return to France, his first. Their emotional "reunion" took place in May 1997. Norbert took Bill to the sites of some of his WWII adventures.

Bill reported that, "Many people were there to greet us, including the press and photographers. They had a champagne reception at the Chaulnes city hall, and the mayor was there. I felt like a movie star!" He was also given some small pieces of his Lightning (P-38J-15, serial #43-28274) that were found where it had come to rest.

Thus was Norbert Greuet's long quest successfully completed. Bill and his wife Deanna enjoyed their visit to France so much that they planned to return there soon.

THE FIRST JET VICTORY
John Stanaway

Captain Arthur Jeffrey was leading the 479th Fighter Group's Newcross Yellow Flight during an escort mission to Merseburg, Germany, on July 29, 1944, when he had the first successful combat with a German reaction-powered fighter—a jet. Although German records dampen the completeness of the victory, Jeffrey is still credited with the first confirmed jet kill.

Newcross, the 434th Fighter Squadron, had rendezvoused with the bombers at about 0940, and Newcross Yellow Flight dropped back to cover one or more straggling B-17s. At about 1145 hours, a stubby little fighter (later identified as an Me 163 rocket) was seen making a pass at the three o'clock position of a B-17 from the 100th Bomb Group. The Messerschmitt seemed more curious than hostile, but Jeffrey and his wingman, Lieutenant Richard Simpson, attacked immediately while the other two P-38s of Yellow Flight climbed to 16,000 feet to provide top cover.

Apparently, the Me 163 was flying with power off and taking a weaving line of flight that allowed Jeffrey to close and open fire, observing strikes. A series of smoke puffs from the jet's tail indicated that the pilot was aware of the enemy P-38 and that he was attempting to restart the rocket engine. The Messerschmitt climbed to 15,000 feet and circled to the left, but Jeffrey's P-38, with aileron boost, was able to turn tighter and get a good deflection shot.

The P-38 was able to close within two to three hundred yards and fired until the 163 did a wild split-ess and spiraled off into an 80- or 90-degree dive. Jeffrey followed, firing all the way down and still observing strikes when the jet went straight down into the clouds at about 3,000 feet. Jeffrey pulled out at 1,500 feet, blacking out in the process of reducing speed from an indicated 500 miles per hour.

Meanwhile, Simpson had trouble following the combat when one of his engines began to malfunction. He didn't see the strikes, but caught up sufficiently to witness the Me 163 dive straight into the clouds and concluded that it couldn't possibly have survived.

The truth of the matter is that the Me 163 was quite capable of making a near right-angle dive recovery from low altitude. There is no doubt that Jeffrey made repeated strikes on his target, but the Me 163—like all other such jet-powered aircraft—was extremely rugged and could absorb terrific damage.

The German jet in question was most likely from the brand-new Jagdgeschwader (Fighter Wing) 400, which was just working up to operations. There is no mention in German records of an Me 163 lost this day, nor is there mention of any being damaged either. Postwar researchers have been quick to deny Jeffrey his confirmed victory.

One enterprising soul even changed history a bit by stating that the jet was claimed and confirmed as *damaged* at the time.

Whatever the truth of the matter, it was a P-38 that first defeated a German jet and, at best, there must have been some major-league chewing outs by the Luftwaffe brass when a battered, top-secret Me 163 was rolled into the maintenance shed.

Major Art Jeffrey with his P-51D "BOOMERANG 'JR.'" that replaced his P-38 named "BOOMERANG," with which he supposedly shot down the first German jet. (Stanaway)

A DEADLY ENCOUNTER
Steve Blake

Among the many roles in which the P-38 excelled was that of fighter-bomber. With its huge load-carrying capability and the deadly cone of fire from the four .50-caliber machine guns and the 20mm cannon in its nose, the Lightning was extremely effective bombing and strafing enemy ground targets.

One of the most successful P-38 units was the 474th Fighter Group, a fighter-bomber outfit that became operational with the 9th Air Force in England in April 1944. The 474th, along with the other fighter groups of that new tactical air force, mostly performed an air superiority role prior to D-Day, escorting the 8th Air Force's heavy bombers to their targets on the European Continent. But once the invasion was underway—and for the next eleven months—the unit really began performing the role for which it was intended: direct support of American ground troops as they marched across France and into the heart of Germany.

Although its forte was ground attack, the 474th FG did meet the Luftwaffe on numerous occasions and shot down scores of enemy planes. Most of these encounters were defensive in nature—the German fighter pilots trying to protect their comrades on the ground and the P-38 pilots protecting themselves. One such mission took place a little over a month after D-Day, on July 6, 1944.

The 474th's pilots took off from their base at Warmwell, England, for the group's second mission that day shortly after two o'clock. The 428th Squadron was assigned as top cover for the other two, the 429th and the 430th. The formation split up over France, and the 428th's Blue Flight, led by Captain John Hewitt, covered the 429th Squadron as it bombed and strafed a railroad yard at Drove.

On the way back to England, around 1615 hours, as the 428th continued to provide cover while the 429th strafed "miscellaneous targets," Hewitt's four-plane flight ran into some Fw 190s near Nogent. Captain Hewitt described what happened in his subsequent report:

"We had started home at 8,000 feet when we saw four Fw 190s coming toward us. We turned over to take a look, identified them and attacked. Before we had turned 180 degrees, out of the corner of my eye I saw my number 4, Lt. Rubel's plane, start to spin down. Eight more e/a then came down from above, and seeing we were badly outnumbered, I called to the flight to hit the deck and run, which I did. When I got down to 3,000 feet I looked back and I was all alone, and back up where the fight was still going on I saw another P-38 spin down in flames. No parachute was seen in either case. I climbed back into the fight and from there I could see the two P-38s burning below us. The other P-38 turned out to be Lt. Frederick, who was flying my number 3."

Stan Huser, Hewitt's wingman, reported:

"Capt. Hewitt and myself jockeyed for position on the tail on an Fw 190. After about 270 degrees of turn we were on him and forced him out of formation into a dive. I followed for a short distance, and looking back over my left shoulder, I saw Lt. Rubel's plane on fire with both engines burning, and he was going down. Later I saw Lt. Rubel's plane explode on the ground. I then broke up and to the right, turning with the three remaining Fw 190s. After about 360 degrees of turn, I looked back to the left and saw Lt. Frederick's right engine burning, and he was going down. Later I saw his plane explode on the ground close to Lt. Rubel's. I saw no parachute."

(As it turned out, Robert Rubel was killed, but James Frederick did bail out successfully and survived.)

Huser was credited with damaging the first 190. As he climbed back up, the dive fillets on his plane popped loose, causing it to buffet severely. Even though he was surrounded by an estimated two dozen enemy planes and could not maneuver his Lightning properly, Lt. Huser stayed in the fight. He dove on the three 190s and shot one of them down, after which the enemy withdrew. Huser was awarded the Distinguished Flying Cross for his actions that day.

They did receive some reinforcements. But as two flights from the 429th went to the 428th's aid, according to the former squadron's history, "approximately 25 more Fw 190s dove down to attack. In short order, almost everyone was in the tangle. Bill Banks shot up one 190. The pilot bailed out and his plane exploded when it hit the ground. Banks turned and jumped another, which he damaged. Bob Milliken got his first enemy plane in the same battle, and the pilot was also seen to bail out of that plane. Frank Reitz damaged one. Ernest ["Larry"] Baillergeon chalked up one probable and one damaged."

Lt. Milliken also described the action in *his* report:

"I was flying in Blue Flight, number 4 man, when we saw one P-38 in a dogfight with four Fw 190s. We climbed to 10,000 feet and attacked. Lt. Banks caught a 190 with a deflection shot and it went down in flames. I broke into a 190 coming in on our tail, but broke off as a 190 came in on me at about 5 o'clock. I racked to the right, and in one turn was on the 190's tail, but after a deflection shot lost him. Then I saw a 190 on the deck. He saw me and weaved to the left and right, and must have chopped his throttle, for I overshot him the first time. I closed to 175 yards and fired, and observed direct hits in his cockpit. The pilot climbed out and his chute opened as he passed below me. The plane burst into flames and half-rolled into the ground. The pilot had not been aggressive, and may have been

Lt. Bob Milliken and his P-38J-25 (serial #44-23663) named "SWAT," with which he scored the second, third and fourth of his five aerial victories. 44-23663 was badly damaged in an accident on the ground on November 28, 1944, while it was parked. (Milliken via John Stanaway)

out of ammunition. In any case, my 'G' suit gave me a great tactical advantage."

Larry Baillergeon recalled his experiences on July 6, 1944, 56 years later:

"After completing our [bombing] mission we were at about 5,000 feet assembling for our return flight to base when an urgent call came in over our radios informing us that enemy fighters were in the area coming in high and heading south. We immediately started a steep, full-power climb toward the enemy. When we reached about 12,000 feet, we sighted about 40 Fw 190s diving into us. We started the engagement in a high nose attitude and fired our guns into the enemy. I don't know what effect that had, but we must have hit some of them, as the enemy flight started breaking up their attack formation.

At this point I was unable to locate my element leader. He seemed to disappear, leaving me alone. Most of us broke off from the blazing 190 guns and went into a descending left turn. As usual, our formation gradually broke up, with everyone going off on their own. I went into a descending left turn to gain airspeed I lost from the climb. With power on full and descending, my speed quickly reached 300 mph or more. Suddenly, I spotted an Fw 190 dead ahead, about 300 yards away. I gave him a short two-second burst and saw hits on the tail and wing. He rolled over and "split-S'd" out of my sight. I became concerned about my speed and altitude and elected not to follow.

I continued my speed and descent with a gradual turn to the right, then I suddenly noticed another 190 about 200 yards ahead. The enemy was not turning right or left and was going slow in a descending attitude, not appearing to be aggressive. Closing fast, I chopped my throttles for fear of running into him—or worse, getting ahead of him and in front of his guns. (This was before we had dive flaps installed to slow our speed.) I came in right behind him very close—about 100 yards—and gave him a burst. I saw hits at his cockpit and his canopy flew off. As I did all this, and closing fast, I knew I would fly past him and into his line of fire. In front of him now, I gave it full power and made a steep left turn. I circled around the area for a few minutes and could see no airplanes, friend or foe. Getting low on fuel, I headed home without further incident."

The 474th FG pilots were credited with three Focke-Wulfs destroyed, one probably destroyed and four damaged.

The initial flight of Fw 190s that was engaged by the 428th Squadron was JG (Jagdgeschwader, or Fighter Wing) 77's 9 Staffel (Squadron), which was attached to I Gruppe (Group) of JG 1. JG 77 was an Me 109 unit that had been fighting in the East and in the Mediterranean. Its 9 Staffel had recently been transferred from Romania to the Western Front, where its pilots had converted to the Fw 190 (an average of six hours flying time per pilot!) prior to joining JG 1.

Ironically, the July 6 mission was 9/JG 77's first over France. The staffel's single flight accompanied two other flights of Fw 190s from I/JG 1. (It is possible that another Luftwaffe unit also became involved in this fight.) When the battle was over, 9 Staffel had lost two of its planes and claimed two Lightnings. One of its pilots, Leutnant [Second Lieutenant] Ernst Hanf, recalled this action many years later:

"The day after our arrival at Alencon [I/JG 1's base], the Staffel took off at around 1535 for a free hunt [fighter sweep]. Some time later we made contact with the enemy—about twenty Lightnings. The Staffel attacked immediately, taking advantage of a slight height advantage. Some P-38s formed a defensive circle, and our Staffelkapitän [squadron leader], Oberleutnant [First Lieutenant] Ernst, went after one of these. However, during this whirling battle his machine received some hits and he had to bail out. His Kaczmarek [wingman], Unteroffizier [Corporal] [Hans] Maximow, fell in this air battle. Already this first mission showed us the degree of enemy superiority we would have to contend with."

205

Leutnant Hanf's wingman, Feldwebel [Sergeant] Loch, was credited with one of the Lightnings shot down in this fight.

Wolfgang Ernst remembered later that "I had just downed a P-38 when I, in turn, was hit. I had to bail out. I got out of the cockpit and the air current caught me and I hit the rudder. My right arm was broken with the impact. Shortly afterwards the parachute canopy opened and I finally landed."

Ernst's victory was his 29th. He had to be hospitalized for a while, so Leutnant Hanf took over command of the staffel, which was re-designated 4/JG 1 the following day. Their Western Front combat debut was an eye opener for its pilots, almost all of whom would be lost in action in the ensuing weeks.

The Lightning pilots had once again demonstrated the P-38's ability to successfully dogfight single-engine German fighters. However, they had also been reminded that the Luftwaffe was still a force to be reckoned with.

The 474th Fighter Group had the distinction of being the only P-38 unit in the European Theater of Operations at the end of the war there. The two other P-38 groups in the 9th AF and the four in the 8th AF had by then converted to P-51s or P-47s. Besides expending tons of bombs, rockets, machine gun bullets and cannon shells on ground targets, its pilots had been credited with nearly 100 enemy planes destroyed in the air.

Postscript: In 2002 former 9th Air Force P-47 pilot Richard Reid published an account of his experiences as an evader in occupied France, assisted by the French underground:

"One afternoon we observed a formation of P-38s overhead as they were attacked by some Fw 190s. Immediately, a P-38 became a flamer and a parachute blossomed. Just as swiftly, an Fw 190 broke from the melee and was shooting at the pilot dangling from his chute. But wait, here comes a P-38 on the tail of the 190! They went down to treetop level. They went into a circle right over our heads, and the Lightning pulled his nose ahead and shot the German down. It looked like the two pilots came down close to each other.

We went to see if we could find the American pilot and found him with a French couple. As we approached, he came forward, sobbing and holding out his badly burned hands, saying 'I *was* a concert pianist.' He was 19-year-old James Fredrickson (sic). We took him with us. James was very bitter in the days that followed."

The young P-38 pilot was, of course, "Jimmie" Frederick. After he was liberated, Lt. Frederick was sent to England for treatment but on August 15 he flew to the 474th's new French base at Neuilly (A-11) to visit his squadron before returning to the States. His arms were still in bandages at that time.

A BROTHER'S SEARCH IS REWARDED
Jim Pavlovsky

Jim Pavlovsky commissioned this painting of his brother Bill and his
P-38, which he named "The Youngun." (Pavlovsky)

From Oprep [Operations Report] No. 75-A for twenty-four hours ending sunset 14 July 1944:

"Killed in action: 2nd Lt. William L. Pavlovsky, O-780381, 401st FS, 370th FG was seen to crash and explode near St. Maure, France—cause uncertain—probably both flak and defective bomb in own or preceding plane on glide bomber run."

On August 4, 1944, Leona Pavlovsky received a telegram stating that her husband was missing in action, followed by a letter written more than a week later assuring her that "any time additional information is received it will be transmitted without delay."

In the meantime, the mission report for July 14, plus statements from three of the pilots who were eyewitnesses, confirmed that Bill Pavlovsky was killed. However, the young widow did not learn of his death until November 23, when a telegram arrived as the family was gathered for Thanksgiving dinner.

Why the delay? And why did his mother, who kept writing letters of inquiry until her death in 1969, never learn the details? And how did his younger brother Jim finally unravel the mystery?

Thanks to Richard Groh, the author of the 367th Fighter Group history, "The Dynamite Gang," Jim Pavlovsky learned that he could obtain information through the Freedom of Information Act. Thus in 1983 he discovered that Bill was one of three P-38 pilots sent to bomb a railroad yard in St. Maure, just south of Tours, France, that day.

Lt. Pavlovsky was the second of the three, and the planes were each armed with two 500-pound bombs with 15-second time-delay fuses. Lt. Marvin Childs went in first and dropped both his bombs, with Pavlovsky right behind and dropping his bombs. Childs' bombs exploded on impact and Pavlovsky's broke and burned.

The two planes were observed to climb in formation, a chandelle to the left, and then Pavlovsky's P-38 suddenly went into a dive. He was seen to eject from the cockpit, but the chute was on fire and did not open. His body struck the roof of a barn and fell to the ground.

There were reports by several witnesses of Germans firing small arms at the planes. However, many were of the opinion that malfunction of the bombs' timing devices caused the crash.

If the delay in forwarding the information to the family seems heartless, one must remember that the action was in enemy territory and there were many such incidents to verify. If the failure of the government to answer Mrs. Pavlovsky's many letters with details seems inexcusable, brother Jim says, "How can you tell a mother that her son was killed by [faulty] weapons or a ground man's mistake?"

Whether Bill Pavlovsky was killed by "friendly" error or by German fire, as several witnesses claim, may remain a mystery. But, by researching into this as a labor of love for a cherished older brother, Jim Pavlovsky reaped a terrific reward: an outpouring of love from the inhabitants of St. Maure de Touraine.

After obtaining all the information possible from our government, Jim contacted the small village, requesting eyewitnesses. To his amazement, there were many, including the wonderful Madame Percheron, who had held the head of "the very tall, very young, handsome blond young man who seemed to me to be covered with bullet holes."

Madame Percheron had cleaned the body and provided the blanket to wrap around him. The Germans took away the body and buried Pavlovsky in the local cemetery, locking the gates. But the French partisans climbed the fence and erected a concrete slab to hold the propellers of his plane. (The Germans, irritated by this display, arrested several of the locals, but they were freed a few days later when the Americans took the town.)

There were other living witnesses whom the Pavlovskys met during their trip to St. Maure in 1984, and everything they were told was heartwarming. Apparently Bill had been the only American to die there in WWII, and the citizens had made him their hero. In the city mall they have his picture hanging and the medals he earned.

Jim Pavlovsky and his wife reported an intense interest in their presence, and an avalanche of affection and friendship which was genuine from the people of the Tours region. A special TV documentary was made of their quest, and invitations were extended to other Americans to visit.

Said Jim of the experience: "It was overwhelming. It was 40 years later and they were still celebrating and wanted to thank someone, and I happened to be there. Any [pilot] who was on that raid would be welcome the same way if they would visit St. Maure."

[According to a recently published history of the 370th FG, "Lt. Pavlovsky flew into his flight leader's bomb blast while dive bombing. The flight leader's bomb detonated early due to a faulty time-delay fuse." Pavlovsky was flying P-38J-15, serial #43-28706.]

The Mayor of St. Maure de Touraine, France, stands by the grave of Lt. William L. Pavlovsky. Partisans erected a monument with P-38 propellers on the grave. (Pavlovsky)

THE CATERPILLAR CLUB
Bob Carlton

The Caterpillar Club was established to recognize those airmen who had to bail out of an airplane to save their lives. I joined it on September 10, 1942, after having bailed out of my P-38 over England. I was then a member of the 49th Fighter Squadron, 14th Fighter Group. We had flown across the North Atlantic via Greenland, Iceland, Scotland and down to our new base in England in July 1942, and had been training there for the past two months. In early September our squadron was put on alert duty, where we kept two aircraft standing alert during the daylight hours.

On this particular day I relieved one of the alert pilots so he could go to lunch. Things had been quiet, and I was not expecting anything to change. However, a short time after I had taken over the alert duties, a red flare was shot off from the control tower and my partner and I immediately took off. The weather was overcast and we soon were climbing into the clouds on a course given to us by the ground controller. We were told to climb on course to 15,000 feet. Just before reaching our assigned altitude, I lost radio contact with the controller. In addition, I also lost my primary flight control instruments—the gyrocompass and the flight indicator. We were still in the clouds, so I decided to climb up above the overcast. I finally broke out above the clouds at 32,000 feet. The outside temperature was minus 40 degrees.

I flew around above the clouds for some time, hoping someone would come up and help me out, but nobody did, so I finally decided that I had to let down and see if I could get below the clouds and find a place to land. Without my gyrocompass and my flight indicator, I was trying to fly a reciprocal course using my magnetic compass and my needle and ball instrument.

Shortly after I started my descent I noticed that my airspeed was increasing, so I tried to bring the nose of my plane up. Instead, it dropped lower and my airspeed increased until it showed 550 mph. At that point it was obvious that I had better get out, so I began to prepare myself to bail. First I released the canopy and then I unfastened by seat belt. I was then sucked out of the aircraft. I went out in a sitting position, and in doing so hit both my knees on the control wheel. I thought I had broken both legs.

I think I went out at about 20,000 feet, and after tumbling around for a while I felt like I had slowed down enough to open my parachute. I should have waited longer, for when I opened it, the jerk dislocated my shoulder. It was really cold at that altitude. When I opened my parachute one of my shoes came off, and I thought that foot would freeze. I wasn't in very good shape at that point.

In the cockpit of his P-38, pilot Robert Carlton. (Carlton)

I finally landed in a farmer's back yard, and he took me into his house and put me on one of his beds. First he contacted the local constabulary to make sure I wasn't a German pilot, then he contacted my squadron and they sent an ambulance and a doctor to pick me up.

My aircraft had crashed 20 miles from where I landed, and when it did it killed about 20 chickens. Later, when we were in operations in North Africa, I was called into our squadron office to sign some Lend Lease papers so that the farmer could be paid for those chickens. Oh yes, I was given a "pilot error" notation for the accident.

THE STORY BEHIND THE CITATION
Reyburn F. Crocker

"Distinguished Flying Cross Awards, Section V. Reyburn F. Crocker, T-2940, Flight Officer, Air Corps, 370th Fighter Group. For extraordinary achievement while participating in aerial flight against the enemy in the European Theater of Operations. On 25 February 1945, when the formation of which he was a member was attacked by fifty enemy aircraft, F/O Crocker unhesitatingly opened fire upon them and destroyed one enemy plane, damaged two more, and assisted in the final dispersal of the remainder. F/O Crocker's devotion to duty and skillful aerial tactics brought great credit upon himself and his organization, and are in keeping with the finest traditions of the military service."

Crocker, who had joined the 370th FG as a replacement pilot just two months earlier, later shared the full story behind that mission and the resulting citation:

"On Sunday, 25 February 1945, eleven P-38s of the 401st Fighter Squadron, 370th Fighter Group, 19th Tactical Air Command, 9th Air Force, took off on an armed reconnaissance mission across the Rhine River (the war front/bomb line at that time) into Germany seeking targets of opportunity. We were carrying a full load of ammunition and two 500-pound bombs on each plane. One plane aborted and one flight (four planes) returned to base.

At approximately 0700 hours, we (the seven remaining P-38s) engaged from 50 to 70 Me 109s at an elevation of 12,000 feet. A head-on pass started the proceedings. Here I speak only of my own actions; I was too busy to notice others.

I shot down one Me 109 and joined my flight leader, Captain Marion P. 'Snuffy' Owens, in destroying another. I then broke onto the tail in a diving pass and destroyed a second. I had just engaged another from the rear and was watching my bullets strike his plane when I noticed an Me 109 on the tail of Owens. The 109 was trying to shoot down Owens. I got behind the 109 and tried to shoot him off Owens. Neither of us succeeded, and he broke off from Owens and I broke off him in pursuit of another plane on which I scored heavy hits and saw him start to smoke and go into a spiral dive. I then went after another Me 109 and damaged him, but I exhausted my ammunition and left to join up with Owens.

Lt. [Wallace R.] Anderson joined up on my wing and radioed, 'Do you plan to take those bombs back to base?' When contact was first made I armed the bombs, hit the release button, pulled the manual release handles and entered the fray. I was unaware that the armed bombs were still attached during the ensuing conflict! This probably explains why I was unable to get a shot at the Me 109 which was pursuing Owens. I freed the bombs manually (and chopped down a couple of trees, I suppose) and returned to base.

As we approached base I asked Owens if we would do victory rolls and he replied in the negative. My score for the day: two and a half destroyed, one probably destroyed and two damaged.

At debriefing Captain [Walter] Johnston, our intelligence officer, separated us for review of the actions taken. I was informed that I would receive credit for one destroyed and two damaged, but only if I agreed to affirm two kills for Captain Owens. I dissented but was told that would be the report, except if I did not affirm Owens I would receive no credit. I acceded. Thereby the 'official' record as stated in the General Orders resulted.

Note: When General Elwood 'Pete' Quesada [the 19th TAC commander] presented my DFC to me, he turned to Major [David] Bayle, C.O. of the 401st, and asked, 'Why is this man still a flight officer?' The next day I was promoted to second lieutenant."

JIM HOLLINGSWORTH—EUROPEAN STRAFING ACE
John Stanaway

434th Fighter Squadron strafing ace Captain Jim Hollingsworth in full flight gear. (Stanaway)

Lt. Jim Hollingsworth was never accused of timidity, and when a flight of Corsairs jumped his P-38 training formation over California on January 16, 1944, he accepted the mock combat and quickly got on the tail of one of the Marine Corps fighters. The pilot of the Corsair was a Marine captain who was quite skilled and aggressive himself, but later testified that he couldn't shake the obviously beat-up old training P-38.

One mistake the pilots made in their friendly tussle was to pass directly over the Marine base Operations office while the base commander was having breakfast there. The Marine pilot was doing everything he could to shake the tenacious Lightning, including some prohibited buzzing at about five feet off the ground. After landing, Hollingsworth was invited to his C.O.'s office.

Pilots who did the sort of thing Hollingsworth did were being discharged from the Army Air Forces. Luckily for Hollingsworth he did such a good job of demonstrating the P-38 that he probably saved himself from a more severe fate. As it turned out he was only admonished and fined $80.

It was fortunate that he was not more severely punished. He had finished one combat tour with the 37th Fighter Squadron of the 14th Fighter Group in North Africa the preceding September, and would fly another fruitful tour with the 434th Fighter Squadron, 479th Fighter Group in England. He had been credited with three aerial victories in the Mediterranean and would get seven more on the ground in his P-38 with the 434th.

The first of Hollingsworth's ground victories was claimed on August 28, 1944, when he was part of a mission to southeastern France. Capt. Arthur Jeffrey led the mission and claimed a Ju 52 in the air, while Hollingsworth confirmed a Do 217 on the ground.

Eight days later, on September 5, Hollingsworth set a record for

214

P-38 pilots in the ETO when he claimed six more aircraft on the ground. He was Newcross (434th) Red Leader on a strafing mission to the Giessen, Germany, area. After attacking the primary target, Newcross Red Flight explored the scene of a previous strafing mission at Ettingshausen Airdrome and found eight untouched aircraft on the tarmac.

The new targets were called out to the group leader, who gave the four P-38s of Red Flight permission to attack. Hollingsworth waded in from the southeast with his four P-38s and made two more passes from different directions. The light flak did little to deter the Lightnings, and Hollingsworth claimed two Do 217s and four Me 410s destroyed.

A Distinguished Unit Citation was awarded to the 479th FG for its strafing and aerial combat successes in August and September 1944. Jim Hollingsworth was an outstanding part of that success in terms of strafing expertise. Unfortunately, his aggressiveness was curtailed in December 1944 after the group had converted to the Mustang and he was downed by flak to spend the rest of the war as a POW.

Hollingsworth was not interested in the glory part of the war and had to be coaxed on occasion to make his claims. He was really a fighter pilot at heart who loved the fine points of the P-38.

When the 479th switched to the P-51 Mustang, he was one of those who regretted the change, perhaps even more so after he was shot down and captured while flying a P-51.

SHOT DOWN BY ALLIES—AFTER THE WAR'S END
Tom P. Petrus

Although what I am about to tell you may sound like a "war story," the incident actually took place, on May 9, 1945, the day following the surrender of the Axis forces in Europe. I was a first lieutenant assigned to the 39th Photo Reconnaissance Squadron, 10th Photo Reconnaissance Group, 9th Air Force, based at Wiesbaden, Germany.

The aircraft we flew was the photo recon version of the P-38, the unarmed F-5. I had completed 39 missions from bases in France, Belgium and Holland, and was very happy to have survived the war in Europe.

Following the cessation of hostilities, our squadron was tasked to fly missions to locate and photograph POW camps, both known and suspected. So, on the morning of May 9th, I, along with wingman Lt. Tom Jackson, took off from Y-10 (Wiesbaden) on a heading for our first target, an air base near Prague, Czechoslovakia. We had been briefed that we would be overflying Russian-held territory, but since they were our Allies we were not to be concerned. Normally we flew our photo missions at high altitudes, but today we were expected to fly at less than 5,000 feet. The weather was cloudless and visibility unlimited. It was a pure delight to view the beautiful European countryside from low altitude.

About two hours later, with cameras running, we started a low pass across our first target, the airport at Prague. As we approached I spotted numerous Russian aircraft on the ground, but assumed our presence over the field would be warmly received. Not so! We were greeted with fairly heavy ground fire. Seeing this, we broke off the run. I turned left and climbed to 2,500 feet. Jackson broke right. Bewildered, but relieved that neither of us had sustained damage, I began to circle a few miles north of Prague waiting for Jackson to rejoin me.

I assumed that the hostile fire we experienced was the result of mistaken identity on the part of the Russians. Boy, was this my day for wrong assumptions, because then it happened! Without warning, I heard a loud bang and the airplane shuddered. Looking to the direction of the noise, I saw a huge, ragged hole in the right wing, trailing fire, and in my rear view mirror I saw three Russian fighter aircraft directly on my tail with all guns blazing! I later identified them as Yaks. Dropping my fuel tanks and adding full power, I started a steep, climbing right turn. It was too late. I continued to take more hits, and I knew the F-5 was doomed when flames came into the cockpit.

I had been taught two procedures for bailing out of a P-38, but that day I think I discovered a new one. I left the airplane at about

Lt. Tom Petrus in the cockpit of an F-5. (Petrus)

2,000 feet, which gave me little air time, but the jump was successful and I lit in an open field. My face and hands were burned.

While trying to decide what to do next, a group of Russian soldiers arrived and made the decision for me. They took my .45 and drove me back to the same air base where we had made the pass earlier. I was treated for my burns by friendly Czech medics and placed in a dispensary under guard.

In the meantime, Jackson had seen the airplane crash and explode. He wisely returned to base as fast as possible and reported that he had not seen a chute. I was presumed dead and reported as missing in action. My parents were notified accordingly.

The following day I asked to see the Russian commander with the hope of getting help to return to American forces. The answer was a belligerent "Nyet," and I was returned to my ward and again placed under guard. No further explanations. It occurred to me that the Russians realized they had made a big mistake and would have preferred that I had gone down with the F-5.

After three days, and with the help of a Czech teenager who was a ward boy in the hospital, I left through a back window and jumped into the sidecar of his motorcycle. It was the middle of the night. We drove through the streets of Prague and headed west toward friendly forces. Late the same day we met two American infantrymen on patrol in a jeep. They took me to a field hospital near Pilsen and from there I was air-evaced to a general hospital near Paris.

I venture to say that I have the dubious distinction of being the last aircraft to be shot down during the war in Europe.

THE DAY THE LIGHTNINGS FELL FROM THE SKY
Steve Blake

The date was July 17, 1944. It was just before noon, and Geoffrey Lyden-Brown's plan was proceeding well. Lyden-Brown, a Royal Navy motor torpedo boat commander, was spending his leave with his girlfriend, Vera "Vicky" Pullen, a professional dancer. They were staying at The Three Cups in Stockbridge, Hampshire, England, a romantic 15th Century inn at which Horatio Lord Nelson and his inamorata, Lady Hamilton, had enjoyed some assignations over two hundred years earlier. It was the perfect place and time for what Lt. Lyden-Brown had planned so carefully: a proposal of marriage.

The moment had arrived. Geoff popped the cork of their second bottle of (carefully hoarded) champagne and reached for the ring. Just then, several loud explosions intruded on this romantic scene, followed by smaller crashing noises. The mood instantly broken, they rushed outside. Geoff and Vicky saw smoke trails in the sky, then heard another explosion and witnessed a pillar of smoke in the distance. It was obvious that at least one aircraft had crashed to the earth. Also, as they soon learned, a large American plane (type unknown) had force landed in a park a few hundred yards from the inn. They jumped into Geoff's car and drove to the site, where they assisted its crew, at least one of whom was injured.

When they returned to the inn with two of the "rescued" American airmen as their guests, they found they had little to offer the latter. Someone had broken into their room, eaten all their food and stolen their supply of booze! The blackguards had also taken the engagement ring and some valuable war trophies that Lt. Lyden-Brown had liberated from a German E-boat. (After a brief investigation, the culprits—some drunken Polish sailors—were apprehended and the ring and most of the rest of the "booty" were recovered.)

They learned later that at about the same time the aircraft force landed nearby, two USAAF P-38s had crashed a few miles from Stockbridge, killing both pilots. It seems almost certain that it was the terrible sounds generated by the Lightnings that had startled Geoff and Vicky.

Lt. Lyden-Brown did eventually get around to asking Miss Pullen for her hand, and she, of course, agreed. They were married in 1945, shortly after the war's end, and remained happily so until Geoff's death in 1988. The story of his interrupted proposal became a popular and often told part of the Lyden-Brown family lore.

Amazingly, while attending an air show about forty years after the tragedy, their son Steve and his wife Rosanne came across a display featuring the crash of one of the P-38s on July 17, 1944. Debris that had been dug up by aircraft archaeologists was its centerpiece. The

Lyden-Browns purchased a small part from the Lightning, which Rosanne describes as a "conrod big end that has been twisted, curved and broken off under the impact stress. It has been highly polished over the years and makes a very fitting family keepsake." This, of course, intensified their interest in the incident and created within them a desire to find out more about it, and especially about the two young American pilots. Their search was successful, due mainly to the assistance of English and American aviation historians and aircraft archaeologists, including *Lightning Strikes* editor Steve Blake and P-38 National Association member Jay Jones, who is writing a history of the 370th Fighter Group.

The P-38 pilots were, it turned out, members of the 370th FG's 402nd Fighter Squadron. They were 1st Lt. John H. Stevens (flying P-38J-15 serial #42-104197) and 2nd Lt. Virgil J. Mary (in J-15 serial #42-104047). Thirty-eight Lightnings from the group's three squadrons had taken off from their base at nearby Andover (Station 406) for a bomber escort mission. After the 402nd had formed up over the Hampshire countryside, it set off toward its target, Rennes, France, at 1145.

Lt. Stevens was wingman to the squadron commander, Major Joel Owens, and Mary was the #4 man in their flight. At 1150, as they made a turn to the left and began climbing around a cumulus cloud, Lt. Stevens suddenly rolled to the left. Then, with the aircraft upside-down, its left propeller tore loose and hurtled into Lt. Mary's P-38. Stevens' plane continued its roll, then straightened out and began a long glide. Trailing smoke, it glided at a steep angle toward a grain field. An eyewitness on the ground stated that the Lightning made a series of maneuvers that appeared to be attempts at leveling out, but each resulted in a stall. It finally did begin to level out about 100 feet above the terrain, but then its nose dropped and it hit the ground in a wheat field near Marsh Court Farm, about a mile north of the village of Kings Somborne. Lt. Stevens was killed instantly.

Meanwhile, Lt. Mary fared no better. Stevens' propeller had dealt his P-38 a mortal blow, and it went into a spin to the left. It turned twice, recovered, and began to level off. Suddenly, the plane burst into flames, slipped off its right wing, rolled onto its back and went straight into the ground on the top of a hill, also near Kings Somborne. (It was from this aircraft that the Lyden-Browns' keepsake came.)

Joel Owens remembered this incident well over 50 years later:

"On July 17, I was leading the squadron on an escort mission... We were off on time and join-up was made below the cloud deck. The weather was scattered to broken cumulus with bases at 1,500 feet and tops at 13,500 to 14,000 feet. The flights were in finger-four formation with each flight in trail as we threaded our way around the open spaces in order to maintain visual contact. We had just cleared the tops of the clouds and I was starting to relax when my wingman spun out and hit one of the other planes. Both planes crashed and the pilots were killed.

My first reaction was one of remorse and panic as I asked myself, 'What the hell did you do to cause your wingman to spin out?' My next thought was to return to base, hopefully to assist in the rescue efforts, since we couldn't report the incident over the radio for security reasons. After the mission, the eyewitnesses reported that the engine of my wingman, Lt. J. H. Stevens, had blown up and the propeller hit the other aircraft, flown by Lt. V. J. Mary. It was difficult to accept that there was nothing that I could have done to avoid the accident. There were a lot of 'what ifs': What if I had been using less power? What if I had flown at a lesser angle? What if I had been carrying ten more miles per hour airspeed? Thus, Lt. John Stevens joined Lt. Larry Pace of the 27th Fighter Squadron as the only two wingmen I lost while flying 147 missions." [Owens had flown an earlier P-38 tour in North Africa.]

As to the official cause of the accident, the resulting USAAF report stated that, "An inspection was made of the wreckage and it revealed that the propeller with the shaft and parts of the reduction gear was still intact. These parts were broken from the engine. It was also noted that the servo valve had become disconnected from the bellows in the left supercharger regulator, which could cause excessive manifold pressure, causing the engine to blow up, and it is possible that the engine overspeeded, causing excessive vibration. It is believed that excessive manifold pressure was built up, causing the engine to blow up, and excessive vibration caused by the engine overspeeding were the direct reasons for the propeller and reduction gearing to be broken off of the engine."

This was just one of so many ironic moments in that catastrophic conflict called World War Two—the union of two vital young people and the concurrent deaths of two others, in close proximity.

Another ironic aspect of this story is that John Stevens' brother, 2nd Lt. Henry J. "Hank" Stevens, who was also a pilot in the 402nd FS, was missing in action at the time of John's death. Hank has been shot down in an air battle over France just two weeks earlier, on July 4. In his case, however, there was a happy ending. He had, as it turned out, survived and was hidden by the French underground until he was liberated by Allied ground forces.

CHAPTER SEVEN

POST-WORLD WAR II LIGHTNINGS

POST-WORLD WAR II LIGHTNINGS

Hardly was the ink dry on the surrender documents signed on board the *USS Missouri* on September 2, 1945, than the USAAF began planning to divest itself of many thousands of suddenly unneeded and unwanted "surplus" aircraft. Unfortunately, near the top of its hit list was the Lockheed Lightning. Although many of its contemporary, single-engine, P-47s and P-51s soldiered on (with the National Guard, at least) for more than a decade after the war, the P-38's future in the USAAF could then be measured in months, this at least partly due to the expense of maintaining those large, twin-engine fighters.

So it was that on foreign USAAF bases around the world, P-38s—along with many other aircraft types—soon began to be cut up for scrap (in some cases after salvaging the engines and/or important flight instruments), crushed, burned, buried and/or dumped in the ocean. P-38s did serve with the occupation forces in Japan into 1946, but by the end of that year they had been completely replaced by P-51s. Few, if any, were returned to the U.S., where there was also a large surplus of Lightnings.

Late model P-38s in the process of being scrapped on Shemya Island in the Aleutians post-VJ Day. (USAF)

In fact, a few P-38s did remain in operational service overseas for a few years—in foreign arms. The Nationalist Chinese Air Force received hundreds of military aircraft from the U.S. during and immed-

225

iately after World War II. These included about 50 Lightnings, mostly F-5s—enough to equip a reconnaissance squadron. The NCAF flew the latter over Communist-controlled territory (solely from Taiwan beginning in 1950) until 1952. An NCAF F-5E had the dubious distinction of being the first victim of the new Soviet MiG-15 jet fighter when a Russian pilot shot it down over China in April 1950.

The Lightning was also utilized for a few years in postwar Europe. France's *Armée de l' Air* continued to operate the F-5s it had received from the U.S. during the war well into the 1950s, to map portions of French West Africa, fulfill its NATO commitments, etc.

The largest foreign user of the P-38 was the Italian Air Force (*Aeronautica Militaire Italiana*), which received 100 Lightnings stored by the USAAF in that country in early 1946. They included some F-5 photo recon ships and one "Droop Snoot" for training purposes. The Italian P-38s equipped two fighter wings (of two fighter groups each) in succession until they were phased out in the early 1950s (the last of them were scrapped in 1956). Several Italian Air Force F-5s were TDY with a NATO force in Italy, one of which crashed during a mission over Communist Yugoslavia.

Back in the States, the elimination of P-38s from the USAAF's domestic inventory proceeded full speed ahead starting in early 1946. They and other surplus military aircraft were flown to War Assets Administration depot airfields around the country for disposal. Approximately 75 Lightnings were sold to individual American civilians for $1,250 each, mostly at Kingman Field in Arizona, before the rest were purchased by scrap dealers. The last one reportedly sold to an individual changed hands in October 1946. Thus, by the end of that year, only a few hundred of the nearly 10,000 P-38s built in the previous five years had survived.

There *were* still a handful of Lightnings left in its inventory when the new independent U.S. Air Force re-designated the type "F-38" in 1948. Not all the occupation P-38s in Japan had been destroyed; a "substantial" number were stored there, including some P-38M night fighters, but they were finally scrapped during the early days of the Korean War.

The National Air Races, which had been cancelled during WWII, were revived in 1946, and their major attractions were the war surplus fighters that were entered, including P-38s—some modified and some "stock." Interest in them had waned by 1949, partly because of the increased fascination with jets, but during those three years at least twenty-seven P-38/F-5s were registered to race, with greatly varying degrees of success. The most successful was the one owned and flown by the famous Lockheed test pilot Tony LeVier. His was reportedly the first P-38 sold at Kingman, in January 1946. Tony's bright red #3 finished second in the 1946 Thompson Trophy Race and first in the 1947 Sohio Race, the best performances by any of the P-38s in these events. (Several Lightnings have participated in a few other air races after that sport was revived—especially in Reno, Nevada—a couple of decades later.)

The main civilian use of the P-38/F-5s in the '50s and well into the '60s was a continuation of one of the photo recon Lightning's primary tasks in WWII: aerial mapping, which important postwar function was provided all over the world (but especially in North and South America) by more than a dozen companies. Most of these F-5s were highly modified for their extensive high-altitude work, the special equipment they carried and their usual two-man crews.

Interestingly, a handful of Lightnings found their way into some Latin American air forces—some legally, some not. The Caribbean and Central American countries that utilized these aircraft in the late '40s and '50s were Cuba, Dominican Republic, Honduras, Costa Rica and Nicaragua. The last combat mission by a P-38 was reportedly flown by the Honduran Air Force (*Fuerza Aerea Hondurena*) during a dispute between that country and neighboring Nicaragua in 1957.

Paul Stiles, pictured here with a Fairchild Aerial Surveys F-5, was a WWII Navy pilot who worked for the company after the war, mapping such places as Alaska and Panama. He eventually accumulated 600 hours in the P-38. Note the radical modification that had been made to the nose of the airplane. (Stiles)

Most of the surviving Latin American Lightnings eventually found their way back to the U.S.

As of this writing (2011) there are seven P-38s currently flying, six in the U.S. and one in Austria. A couple dozen others are displayed statically in air museums around the world, some little more than wrecks and others in good to excellent condition, several of which are potentially airworthy. The amazing Lockheed P-38 is still a huge attraction to World War II aviation buffs, at museums and air shows and in books and magazine articles. Vive le Lightning!

Chapter Seven title page photo: P-38s after the war, towed to a pit and dropped over the edge by crane at Tinian Island. (Robert Osheim)

RAY'S P-38 TALES
Raymond H. Miller with Gloria Osberg

Flying airplanes has been a lifetime career for Ray Miller. Starting as a teenager, he took flying lessons at a gravel airstrip, known as Pangborn Field, at Wenatchee, Washington. Those were Depression years, so Ray paid for his lessons by raking the gravel. He earned his license before he graduated from high school in 1936. During World War II he attempted to join the Army Air Corps but was rated 4-F due to a dental problem. For one year he taught Navy Cadets to fly.

With the war still on, Ray went to work for an aerial mapping company, Aero Exploration, based in Tulsa, Oklahoma. The company had contracted to furnish aircraft and crews to the USAAF's First Photo Wing to do aerial photography for its photogrammetric mapping programs. When the war ended, Ray was still in Tulsa working for Joe Turner, the Aero Exploration Co. president. Joe wanted to map at higher altitudes, which is more efficient. He figured that a P-38 might be capable of doing the job. Joe learned that some 6,000 surplus WWII military airplanes were stored at the Army Air Base at Kingman, Arizona, and that about 500 of these were P-38s.

Joe also knew that the P-38s were brand new, and that they had been transported from the Lockheed factory in California to Texas to have the armament nose removed and for the installation of new, broader noses with room for three cameras and windows to shoot through. Later these airplanes were transferred to Kingman for storage. These models were the F-5 version.

Joe ordered ten of these airplanes and a Tulsa businessman ordered twelve. This happened sometime in 1946. Joe and Ray, along with another pilot, Gary Noble, flew the company Cessna to Kingman. There they planned to buy the ten planes to be flown back to Tulsa in shifts. Now Ray picks up this narrative:

"The P-38s were parked in a dirt field. Joe paid for two planes then and said he would come back for the remaining eight later. He paid $1,250 each for the airplanes, which the agent in charge said was 1% of the original amount paid to Lockheed of $125,000. We took possession of two airplanes, planning to come back for the rest.

I had never been in the cockpit of a P-38 before. Full of confidence, I climbed aboard. I got the engines started, but when I tried to turn on the radio, I couldn't find the switch. This is some complicated airplane! Right away I started to taxi to the tarmac, without benefit of a contact with the control tower. Upon contact with the edge of the concrete, which was a higher surface than the dirt parking area, the nose wheel spun the wrong way, and I was stuck. The Army came to my rescue with a tow truck and pulled the airplane onto the concrete, where I decided to practice taxiing. It wasn't too

August 1946: Ray Miller in the cockpit of an Aero Exploration Co. P-38 at Pangborn Field in Washington. (Miller)

long before the gentleman in the control tower got fed up trying to contact me, and thinking that I was trying to take off, shined his red light on the aircraft and its pilot. The end result was that I flew the Cessna back to Tulsa and Joe and Gary flew the P-38s. I studied the manuals before trying to fly the airplane again.

Much to Joe's surprise, the Air Corps sold all the surplus airplanes before Aero Exploration could take delivery on the other eight P-38s. An entrepreneur bought the airbase and the airplanes. He sold the airplanes for scrap metal (aluminum). The sale was handled through a government agency, the War Assets Administration.

I remember that at this time (1947) there was only one other aerial mapping company in the U.S. and one in Canada besides Aero Exploration who were working on including P-38s in their mapping business.

I contacted the businessman from Tulsa, who sold me two P-38s from those he had bought in Kingman. I paid for these airplanes from savings (I had had a good night at the crap table in Reno). One was put into storage in Tulsa, and I didn't fly it until 1948. The second was dismantled for parts.

The P-38s that Aero Exploration owned were flown as NX (Experimental) aircraft. In 1948 the FAA decided that ex-military aircraft could be licensed under a classification of NL (Limited). I provided the engineering data and flight testing to the FAA. The plane type class was then registered in the FAA files as the 'Raymond Miller Lightning.' About a year later, the Lockheed Aircraft Corp. did what was necessary to get the name changed to 'Lockheed Lightning.' My aircraft mechanic pointed out to me that the aircraft maintenance manual, issued to licensed mechanics, referred to the Raymond Miller Lightning.

Also in 1948, I left Aero Exploration for an opportunity to take a one-third interest in a Minnesota company called the Mark Hurd Mapping Co. It soon incorporated and changed the name to Mark Hurd Aerial Surveys. This new company was formed to conduct 'high-altitude photography' that would be possible using a P-38. The one I had put in storage in Tulsa was the aircraft that could do the job.

We conducted a test project for the U.S. Army Map Service, and since it was a success, they gave us our first contract covering three Midwestern states. I must comment that blocks were also given to two of our competitors, and they failed to perform. We later flew their blocks for the Army after our job was completed. Subsequently, the Army Map Service contracted to have our company map the entire U.S. We also mapped many developing countries around the world.

This P-38 and four additional P-38s were the new 'work horses' for the next 20 years. The fleet of five P-38s went through many modifications during this period to make them more effective. Several were:

1A—The aircraft cockpit was overhauled to make it 24" longer to provide seating for two men. The cockpit was sealed for two psi differential cabin pressure from the engine turbo superchargers.

1B—The Curtiss Electric propellers were removed and four-blade Aero Products props were installed.

1C—The intercooler door was reversed to reduce drag when

Ray and an unidentified friend pose with an Aero Exploration Lightning. (Miller)

The five Mark Hurd Aerial Surveys Lightnings. The two on the right already have the bulges on their noses that were part of the modification allowing them to carry two huge cameras there. (Miller)

opened.

As a result of these modifications, the aircraft were used successfully for projects that required photos taken at 36,000 feet above mean terrain that reached over 10,000 feet above sea level (the Rocky Mountain states, the Andes in South America, etc.).

These aircraft had the nose modified to encompass the installation of a dual-camera system. This system required a 12-inch blister on each side of the nose to use two cameras mounted on a gimbal, shooting vertical. This did not change the performance of this wonderful aircraft.

Ray is the pilot in the cockpit of the Mark Hurd F-5 in the foreground; the photo-navigator is Cliff Kristofferson. (Miller)

232

During the 20 years we operated this fleet we had no serious problems. Three of the P-38s had remotely controlled camera systems. The crew (pilot and photo-navigator) worked together.

Our company retired all five P-38s in 1970. They were replaced by three Model 24 and 25 Gates Learjets. For the next 17 years (1970-87), I flew 6,000 hours in this aircraft on world-wide mapping projects."

Addenda: The Hurd Lightnings eventually received new civil registration numbers after being acquired by the company. They were: N501MH (for Mark Hurd), originally USAAF serial #44-27183; N502MH (44-27083); N503MH (44-27002); N504MH (44-54078); and N505MH (44-53186). They were all built as P-38L-5s but except for N504MH were converted to F-5G-6 photo recon configuration. The former N505MH now resides at and flies from the Evergreen Aviation and Space Museum in McMinnville, Oregon, and the former N501MH is the Yankee Air Museum's F-5G, which it displays—statically only—in its facility at California's Chino Airport.

TO OWN A LIGHTNING
Mary Lou Neale

When there was a surplus of military planes right after World War II, pilots looked for practical aircraft easy on fuel consumption. Even wealthy, diehard fans of military surplus planes rarely gave a thought to buying a fighter. Acquiring a twin-engine, gas-guzzling airplane like the P-38 was deemed ridiculous.

Yet Nadine Ramsey, who was neither wealthy nor foolish, purchased a surplus P-38. For at least a brief, happy time, she was able to afford to keep the plane she loved by flying at airshows.

But the amazing part of this story is not that Ramsey, a former WASP (Women Airforce Service Pilots), bought the impractical Lightning, but that she was able to fly anything, much less walk again, after a terrible plane crash in the early 1940s. She was bedridden for more than four months, declining the doctor's recommendation that her injured leg be amputated. Ramsey recovered, was accepted into and graduated from WASP training, and was selected for the USAAF Ferry Command.

Ramsey was already an accomplished pilot when WWII began. Before becoming a WASP, she had flown and sold aircraft. As a WASP, she wanted to fly fighters and bombers, so requested a transfer to Long Beach, California, where she could accomplish her goal under the command of Barbara London.

The fast, maneuverable P-38 was one of Ramsey's favorites. She liked the way the twin-engine fighter responded to fingertip control.

After the war she borrowed $1,250 from her brother and bought a P-38 that was sold as surplus by the military along with acres of other military aircraft at Kingman, Arizona. Her new purchase had only 22 hours of service and was then estimated to be worth more than $165,000.

At the time she was the only woman in the nation who owned a fighter aircraft. She was met by photographers and newsmen at the Long Beach Airport when she flew it in. She kept it at that airport for more than two years and attempted to pay for the upkeep of it by making appearances at airshows. She sold it for $4,000 when she could no longer afford the maintenance and fuel bills (it used 100 to 120 gallons of high octane fuel each hour).

Nadine Ramsey's story is more than just an answer to a trivia question—"Name the only woman to ever personally own a P-38." Her story is a lesson in true grit—working hard to pay for flight instruction and flight time to get her pilot's license, and overcoming terrible injury and enormous odds to reach her goal to fly the P-38.

After a long illness, Nadine Ramsey passed away on February 16, 1997, the first, and perhaps the last, woman to own a P-38.

Nadine Ramsey with her P-38 at the Long Beach Airport. (Ramsey)

CHAPTER EIGHT

MISCELLANEOUS
P-38 STORIES

THE YOUNGEST P-38 PILOTS
Steve Blake

Over the years there has been some spirited discussion amongst members of the P-38 National Association as to who the youngest military pilot to fly the Lightning was. Although it is likely that no clear-cut winner of this "contest" will—or could—ever be decided, two very likely candidates have surfaced.

Lincoln D. Jones was born on December 4, 1923. He received his wings and commission at Luke Field, Arizona, as a member of Class 42-I on September 29, 1942, at the age of 18 years and 300 days. His first flight at the controls of a P-38 took place on October 16, at Muroc Army Air Base [now Edwards Air Force Base] in California's Mojave Desert, age 18 years, 317 days.

In December, Second Lieutenant Jones was sent to North Africa with a group of P-38 replacement pilots and assigned to the 49th Fighter Squadron, 14th Fighter Group at Berteaux, Algeria. He flew his first combat mission on January 16, 1943, at age 19 years, 43 days. When the 14th FG was relieved from combat temporarily at the end of that month due to heavy losses and being short one

Lt. Jones (on the far right) and three of his 96th FS mates in North Africa, mid-1943. (Jones)

Stan Ordway in the cockpit of a 370th FG P-38 in Europe. (Ordway)

squadron, "Linc" was reassigned to the 96th Fighter Squadron, 82nd Fighter Group. He scored his first aerial victory on April 5, during a huge air battle north of Cap Bon, age 19 years, 121 days.

Lt. Jones was credited with shooting down one more enemy aircraft before completing his 50-mission combat tour on July 16, 1943, age 19 years, 223 days.

Stanley I. Ordway was born on March 26, 1925. He soloed in a P-38 on January 13, 1944, at the age of 18 years and 293 days. This was before he was awarded his wings, which occurred on February 8 at Williams Field, Arizona, with Class 44-B—age 18 years, 319 days.

Second Lieutenant Ordway went to England as a P-38 replacement pilot and was assigned there to the 485th Squadron of the 370th Fighter Group, a 9th Air Force fighter-bomber unit, in July 1944. By the time he finally flew his first combat mission he was several months older than Linc Jones had been when he flew his first. And unlike Jones, Stan did not complete his combat tour; he was shot down by anti-aircraft fire on December 27, 1944, during his 36th mission. He spent the rest of the war as a POW and was liberated from Stalag Luft III in April 1945, about a month after his 20th birthday.

So, as to who was the youngest military pilot to fly a P-38, as far as we know it was Stan Ordway, by a little over three weeks. But

Linc Jones was most likely the youngest pilot to fly a combat mission and to shoot down an enemy aircraft in the Lightning.

There is little doubt, however, as to the identity of *the* youngest person to fly a P-38. It was a teenage civilian by the name of William P. Lear, Jr., son of the designer of the famous Learjet. Bill tells us that, "On May 20, 1946, at age 17 years, 321 days, I purchased P-38/F-5G serial #44-53026 from the War Assets Administration at Kingman, Arizona, for the grand sum of $1,250. On that day I flew my newly acquired Lightning from Kingman to Compton, California, where I made my first landing [in it] on a 3,000-foot dirt strip." He flew his F-5 (actually two of them) at numerous airshows and other aviation events for the next two years.

Self-described airshow "gypsy" Bill Lear, Jr. shows off his Lightning and his fancy pilot's uniform in 1947. This was Bill's second F-5G, his first having been badly damaged in a crash landing in September 1946. (Lear)

HONDURAN AIR FORCE P-38s
Mike Alba

I was assigned by the USAF to the Honduran Air Force (HAF) as a "combat operations advisor" from 1953 to 1956. My mission there was simple: Make the Honduran Air Force combat ready. When I arrived, the HAF (in Spanish the Fuerza Aerea Hondurena, or FAH) had seven P-38s and an assorted lot of other aircraft, including a couple of P-63s, several C-47s and a bunch of T-6s and Stearmans. Of course, the P-38s immediately caught my attention! It took a while before my flight training program reached the P-38 level. First, I had to train them (in T-6s) in instrument flying and night flying. Then, still in T-6s, I took them into combat formation and tactics, fighter gunnery and all that "sexy" stuff.

I must make it clear that Col. Hernan Acosta Mejia, the Chief of the HAF, had developed an outstanding group of basic pilots. But they had absolutely no notion about instrument flying and therefore no notion about night flying. They had never flown at night! But they were eager to learn and none more so than Col. Acosta.

Finally, we could graduate to the P-38 and repeat the combat program with it. There was a slight difference in this combat training phase from my combat days with the 55th Fighter Group (8th Air Force). The HAF Lightnings did not have the 20mm cannon, and we had only 500-pound bombs instead of the 1,000-pound bombs we had used on tactical missions in Europe. Toward the final phase of this combat training I had them plan and fly simulated missions. This included the P-38s being fully loaded (bombs, ammo and fuel) for the selected targets. Of course, no actual firing and bombing was done. I would fly "tail-end Charlie" to evaluate. And darn it, I would have to fly in a P-38 to do this! During one of these missions my dear friend Col. Acosta was killed in a takeoff accident in his P-38. Now the HAF had only six P-38s—and no commander. I was asked by the president of Honduras to take over as chief of the HAF, which I respectfully declined.

I flew the HAF P-38s (which had been acquired in the late 1940s) for a total of at least two years. And I wasn't just flying them around the pattern; I was flying them in the combat mode. Just about every time—if not *every* time—I flew an HAF P-38, it was a different one.

Unfortunately, just before I completed my tour with the HAF it became clear that the lack of spare parts for the P-38s was becoming an impossible problem in maintaining the aircraft in combat mode. Gordon Maddox had been contracted from Lockheed to supervise the maintenance of the '38s. We concluded that we had to replace them. Since the primary mission of the HAF was tactical, I recommended the Corsair as their replacement. This is what was available and that

242

is what the HAF got. I had completed my tour at about this time, so I never knew where the HAF P-38s went.

[Lt. Col. Michael Alba, USAF, Ret., served a full combat tour with the 55th FG's 338th FS, flying both P-38s and P-51s, and was credited with shooting down two Me 109s. Three of the former Honduran P-38s have survived. One, the FAH's #503 (USAAF serial #44-53097) is on static display at the Museum of Flight in Seattle, Washington; FAH 505/44-53232 is also on static display, at the Air Force Museum in Dayton, Ohio; while FAH 506/44-53095, the only one still flying, is the Friedkin Family Warbirds' *Thoughts of Midnite*.]

USAF Captain Mike Alba (center) checks the "cruise control" forms of Honduran Air Force pilots after returning from a P-38 navigation mission. The man on the left, standing, is HAF Commanding Officer Colonel Acosta. (USAF via Alba)

P-38 RAIN MAKER
Steve Blake

Among the many uses to which the Lockheed Lightning has been put during the past 70 years, both military and civilian, none was more unusual than "rain maker." That was how war surplus P-38 serial #44-53242 (civil registration number N57496) was utilized in the late 1940s and '50s, over the Sierra Nevada mountain range in California.

44-53242 was built at Lockheed's Burbank plant as a P-38L-5 in 1945 but was then modified at its facility in Dallas to an F-5G-6 photo reconnaissance configuration. By 1947 it was owned by civilian Tom P. Mathews, who entered it in that year's National Air Races at Cleveland, Ohio. It was unable to compete, however, due to mechanical problems. Mathews then sold it to the Ball-Ralston Flying Service in Hillsboro, Oregon, where it was modified by moving the pilot's seat forward five inches to make room for a passenger. Shortly thereafter Ball-Ralston sold N57496 to the California Electric Power Co., which based it at the Bishop Airport in California for weather-related work, specifically for cloud seeding, or "rain making."

Cal-Electric's primary pilot, Robert F. Symons, became somewhat accidentally involved in what was later the U.S. government's Sierra Wave Project, the investigation of a weather/wind phenomenon that is unique to the eastern Sierra Nevada. A now-famous photo Symons took of the Sierra Wave and the distinctive lenticular clouds it produced was a major impetus for this program. Writer Bertha Ryan described Symon's coup in her article entitled "A Brief History of Soaring at Inyokern Airport" on the latter's website:

"On March 5, 1950, Bob was flying his P-38 and took advantage of this little understood weather phenomenon to try something new. He soared the P-38 with both engines dead and propellers feathered for more than an hour between 13,000 and 31,000 feet. Maximum climb was 3,000 feet per minute. The ground winds were strong and blew the roof off a hangar at Bishop Airport. It was on this flight that he took the famous picture that has appeared in many publications."

Symons, who was then 40, had been a fixture among the aircraft and glider pilot community in the Owens Valley for more than 20 years. He had been bitten by the glider "bug" while a student at Riverside Junior College in California and was at one time co-holder of the world two-place altitude record. During WWII Bob was a civilian glider instructor for the Army at Wickenburg, Arizona, and then worked at a company in San Francisco building large military gliders. He was also an aviation mechanic, an accomplished photographer, a warrant officer in the Civil Air Patrol—with which he flew many search and rescue missions in the Sierra Nevada—and ran the FBO at Bishop

Airport. He managed all these activities despite having lost a leg in a farming accident in 1936 and to fly with a wooden replacement.

Bob Symons' main job as pilot of the Cal-Electric P-38 was cloud seeding. He had previously used several other types of aircraft for this purpose, including the AT-6 which the Lightning replaced. It was definitely a case of the right plane for the right job. Bob described some of his experiences flying the P-38 in an article for *Skyways* magazine's June 1950 issue, beginning with picking it up in Portland, Oregon, in early 1948:

"The only twin-engine airplane I'd ever flown before was a twin-Cessna. The first hop I made in the P-38 came near being my last. I had one of the pilots on the field show me how to start the engines, and then I took off for Reno, Nevada. It began to get cold at 15,000 feet so I hunted around in the cockpit for the cabin-heater control. The whole cockpit began to smell of exhaust smoke and gas fumes so I shut off the heaters in a hurry. There was still exhaust coming in through the vent so I used a map to scoop fresh air into my face from the cabin intake. I darn near froze all the rest of that trip. When I finally had the airplane safely in the hangar at Bishop, I began checking through the tech manuals of the P-38 and found that the mechanics who had replaced the superchargers had sawed off the heater intake tubes so that I was getting pure exhaust gasses in the cockpit.

That's the only trouble I've had with the ship aside from losing engines from icing while flying on instruments inside the clouds. Above 20,000 feet you're supposed to use electrical boost pumps in addition to the regular engine-driven fuel pumps, but even then we'll sometimes pick up a vapor lock at high altitudes when it is extremely cold outside.

I've been as high as 39,000 feet with the P-38, and it doesn't take me all day to get there. Clouds develop fast in these high mountains, and if I'm to get the moisture out of them where I want it, I've got to have a ship that will go upstairs in a hurry. Aside from the fast climb, the P-38 is ideal for this work because of its rugged construction and ever-lovin' twin-engine safety. The turbulence in some of these clouds is really rough."

During the seeding flights, a technician in the modified nose of the plane would dispense silver iodide into the cloud, thereby hopefully producing some rain, which would increase the water flow in Bishop Creek that powered the generators in the plants along its banks that produced the hydroelectricity that the company sold for its profits. The theory of seeding clouds from aircraft was proven in 1946, and Symons was one of its first proponents.

In 1955 Cal-Electric sold the P-38 to Weather Modifications, Inc., for which Symons and other pilots continued to utilize it for rain making in the Bishop area. Sadly and ironically, Bob was killed in a glider accident in April 1958. Six months later, N57496 crashed near Bishop Airport, killing its pilot, Chester A. Janes. Its remains were salvaged and later used to rebuild or repair other P-38s.

Bob Symons pilots Cal-Electric's P-38 over his beloved Sierra Nevada. It was still painted in its old racing colors and number "47".

THE SAGA OF THE SHIPWRECKED YIPPIES
Ernie Cromie

In September 1942, a number of Lightnings that were earmarked for the 8th Air Force in England were flown in stages from Lockheed's Burbank, California, factory to Newark, New Jersey. A relevant USAAF aircraft history document provides the serial numbers of five of them, all P-38G-5s: 42-12802; 42-12810; 42-12811; 42-12812 and 42-12818. They were taken to Newark Harbor, where they were destined to become part of convoy HX 212.

One of the ships making up this convoy was the 17,000-ton Norwegian former whale factory ship KOSMOS II, which, interestingly, was built in Belfast, Northern Ireland, in 1931. Her main cargo was 21,000 tons of crude oil. Another of the convoy vessels was the tanker SOURABAYA. Such was the pressure to make use of all available space, both ships carried additional cargo in the form of US-built LCT (Landing Craft, Tank) vessels that were being supplied to the Royal Navy as Lend-Lease equipment. Each LCT was of a type that could be disassembled into three sections for shipping as deck cargo, and the opportunity was taken to lash a P-38 to each section.

Tragically, this convoy, like many before and after it, was ill fated, for both SOURABAYA and KOSMOS II were sunk by German U-boats a few hundred miles southwest of Iceland, on October 27 and 29, respectively. Consequently, the USAAF document mentioned above was endorsed on November 3, 1942, with a note to the effect that the subject Lightnings had been "destroyed en route." Remarkably, though—and unknown to the endorser—a few of the LCT sections had broken free and continued their eastward passage, drifting helplessly, some of them still carrying a P-38. This was apparent from at least as early as November 17, on which date the crew of a Sunderland flying boat of 423 Squadron from RAF Castle Archdale in Northern Ireland reported sighting a P-38 on a raft adrift in the North Atlantic. On November 21, another of the squadron's flying boats reported seeing the same or a similar combination, the precise identity of the P-38 on either occasion having been impossible to obtain.

During succeeding weeks, intriguing evidence that more than one of the Lightnings had "escaped" accumulated in a variety of ways. On November 23, an employee of Lockheed Overseas Corporation at the Langford Lodge Air Depot in Northern Ireland, the late Douglas Eastwood, noted in his personal diary: "P-38 came in today with the front and back of the pilot's compartment bashed in. Was supposed to have been found floating on the ocean on a landing barge." Around the same time, a member of the U.S. Signal Corps photographed an actual LCT/P-38 combination in Belfast Harbor. Two of the photos he took are in the National Archives at College Park, Maryland, one of which is captioned: "A damaged Lockheed P-38 on part of an assault barge is brought into port at the Dufferin Docks, Belfast, Northern Ireland. Plane and assault barge were damaged when ship which they were on was torpedoed. Both were found floating, and an English corvette towed plane and barge 300 miles to harbor. 25th November 1942."

In none of the cases of sighting referred to thus far was evidence recorded confirming the serial numbers of the subject Lightnings, but the identities of two "escapees" were about to emerge. On December 7, 1942, yet another P-38/LCT combination, which had also been taken in tow by a Royal Navy warship, arrived at the mouth of Lough Foyle and was anchored off Magilligan Point in Northern Ireland. There it remained until January 9, 1943, when it broke adrift, only to be washed up later that day on the opposite shore of Lough Foyle, in County Donegal, Eire. Records in the Irish Military Archives in Dublin identify the aircraft as 42-12802, one of the Lightnings embarked in HX 212. Subsequently, permission having been given by the Eire authorities, several attempts to re-float the combination were made on January 13 by British vessels. The attempts were unsuccessful, but on January 21 the LCT, with the P-38 still attached, floated free on a high tide and was towed away to an unspecified destination.

The question arises as to whether or not any of the "escapees" were returned to serviceable condition. At this point, the evidence is somewhat frustrating. In his book *THE LOCKHEED P-38 LIGHTNING*, Warren Bodie claims that the example photographed in Belfast on November 25 was repaired at Langford Lodge and returned to service. Provided the P-38 concerned was 42-12811, that is correct, for according to LOC records for Langford Lodge, work described as "reassembling and major repairs" commenced on that aircraft on March 9, 1943, and was completed "51 work days (2,764 man hours)" later, on April 29.

Unfortunately, the LOC records in my possession do not explain when or in what circumstances 42-12811 arrived at the depot, nor do they contain diagrammatic or photographic evidence of the nature of the damage that was repaired. Nor has it been possible to prove the identity of the "escapee" seen by Douglas Eastwood. If the date on the National Archives photos is the date the captions were written and not necessarily when they were taken, the damaged P-38 seen by Doug was almost certainly 42-12811. Sadly, of 42-12802 there is no mention, not even as a salvage item.

[The author, a prominent Irish aviation historian, was assisted in his research by fellow Irish aviation historian Martin Gleeson. He borrowed his title from an article in the *LOC Magnet*, the Langford Lodge Air Depot's daily news sheet, warning its employees not to talk about these incidents. "Yippee" was the unofficial name given by Lockheed employees to the thirteen pre-production model YP-38s that were built by the company in 1940-41 for service testing. The name stuck and was often applied to later production models of the Lightning as well.]

This is one of the two National Archives photos of the shipwrecked Yippee to which the author refers in his article. The other photo is shown on the Chapter Eight title page.

Made in the USA
Middletown, DE
23 May 2021

40273219R00139